# K·I·T·C·H·E·N  S·C·I·E·N·C·E

# K·I·T·C·H·E·N

*A Guide to Knowing the Hows and Whys*

**Revised Edition**

*Illustrations by Jill Kampmier*

BOSTON

# S·C·I·E·N·C·E

*for Fun and Success in the Kitchen*

## HOWARD HILLMAN

COAUTHORS   Lisa Loring
Kyle MacDonald

HOUGHTON MIFFLIN COMPANY

For information about permission to reproduce selections from this book,
write to Permissions, Houghton Mifflin Company, 2 Park Street, Boston,
Massachusetts 02108.

Library of Congress Cataloging-in-Publication Data

Hillman, Howard.
    Kitchen science : a guide to knowing the hows and whys for fun and
success in the kitchen / Howard Hillman ; coauthors, Lisa Loring, Kyle
MacDonald ; illustrations by Jill Kampmier.
        p.    cm.
    "Revised edition" — Foreword.
    Bibliography: p.
    Includes index.
    ISBN 0-395-48072-8
    1. Cookery.    I. Loring, Lisa.    II. MacDonald, Kyle.    III. Title.
TX651.H544    1989
641 — dc20              89-34551
                        CIP

Printed in the United States of America

BP 13 12 11 10 9 8 7 6 5

## DEDICATION

*To creative, intellectually curious cooks
because they make cooking and dining
more fun, and more exciting and delicious.*

# Contents

# Foreword to the
# Revised Edition

By popular demand, we've expanded *Kitchen Science*, by 25 percent. It was fun because we love to eat, cook, and experiment (a friend affectionately nicknamed us "mad scientists in the kitchen").

Our new book is a substantive update. We wrote a new chapter. And we added at least several new Q&A's to each existing chapter — and revised many of the Q&A's. Overall, we've added more than one hundred new Q&A's and revamped over seventy-five existing ones.

We selected the new questions based mainly on the suggestions we received from you, our readers. We listened. For example, we've added many new Q&A's on diet, health, and nutrition because many of you have a growing interest in those topics.

My staff and I hope you will enjoy the new *Kitchen Science* as much as you did the original one.

HOWARD HILLMAN

# *Preface*

An ancient Chinese philosopher once advised his assembled followers,

> Give a man a fish, and you feed him for a day. Teach a man to fish, and you feed him for a lifetime.

There is a parallel in cooking:

> Find yourself a recipe, and you can cook one dish. Teach yourself the science of cooking, and you can cook creatively forever.

Creative cooking requires love, imagination, art, and science. The love and imagination can be encouraged but not taught, the art is acquired from experience and through helpful guidance from other cooks, and many of the practical scientific principles can be learned from this book. As a quick thumbing through its pages will show you, *Kitchen Science* takes the mystery out of cooking, and does so in nonacademic language. You will learn why baking powder leavens, why freezing ruins the texture of meat, why some pots are superior to others, why some people can eat more hot chilis than other people, why sauces thicken, why new potatoes are best for making potato salad, why a "bloody rare" steak is not really bloody, why a soufflé rises, and hundreds of gutsy answers to other practical questions.

*Kitchen Science* will help you become a more creative cook because you will not only be better able to adapt recipes but will also need to rely less on them. When your kitchen or market lacks a specific ingredient, you will be able to improvise with greater flair. In short, you will be able to create new dishes and modify old ones more freely because you will know what can and cannot be done — and why.

The "whys" have been well researched. In addition to having devoured hundreds of weighty tomes and thousands of academic articles that explore the world of food science, my staff and I have interviewed a wide variety of food scientists and have conducted countless experiments in the kitchen in order to separate food facts from myths. Supplementing that information is my knowledge, which comes from having written other food books and from having a lifelong interest in discovering the "whys" of cooking.

I enjoyed researching and writing *Kitchen Science* because it was an exhilarating, mind-stretching experience that has further increased my own creativity in the kitchen. I hope you share my enthusiasm for kitchen science.

# K·I·T·C·H·E·N  S·C·I·E·N·C·E

# 1

## C·O·O·K·I·N·G

## E·Q·U·I·P·M·E·N·T

**Why are dull knives more dangerous than sharp ones?**

The sharper the knife, the less likely cooks are to cut themselves. This may sound like dull-witted reasoning, but the point is valid for two pragmatic reasons. First, people tend to be more careful when using sharper knives because the potential harm is more vivid in their minds. Second, a duller knife is more apt to slip when cutting because it requires more downward pressure to do the job.

There are more benefits from a sharp knife than just safety. It will make cutting quicker and more efficient, will minimize ripping and tearing of the food, and — when appropriate — will make thin slices.

Two of the wisest rules for any kitchen are to buy quality carbon steel (or, at least, high-carbon stainless steel) knives and to keep them well honed.

**How do carbon and stainless steel knives differ?**

Both knives have blades of steel, an alloy consisting mainly of iron mixed with carbon and a smaller portion of other elements. The critical difference between carbon and stainless steel alloys is that the first has a higher carbon content, whereas the other amalgamation contains more chromium, and often nickel.

The relatively new high-carbon stainless knife is betwixt and between the two — its carbon, chromium, and nickel proportions lie somewhere in between those of the standard carbon and stainless steel varieties.

Yet another variation of the theme is the superstainless knife, the one with the scintillating silvery look. Its alloy — at least its plating alloy — is impregnated with relatively large quantities of chromium and nickel.

An alloy's precise make-up determines to a considerable extent a knife's advantages and disadvantages for a cook.

### What are the pros and cons of each knife blade alloy?

A knife made with carbon steel is unequaled in its ability to take an extremely sharp edge, and therefore it is preferred by most serious chefs. The major drawback of carbon steel is that unless the blade is promptly wiped dry after each use, it will rust. The alloy is also vulnerable to attack by the acid in foods like citrus fruits, tomatoes, and onions. If the knife is not washed soon after contact with these ingredients, the acid will react chemically with the metal, blemishing the blade's surface with blackish stains. Moreover, that discoloration and its attendant off-odor can be transferred to the foods you are cutting.

Superstainless steel is the least efficient of the four basic knife alloys. It is all but impossible for a cook to restore its sharpness once the knife loses its original well-honed edge (if the manufacturer gave it one in the first place). Kitchenware demonstrators speak hokum when they claim that superstainless steel knives never need to be sharpened. What they should tell you is that their products can't be sharpened.

Stainless steel, like its supercousin, resists rust, stains, and corrosion caused by water and acid. Though it takes a sharper edge than a superstainless one, a stainless steel blade will still be annoyingly dull in the hands of a busy cook.

A high-carbon stainless steel knife — by far the most expensive of the four types — will neither rust nor stain. Consequently, it is the answer for a cook who lives by the sea or in a humid climate, because salt can corrode and moisture can oxidize (rust) nonstainless steel. High-carbon stainless steel is also recommended for cooks who do not want to be bothered with having to wash the knife and wipe it dry promptly after each use — or who do not want the knife and food to become tarnished because the chore was neglected.

Although a blade made from high-carbon stainless steel can be honed to a fairly sharp edge, do not believe the food writers and salespersons who tell you that its sharpness will match that of a knife made with carbon steel. As our kitchen tests verify, this is physically impossible.

## What should I look for when buying a knife?

Selecting the right blade alloy is not enough. You should buy only a knife produced by a quality manufacturer because fine knife making requires skilled workmanship involving a myriad of precision tasks, such as tempering the steel. In fact, unless you can buy superb carbon steel knives (they are becoming difficult to find in America nowadays), we recommend that you purchase the top-of-the-line, high-carbon stainless steel knives of a quality manufacturer, such as Wüsthof (Trident trademark) or Henckels.

The tang (the part of the metal enclosed by the handle) should run the full length of the handle and should be well secured with at least three rivets. Otherwise, the handle and the metal part of the knife may separate within a matter of years (a top-caliber knife should last a lifetime). The full tang also contributes weight and balance, two essential qualities that inexpensive knives usually lack.

A knife's handle should be easy to grasp and should feel comfortable in your hand. Its material should be durable, nonslippery, and — for your hand's sake — a poor conductor of heat. Nearly all hardwood and many modern plastic-and-wood composite grips fit the bill; plastic hilts do not.

There exist many styles of knives to choose from — some functional, some fanciful. It is wiser and more economical in the long run to invest in a few quality knives than to purchase a broader assortment of less expensive and inferior implements. Our recommended six-unit starter's set performs a wide variety of tasks. It comprises a three- to four-inch (blade length) paring knife, a six-inch utility knife, an eight-inch serrated slicing knife, an eight-inch chef's (chopping) knife, a ten-inch nonserrated slicing (carving) knife, and a ten-inch butcher's steel for honing. Of the group, the indispensable quartet consists of the butcher's steel, the paring knife, and the chef's and nonserrated slicing knives.

As the accompanying illustration shows, there is a notable difference — for reasons of function — between the cross-sectional blade of the slicing and chef's knives.

Because the first blade is relatively thin, friction and food crushing is minimized as the knife slides through the food. Just as important, the thinner design allows the carver to cut narrower and more uniform slices because the blade stays reasonably parallel to the face of the cut.

The wedge shape of the chef's knife is, by contrast, broader on the top of its cross section. That extra weight gives the blade extra momentum and therefore more power to help the cook chop through firm food.

**What are the best and worst ways to sharpen a knife?**

Honing a knife on one of those extremely coarse grinding wheels or belts that are commonly used by peregrinating peddlers or key makers is one of the most unsatisfactory methods. Repeated sharpenings on these instruments will wear away your blade within a few years. Almost as bad are those small pairs of steel rotating disk-cylinders that are supposed to be attached to a kitchen door or cabinet. Not only do these gadgets devour the metal of the blade faster than need be, they tend to scratch the blade too much and throw it out of alignment.

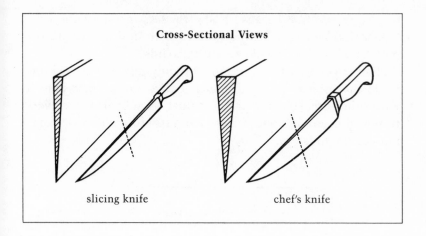

**Cross-Sectional Views**

slicing knife          chef's knife

The best day-to-day sharpening implement is the butcher's steel, a rough-surfaced, hard metal rod equipped with a handle. However, unless you use the steel frequently to sharpen the knife, as a butcher is wont to do, the edge of your knife may dull beyond the restorative powers of the honing rod. In that case, you will need to sharpen the knife periodically with a whetstone, a small, abrasive, bluish-black block made of the exceptionally hard silicon carbide, Carborundum (available in most hardware stores).

Some food authorities say that 15° is the correct honing angle, whereas other estimates place the number at 25° or even 30°. For the record, approximately 20° produces the best results.

### Does the cutting surface affect a knife's sharpness?

The harder a cutting surface, the more quickly a knife dulls. Hard surfaces include metal, marble, china, crockery, enamel, glass, and most kitchen countertops. The softest, and therefore the most desirable, of the popular cutting surfaces is wood. Though softwood does less harm to the knife's edge, hardwood is used most often because it absorbs less moisture and lasts longer. Ranking just behind hardwood in desirability are the molded white polyethylene cutting boards.

Hard cutting surfaces are not the only anathemas. A knife blade that nicks too many bones, bangs around in a drawer with other utensils, or scrapes against a hard substance every time you insert and withdraw it from its storage slot also may not cut the mustard.

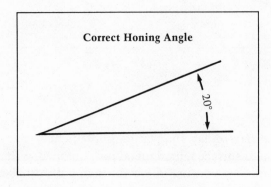

Correct Honing Angle

20°

**Why is fast heat distribution a virtue for a stove-top pan?**

Unless heat can quickly spread through the entire bottom of a pan, hot and "cold" spots will develop. The hot spots will be directly over the places where the flames or electric coil come in contact with the pan. Thus, if the gas burner is starfish-shaped, or if the configuration of the electric coil is a spiral, the hot spots will follow those patterns.

The problem of frying or braising in a pan that has hot and cold spots is that you cannot cook the food properly — unless you do nothing else but constantly and thoroughly stir the contents (and when braising, you could not do that even if you wanted to). Either the food over the hot spots will scorch, or if you lower the heat to prevent scorching, there will probably be insufficient heat to cook the other portions of the food.

When cooking food in a generous quantity of boiling or simmering water, you need not worry so much about the negative effects of hot and cold spots on the bottom of your pan. By the time the heat reaches the food, the cooking medium (water) will have more or less equalized the two temperature extremes. The same principle holds true for steaming.

The speed at which heat can travel through a pan's bottom is a function of how well it conducts heat (see "How Is Heat Transferred to Food?" pp. 27–29). Conductivity varies mainly according to the type of metal as well as the thickness and finish of the metal.

### Is there a way to test a pan for hot spots?

The quickest and surest method we know is to pour a uniform layer of four or five tablespoons of sugar mixed with a couple of tablespoons of water into the pan, then turn the heat to a low-to-medium setting and wait for the sugar to start to caramelize. If the pan has no hot spots, the sugar will caramelize evenly. If the pan has hot spots, the sugar directly over them will caramelize first, forming a pattern that maps your pan's hot spots.

If you discover that your pots have hot spots and you do not wish to replace the equipment, you can minimize the defect by using as low a heat setting as possible or by using a heat diffuser.

### Of the popular pan materials, which are the fastest heat conductors and which the slowest?

The fastest guns in town are silver, tin, and copper. Aluminum is quick on the draw, too.

Middling-speed substances include cast iron and carbon (rolled) steel, the type of sheet metal that is used to fashion traditional woks and crêpe pans. Stainless steel ranks even lower in heat-flow efficiency.

Even poorer conductors are glass, porcelain, earthenware, and pottery in general. The sluggish attributes of these materials, however, can be a plus for your serving dishes. Providing that such a vessel is covered and has thick enough walls, it will absorb and give up heat so languidly that it should keep your food warm for a long time.

Factors other than the type of metal also determine how evenly a pot heats food. The thicker its gauge, the more uniformly a pot will distribute heat throughout its interior surface. However, though a thicker gauge will help compensate for the mediocre heat-conducting properties of iron, the weight of the extra metal usually makes the pot unwieldy. A metal's finish also affects cooking efficiency.

### Are copper pots worth the money?

It depends.

We do not recommend purchasing mass-produced pseudo-copper pots and pans — the lightweight, stamped stainless steel type with copper-coated bottoms. The buyer gets the headache of the genuine copper equipment (keeping the metal polished) without enjoying the heat distribution advantage. The copper coating that is used to produce this lower-priced equipment is typically less than 1/50 of an inch thick, too thin to distribute heat uniformly. Even the stainless steel is deplorably thin.

Authentic copper pots and pans, which are quite dear, are excellent because the thick copper metal distributes the heat evenly throughout the base and the lower sides of the cooking utensil. However, if the copper base becomes mottled with black carbon deposits, the even heat distribution is greatly impaired and hot spots develop, turning a positive into a negative. This is why we never recommend copper cooking equipment to anyone who doesn't have the time and inclination to keep it clean and polished — and it is a chore, to be sure.

Another drawback of authentic copper pots is that they must be periodically relined with tin, an expensive process. The pan must be relined once the tin starts to wear away appreciably because if too much copper leaches into your cooking foods, your liver won't be able to remove the excess from your blood. The results can be noxious. However, the amount of copper from a few scratches in the tin lining shouldn't prove to be dangerously toxic — that is, if you minimize or avoid cooking foods that are high in acid or highly pigmented, which chemically hastens the release of the copper and its oxides. Finally, fat-based cooking (frying) will release less copper than will water-based cooking (boiling, braising, and stewing).

## Why does an aluminum pot give a red tomato sauce a brownish tinge?

If an unlined aluminum vessel is used to cook a high-alkali food such as potatoes, or if the cooking medium is hard water, or if the pot is washed with high-alkali cleanser, the metal's surface becomes stained. When the pot is subsequently used to cook tomato sauce or any other high-acid ingredient, such as onions, wine, lemon juice, or cabbage, the acid chemically removes some of the stain from the pot and transfers the discoloration to the food. Although the brownish tinge diminishes the aesthetic appeal of the food, it poses no threat to your health.

Another drawback of aluminum pots is their propensity to warp when subjected to abrupt changes in temperature extremes (more so than, say, stainless steel of identical gauge). And aluminum implements dent easily, especially if they are thin-gauged.

On the plus side, the heat-flow efficiency of a thick-gauge aluminum pot nearly rivals that of a copper pot of similar gauge, which is noticeably heavier and many times more expensive. Unlike cast iron or carbon steel, aluminum doesn't rust (though it does oxidize slowly). If treated with care, aluminum pots will last for decades.

**Why must I season a cast-iron or carbon steel pot before using it for the first time?**

The surfaces of both of these nonstainless iron-based metals are rather porous and have microscopic jagged peaks. You season a pot by rubbing it with oil, heating it for thirty to sixty minutes in a 300°F oven, and then cooling it to room temperature. The oil fills the cavities and becomes entrenched in them, as well as rounding off the peaks. Two culinary benefits result. First, the cooking surface develops a nonstick quality because the formerly jagged and pitted surface becomes smooth. Second, because the pores are permeated with oil, water cannot seep in and create rust that would give food an off-flavor.

**Once my carbon steel wok or omelette pan is seasoned, can I wash it with soap?**

Many cookbooks say "never," but that advice can run counter to sound hygiene and pleasing taste. Unless you use these metal utensils daily, they should be washed briefly with a little soapy water (then rinsed and thoroughly dried) in order to rid them of excess surface oil. Otherwise, the surplus oil will become rancid within two days or so, giving cooked foods an off-flavor. And, washing your wok or omelette pan gently with a cleansing agent need not ruin your prized possession.

Some cookbooks recommend an alternative method: Scour the pan with dry salt. Since that technique can also chemically precipitate rusting, we do not follow that advice.

**Why do pans sometimes become deseasoned?**

One common reason is that the pan has been scratched with a sharp metal tool, such as a spatula. Sometimes the cause is indirect: If one lets a pan rust, it probably needs to be washed and very likely scoured with soap or detergent. When cleaned in this way, some of the oil that coats the pores and minuscule jagged peaks of the metal bind themselves chemically to some of the cleansing agent's molecules and flow down the drain with the dishwater.

Naturally, the more fiercely one scrubs, the stronger the cleansing solution, and the longer the pan is soaked, the more the pan becomes deseasoned. If damage done by the cleaning is not too great, the pan will automatically reseason itself the next time you fry in it — so no harm done. If the damage is severe, you will have to start the seasoning process over again from the very beginning. If rust has developed deep inside the pores of the interior surface, dump the pan into a trash bin — all the king's cooks couldn't put it back in serviceable order again.

### How do the Teflon and Silverstone nonstick surfaces work?

Teflon is an easy-to-pronounce trade name for polytetrafluoroethylene, a solid, slippery, chemically inert fluorocarbon plastic that is baked onto the cooking surfaces of pots and other culinary paraphernalia. Silverstone is similar but lasts slightly longer. These substances cover the pores and microscopic jagged peaks of the metal (usually aluminum) and therefore deny food the opportunity to latch on to something.

Teflon and the coatings of competing brands in effect season the pan. The commercial "seasoning" method produces a much slicker surface than the home method — so slick that you can, if you want, fry foods with little or no oil or butter.

### What are the pros and cons of nonstick coatings?

The nonstick surface is a blessing to people who must drastically restrict their fat intake. However, for others, the main selling point of the nonstick lining can turn out to be a drawback. When one cooks without oil or fat, the taste buds and olfactory receptors are deprived of rich flavors that are essential to superb dining.

An indisputable positive feature of a nonstick pan is that its smooth surface can be washed free of food quickly and with minimum effort. However, should metal utensils and scouring pads be used, they can easily scratch, making it more likely that food will stick to the pan. A nonstick lining also discolors with misuse or, in time, even with proper use. Too many of the nonstick coated pans are too thin and thus — because of the resulting uneven heat distribution — are not ideal for stove-top cooking.

Finally, the nonstick coating is not truly nonstick ("low-stick" would be a better appellation), and its surface will eventually wear away, despite what some kitchenware ads and salespersons profess. Since the hapless buyers will have to keep replacing the equipment, they would have been better off to invest in a quality, thick-gauged, lifelong-lasting set of pans in the first place.

### How does an anodized aluminum pan compare with a Teflon-type aluminum pan?

An anodized pan will likely be thicker gauged and better built but, like a Teflon-type pan, can be easily scratched and impaired by a careless cook or dishwasher. Both pans have nonstick properties, though those of the Teflon-type pan are demonstrably superior. Unlike the Teflon variety, an anodized pan usually needs to be seasoned occasionally.

The anodization process is based on the principle that an oxide layer forms naturally on aluminum and that this oxide helps prevent food from sticking to the metal. The thicker the layer, the more effective the defense. Manufacturers discovered that they could artificially create a reasonably thick layer by means of electrolysis.

### Why are pans that are constructed with multi-ply bottoms so highly touted?

Their bottoms have three layers: a middle ply (generally aluminum) sandwiched between two stainless steel ones. The purpose of this design is to give the cook the best of both worlds by eliminating each metal's disadvantages.

The aluminum layer cannot become discolored, nor can it color or flavor foods, because it is completely enclosed within the stainless steel. The upper stainless steel layer does not have the hot spots that are common in 100 percent stainless steel pots, because by the time it reaches that stainless steel tier, the heat from the burner has been more or less evenly diffused by the aluminum (which is, unlike stainless steel, an excellent conductor of heat). And, because the pan's entire metal surface is stainless steel, it has an attractive shiny finish and is easier to clean. Still another bonus is that multitiered construction has much the same effect on the pan's bottom as it has on plywood: The possibility of warping is decreased.

## Is enamel cookware practical?

Enamel cookware resists corrosion, and its shiny, often colorful veneer can make it quite attractive, on the range and the dining room table. Unfortunately, its beauty is only "skin deep." Enamelware (a misnomer) is a metal, not an enamel, pan. The enamel is no more than a thin coating produced by fusing a powdered glass onto the metal (often cast iron) pan in a kiln. This sheer layer can chip easily if the cook accidentally bangs the pan against the hard sink. Thermal shock is another hazard; a stove-hot enamelware pot can shatter if the cook sets it in cold water.

## Why can a quick temperature change shatter glass?

The natural brittleness and poor conductivity of glass make it susceptible to cracking when it experiences a rapid change in temperature from hot to cold or vice versa. Contemplate what happens, for instance, when boiling water is poured into a cold glass jar. Because glass has a low heat-flow efficiency, the heat that is transferred from the water to the jar's bottom travels relatively slowly (by conduction) to the top of the jar. Since glass (or any other material) expands when heated, the jar's bottom will quickly swell, and — what is most critical — without a corresponding expansion in the upper part of the jar. This disparity creates a structural stress that cracks the doomed glass.

Treated glass, such as Pyrex, is much less vulnerable to shattering than is regular glass, though it, too, has its limits. Even less susceptible is Corningware. Standard porcelain, earthenware, and other pottery, however, do indeed have glass's "Achilles' heel," so it is a good idea to preheat (with, for instance, hot tap water) a vessel made with one of these materials before placing it in a preheated oven.

### What makes a pan warp?

A metal will not shatter like glass, partially because it has a higher heat-flow efficiency, but chiefly because it has a sturdier intermolecular structure. Metal does, nonetheless, warp for the same reason that glass cracks: structural stress caused by a sudden and significant change in the relative temperature of two adjacent or nearby areas of the cookware.

The metal of inexpensive metal pots and pans (except for the cast-iron variety) is typically thin-gauged, and that of higher-quality utensils is thick-gauged. The thicker a sheet of metal, the greater its structural strength, and therefore the less likely it is to warp. Since warped cookware conducts heat unevenly, cheap pots are seldom a bargain.

### Are there essential differences between a skillet and a sauté pan?

Though many cooks freely substitute one for the other, each pan is designed with specific functions in mind.

A skillet's sloping side allows you to turn and remove food such as scrambled eggs more easily. In contrast, the comparatively high, vertical wall of a sauté pan interferes with these cooking tasks. The rationale behind its construction is different: The design is meant to reduce the amount of oil that splatters beyond the sauté pan's rim when, for instance, the cook pan-fries chicken.

The sides of a sauté pan, incidentally, should not measure more than two and one-half inches. Higher walls cause excess steam to build up in the pan as gaseous water molecules are released by the frying foods. Moreover, some of the imprisoned steam molecules then condense and fall into the oil, needlessly causing extra splatter and lowering the oil's temperature at the same time.

skillet

sauté pan

## Which is better, a gas or electric range?

The ideal range would have gas burners atop an electric oven/broiler — range makers of America, are you listening?

Gas burners are preferable to electric stove-top units principally because they respond to temperature adjustments more quickly. That advantage is critical when, for instance, something starts to boil that shouldn't. With a gas burner, you need only reduce the flame and, if necessary, briefly lift the pan off the stove for a few seconds. With an electric element, chances are that, in addition to adjusting the heat, you will have to remove the pan from the stove for a minute or two because the element takes that much time to cool to the reset temperature.

Some stove-top electric heating units have another failing: You cannot adjust the temperature controls to in-between settings, and sometimes a food needs to be cooked at a temperature somewhere between the fixed settings dictated by the manufacturer.

Electricity is by far the best energy source for the oven/broiler unit for many reasons. An electric oven reaches the desired temperature more quickly, and if the oven has cooled because the cook opened its door, it regains the programmed temperature in less time. Generally, an electric oven is more accurate (particularly at low-temperature settings) and maintains a relatively steady temperature. (Many gas ovens, unless turned on full blast, fluctuate by 25°F or more around the programmed temperature in a roller coaster fashion.) Because many electric ovens can reach a very high temperature, they can be self-cleaning (see next Q&A). Since the broiler is built in to an electric oven, it is easier to reach and can accommodate thicker foods. Finally, an electric oven heats the kitchen less (a boon when the room is hot; not so when it is cold).

Odds are you will be forced to choose between an all-gas and all-electric range. In that case, consider these facts. With a gas unit, you face the potential headache (possibly quite literally) of having the burner blow out — or worse, having an explosion, though this occurrence is quite rare. With an electric unit, you are at the mercy of blackouts, brownouts, and blown fuses; historically, gas supply has been more dependable. You also may need to rewire your house to accommodate the increased current requirements. And electric ranges usually require more maintenance and are shorter-lived than gas ovens.

### How does a self-cleaning oven work?

When the oven is heated to nearly 1000°F, at the "self-clean" setting, any clinging grease on the walls disintegrates into fine particles that either free themselves or can be easily wiped away with a damp cloth. Don't expect to find such a feature on the gas ovens found in today's market because, unlike electric ovens, they cannot be heated to the required minimum self-cleaning temperature.

**Are smoke hoods a good investment?**

Two basic types of smoke hoods exist, both equipped with exhaust fans. One sucks the polluted air out of the kitchen into the great outdoors, as a fireplace chimney does. The other — a less efficient device — simply filters and recycles the adulterated air in your kitchen. Both reduce grime build-up in your kitchen, minimizing the need for elbow grease and redecoration.

According to the results of a study conducted by the Lawrence Laboratory in Berkeley, California, there seems to be an even stronger reason for having a smoke hood, at least in restaurants where a clutch of ovens bakes or roasts continually. The researchers found that oven exhaust can contain excess levels of nitric oxide and nitrogen dioxide (both can create respiratory disorders), carbon monoxide (capable of producing headaches and nausea), and vinyl chloride (a cancer-causing agent).

**Why don't the wok-cooked dishes that I prepare at home equal those made in a topnotch Chinese restaurant?**

Even assuming that your cooking talents and ingredients match those of a professional Chinese chef, your stir-fried food can't have the same intense color, elegant flavor, and crisp texture. A difference in the heat power available to you explains the disparity. A typical home stove-top gas burner generates fewer than ten thousand British Thermal Units. (A BTU defines the quantity of heat required to raise two cups — one pound — of air-free, 60°F water by one degree at normal atmospheric pressure.) The BTU output for a gas range found in a first-rate Chinese restaurant is at least twice as high because of the stove's special design features. It has much more gas to burn because the gas line that supplies the fuel to the burner is much larger in diameter. Moreover, the heating unit itself consists of many concentric burner rings; the normal home gas burner has but one. Finally, the restaurant burner apparatus is normally several times wider.

The higher heat more effectively seals in the juices of the ingredients and therefore helps lock in flavor and nutrients. Just as important, since fewer of the internal juices in the cooking food emerge, the pan sauce better clings to the food, making the dish more appetizing. A crisper texture results because the higher heat can better firm the surface of the food before the interior becomes overcooked. In addition, the higher heat more effectively triggers the chemical reactions that heighten the color of the vegetables as they start to cook. And because the cooking period is very brief, the vivid colors developed do not have a chance to fade.

### Can I use a wok on an electric range?

Unfortunately, the highly functional configuration of an authentic wok is incompatible with the heating surface of an electric stove-top element. The area of contact between this rounded vessel and a flat electric element is small, and therefore heat conducted from the element to the pan is limited. Yet, a genuine wok must have a rounded bottom as a matter of practicality. Stir-frying is best executed with a small amount of cooking oil concentrated in the hottest zone, the heart of the wok, and a concave pan accomplishes these goals. In addition, the combination of the height and slope of the sides facilitates tossing, an essential stir-frying procedure.

Electric ranges (and electric woks, too) are ill-suited for stir-frying for yet another reason. Many a stir-fry recipe calls for a quick lowering or raising of the temperature in the middle of the cooking period. Electric heating units, as we note in a previous Q&A, respond slowly to temperature adjustments.

Do not buy one of those "woks" that has been designed with

a flat bottom specifically for use on an electric unit. You cannot properly stir-fry in one of these vessels, which are essentially high-walled skillets. The rounded bottom is required for true Chinese stir-frying.

**Is a convection oven better than a traditional one?**

Both the convection and traditional ovens depend on convection heating. The salient difference between the two is that the convection oven uses the principle of convection more effectively. It has a built-in electric fan that increases the circulation of hot air molecules within the oven. This increase in air circulation is a boon when you roast meat (including birds) or bake breads and pastry. Since the oven temperature is uniform throughout, the food's surface will be more evenly cooked and browned (though the outside of a meat does not develop as appealing a crusty texture). Another advantage of the convection oven is that the required cooking temperature is lower, and therefore meat shrinks less. Furthermore, most meats do not require basting, and so the cleanup chore is less bothersome because there is less splatter. Energy cost savings are often realized because of the unit's efficiency and generally more compact size.

**How does a microwave oven work?**

A tube within the oven, called a magnetron, emits high-frequency electromagnetic waves (similar to radio waves). This radiation is scattered in the oven by a fanlike reflector (called the "stirrer"). When the waves penetrate the food, they reverse the polarity of the water and other liquid molecules, billions of times a second. This oscillation causes the molecules to vibrate and bounce against each other. These collisions create friction and, as a by-product, the heat that cooks or warms the food.

The plate holding the food is not heated by the microwaves because it is solid and its molecules do not become agitated.

When a plate does become warm in a microwave oven, it is due to the heat that is transferred to it from the cooking food.

**What are the pros and cons of microwave cooking?**

Speed is the name of the game in microwave cookery. Most foods cook in one-quarter to one-half the time that it takes with the other basic cooking methods, because the food cooks from within. Microwave cooking costs less because it requires about one-quarter the power that a traditional oven uses. A microwave oven also causes less splatter and hardly heats up the kitchen.

Baked goods rise higher in a microwave oven. On the other hand, bread, rolls, and other baked goods do not brown as well as they do in a traditional oven. Neither does meat, which means the food won't develop the desirably flavorful crust caused by the Maillard (browning) reaction. Some microwave producers deal with this problem by adding convection fans and electrical heating elements. These devices do work but their results pale compared to those of dedicated conventional and convection ovens.

Cooks face other problems. Microwave cooking tends to give meats a dry, mushy texture. It's also a more iffy process when trying to predict the proper cooking time, especially for a large cut of meat. Consequently, microwaved food is more likely to come out of the oven undercooked or overcooked.

Frozen foods can take a long time to cook in a microwave oven. Since the water molecules are frozen solid, the electromagnetic waves can't agitate them. Until enough water molecules liquefy and then become hot enough to thaw the adjacent frozen water molecules, the cooking process proceeds at glacial speed.

Another inconvenience is that of not being able to use your metal pots and pans or aluminum foil containers in a microwave oven. Oven manufacturers warn against the use of metal because of the possibility of arcing — an electric spark jumping between the metal pot and microwave oven wall when the pot is placed too close to the wall. Arcing can damage the unit's magnetron tube. Although the chance of arcing has been reduced in some new oven models, there is still a strong reason not to cook in metal: It reflects electromagnetic waves and therefore causes uneven cooking.

Finally, there is always a chance of radiation leakage, though the possibility of its occurring with today's equipment is remote.

## Why are budget-priced food processors seldom a good value?

If you are planning to use your food processor only for tasks that require relatively little power (such as slicing a cucumber or other soft vegetable), then a budget-priced model may serve your purposes. Chances are, however, that you also want your machine to perform more arduous chores, like chopping meat, in which case a budget model is no bargain.

A key reason that a budget-priced food processor is ill-suited for chopping foods like meat is that it does not have enough horsepower. If the motor is not powerful enough, it is apt to balk momentarily, or even permanently, when you process a heavy load.

Another reason for poor performance is that nearly all budget-priced models are belt-driven. (In other words, the motor turns a belt, which turns the cutting-blade unit.) The belts in inexpensive models tend to slip when you process a heavy load. This problem doesn't occur when the motor's drive shaft directly rotates the cutting blade, as is the case with most of the better processors.

Motor-balking and belt slippage are major mechanical deficiencies because they make it impossible to chop a batch of food uniformly. What inevitably happens in the case of beef, for example, is that when some of the meat is properly chopped, the rest of the meat is too lumpy (underchopped) or too pasty (overchopped). As good cooks know, a pasty grind guarantees a heavy and compact, and therefore inferior, meat loaf or hamburger patty.

### Is a pressure cooker worthwhile?

For someone who lives at a high altitude or who cans and preserves foods, a pressure cooker is an asset. In Denver, for instance, water boils at 203°F instead of 212°F, as it would, say, in San Diego. Consequently, any given ingredient takes longer to cook in Denver. The predicament of having a relatively low boiling point for water can be solved with a pressure cooker, since it allows water to reach a temperature of up to about 250°F.

Water inside a pressure cooker boils at a high temperature because the atmospheric pressure within the pot is increased. The ingredients also cook faster because the steam — most of which does not escape the pot — is a better heat conductor than air. And thanks to the increased pressure within the pot, that steam more aggressively penetrates the food.

The higher temperatures of pressure-cooking also benefit the home canner because the heat can more effectively destroy pathogenic microorganisms that contaminate the food. This capacity is particularly critical when canning low-acid ingredients.

For other cooks, a pressure cooker can shorten the cooking process and thereby reduce fuel expenditure, compared with the nonpressurized boiling method. From a gourmet's viewpoint, however, the texture of pressure-cooked foods like meat still resembles that of ordinary boiled food.

### Why should barbecue coals not be flaming when I cook the meat?

If flames are still erupting from the coals when the food is placed on the grate, the chances of flare-ups are greatly increased. Flare-ups should be avoided because they char the food, ruining its flavor, taste, texture, and color. They also generate dirty and noxious smoke. Therefore, before beginning the cooking process, allow sufficient time (thirty to fifty minutes) for the flames to cease completely and the briquettes to acquire a grayish coating.

There are other precautions for eliminating, or at least minimizing, flare-ups. Trim off excess fat because it flares up when it melts and drops into the hot coals; but don't overdo this — fat contributes flavor and helps baste the meat as it cooks. And do not cook with a higher heat than is necessary.

## How can I increase barbecuing temperature?

The most common and obvious way of increasing the heat that reaches the food is to place the food closer to the coals. Alternatively, you can increase the heat output by using extra briquettes or by packing them more closely together. Briquettes will also burn better if they are dry and of quality manufacture (the quality brands use a denser, more combustible material).

You can also augment the heat by increasing the speed of the fresh air flow to the briquettes (open the air vents under the barbecue pan, if your unit has them). However, be aware that air flowing over the food will both cool the food and carry away some of the heat rising from the coals. (Try to shield the food from any passing breeze.)

Another way to raise the temperature is to minimize the heat that escapes through the walls of the barbecuing pan. Buy a unit that has a pan made of thick-gauge metal or insulate a thin-gauge pan by lining it with a layer of ashes or aluminum foil. The aluminum foil also reflects heat upward to the food.

The final factor is outdoor temperature. As the mercury drops, less heat reaches the food because more of the generated heat is absorbed by the cold outdoor air.

## Why is a small instant thermometer better than a traditional large one for checking the temperature of a roasting meat?

An instant thermometer is not only more accurate, it also makes a thinner hole in the meat. Fewer of the meat's internal juices, therefore, can exit through that aperture. Although it is true that you make many holes when using an instant thermometer, as opposed to only one with the larger instrument, these holes are so small that they quickly seal themselves.

Because you leave the larger type of thermometer in the meat as it roasts, heat is quickly conducted to the flesh surrounding the metal spike. This rapid heat transfer cooks the meat surrounding the spike faster than it should, and, consequently, uneven roasting occurs. A small instant thermometer does not pose this problem because it is not left in the roasting meat (if it were, the mechanism would be ruined).

An oft-overlooked advantage of a small instant thermometer is that it allows you to test-probe the meat in more than one place.

### What's wrong with peeping over the rim of a measuring cup to read its units of measure?

When you look over the rim, you'll be reading the units of measure at an angle through the cup's thick glass. You'll get a false reading because refraction will make the units of measure appear farther up than they actually are. To eliminate the refraction problem, you must read the units marked on the near side of the cup and keep your eyes level with the ingredient's surface.

### Should I operate my kitchen appliances during a brownout?

A 5 percent or so voltage reduction may cause your television or computer tube to flicker, but it shouldn't cause a serious problem for your kitchen equipment. Likely, your worst setback will involve heating appliances like toaster ovens. They will generate a little less heat than normally.

A 10 percent or greater reduction, however, could cause some motor-driven appliances like an electric mixer to struggle and overheat. Since this harms the equipment, and you probably have no way to measure accurately the drop in voltage, caution is in order. When you see the lights dim, don't use your motor-driven kitchen appliances unless absolutely necessary.

If you cook and live in a brownout prone city, keep in mind that the peak brownout period is typically just after five P.M., when most offices let out en masse. The electricity-hungry elevators tax the local utility's capacity.

**Why shouldn't I use a brown paper grocery bag for cooking purposes?**

Some years ago, it became popular among some ecology-minded cooks to use brown paper bags for various cooking roles, such as lining a cake pan or cooking food inside the bag (*en papillote*). A large share of brown grocery bags are now made from recycled paper. If you heat food in or with these bags, the inedible chemicals that were mixed with the material during the recycling process will infuse the food and subsequently your body.

# 2

## C·O·O·K·I·N·G
## M·E·T·H·O·D·S

**E**xactly **what role does heat play in cooking?**

Heat performs more functions than is commonly recognized. It can:

- enhance, intensify, or alter a food's flavor, aroma, and color.
- improve a food's psychological appeal by increasing its temperature.
- make food more chewable or digestible by softening it.
- firm a food by coagulating its protein or by playing a key role in an emulsifying, gelatinizing, or leavening process (more about these subjects later).
- change a food — butter, for example — from a solid to a liquid.
- reduce a food's volume by vaporizing some of its moisture content.
- preserve a food by eliminating almost all of its water content.
- destroy pathogenic microorganisms.

**What generates heat?**

Nuclear energy is by far the most potent generator of heat, though it obviously cannot be directly applied in your kitchen — at least, not at present.

The two heat-generating modes commonly used in the home are combustion and electrical resistance. Combustion — the most popular of the two — occurs when rapid oxidation of a fuel like gas or wood produces heat and light. Electric ranges and toasters warm up and glow as electricity flows through and encounters the resistance of their metal coils, creating heat and light.

**Why does a higher temperature cook foods faster than a lower one?**

Heat cooking is chemistry. When you increase the heat, you increase the velocity of the molecules in a food. The greater the speed, the more the molecules collide. These microscopic crashes can alter the molecular structures, creating new molecules and changing the color, flavor, and texture of the cooking food. Chemical reactivity more or less doubles for each rise in temperature of 20°F within the normal cooking range.

**How is heat transferred to food?**

Radiation, convection, and conduction are the three principal means of transferring heat from a hotter object to a colder one. Most cooking simultaneously involves two, or all three, of these processes.

Radiant heat is transferred in the form of electromagnetic waves or particles from a hot object, such as the heating element of your broiler or toaster, to food. This transmission does not need the help of a medium like water or air. The food is heated when it absorbs this radiant energy, which travels at the speed of light (186,000 miles per second).

The sun, too, emits radiant energy. On a subzero January day, it is possible to heat a glass hothouse filled with growing spring vegetables by means of solar rays that have journeyed through a frigid void of 93 million miles.

You are cooking by convection when circulating molecules of a gas or liquid transfer their heat directly to your food. These gas or liquid molecules are set in motion by a heat source, which is usually at the bottom of your oven or pot. As the assemblage of molecules closest to the heat source is warmed, it becomes lighter and rises above the heavier, cooler batch of molecules which is simultaneously sinking. The cooler molecules, upon reaching the oven or pot's bottom, are heated and begin their journey upward, displacing the top molecules, which have cooled slightly. This ongoing process creates air or water currents, an essential for convection cooking.

Food cooked in an oven or pot of liquid, incidentally, is also heated by radiation (emitted by the heated interior surfaces of the oven or pot) and by conduction.

When hot molecules transmit some of their heat to cool ones in direct contact with them, the type of heat transference called conduction occurs. Pan-frying a fish fillet exemplifies this principle. The heat of the flame is transferred — on a molecule-to-molecule basis — first through the pan, then through the thin oil layer, and finally through the fish. Another illustration is a metal spoon in a hot cup of coffee. At first the utensil's handle is cool. It then grows warm, and eventually hot.

The speed of conduction is relatively slow, and it varies by substance. Metal conducts heat more quickly than does wood, which helps explain why wood is a popular material for pot handles and cooking spoons.

Boiling (or deep-frying) is chiefly a process of convection, but since heat is simultaneously transferred directly from one water (or fat) molecule to another, conduction is part of the process, too.

Conduction heating takes place inside the food, as well. When cooking a potato or other solid food in a pot of boiling water or hot fat, or in a hot oven, none of the circulating water, fat, or air molecules touch the subsurface molecules of the food. So if the potato's interior is to be cooked, conduction heating must take over where convection heating leaves off. In other words, the surface molecules of the potato will pass along their acquired heat to the next layer of molecules in the potato, and so on. Inserting a metal spike or nail into a potato shortens the baking time by increasing the rate at which heat travels by conduction to the potato's center, because metal, of course, is a better heat conductor than are plant cells.

**What are the basic cooking methods?**

All cooking methods fall within one of two categories: moist and dry.

Moist-heat cooking methods include:
• Boiling/Simmering/Poaching/Stewing
• Steaming
• Pressure-cooking
• Braising

Dry-heat cooking methods include:
• Roasting/Baking
• Broiling/Toasting
• Microwave cooking
• Pan-frying
• Deep-frying

Discussions of each of the above cooking methods appear in Q&A's in this or other chapters (consult the index).

**What determines whether a food should be cooked with moist or dry heat?**

As a rule of thumb, use one of the moist cooking methods if the food is not naturally tender. Thus, meat that contains a large quantity of connective tissue, and plant food with ample or tough fiber call for moist heat. Borderline meat cases can be tipped in favor of dry-heat cooking if the meat is well marbled or its exterior is protected with fat by basting, barding (wrapping solid fat around the meat), or larding (inserting solid fat into the meat).

Of course, recipe specifications, dietary restrictions, time limitations, and personal tastes and whims may overrule these guidelines, as may the lack of cooking equipment. If your oven is occupied by a baking blueberry pie, for instance, you may be forced to braise on top of your stove a U.S. Prime Grade cut that is tender enough to roast.

## Is there a difference in temperature between lightly and vigorously boiling water?

Once water reaches the boiling point, its temperature remains constant (within 1°F), whether it is lightly or rapidly boiling. That temperature at sea level under normal atmospheric pressure is 212°F (100°C). However, a food usually cooks a trifle faster in vigorously boiling water because the faster the heat-carrying water molecules move about the pan, the more heat is transferred to the food by convection.

For most foods, the ever so slight saving in cooking time hardly compensates for loss of fuel, nutrients, flavor, and texture. (Texture suffers because the tempestuous boiling water violently knocks the food pieces against each other and the pan.)

This water turbulence is not detrimental for all foods. Take pasta — the stormy liquid helps keep the individual units from fusing.

## Does salt raise the boiling point of water?

Yes. Salt, sugar, and practically any other substance elevates the boiling point and therefore shortens cooking time. The difference in temperature between unsalted and salted water (one teaspoon of salt per quart of water) is about 1° to 2°F, a difference that can be critical in cooking situations demanding exactness.

## Does hard water boil at a higher temperature?

"Hard water" defines water with a high level of dissolved mineral salts. Therefore the answer is yes. The difference in the boiling point between typical supplies of hard and soft water is about a degree or two.

## Does alcohol lower the boiling point of water?

Alcohol has a lower boiling point than water (about 175°F as compared with 212°F). If you dilute water with alcohol, the mixture will have a lower boiling point up until the alcohol completely evaporates. Should you decide to alter an existing recipe by substituting a fair portion of wine for some of the water, remember to extend the cooking time by 5 to 10 percent, depending on the alcohol strength of the wine and the heaviness of your touch.

The preparation for cheese fondue is a good illustration of the principle that alcohol lowers the boiling temperature of a liquid. The originators of this popular dish added wine and kirsch for more than just their flavors. The alcohol lowers the boiling point of the melting cheese, preventing it from curdling.

## Why does the boiling point of water decrease with altitude?

The higher the altitude, the lower the atmospheric pressure. The less atmospheric pressure that bears down on the surface of the liquid, the easier it is for water molecules to escape into the air. Thus, the water comes to its full rapid boil at a lower temperature in the mile-high city of Denver than it can in coastal Miami.

For each thousand feet above sea level, the boiling point of water drops almost 2°F (or approximately 1°C).

| Altitude (in Feet) | Boiling Point of Water (Under Normal Atmospheric Conditions) | |
| --- | --- | --- |
| | FAHRENHEIT | CELSIUS |
| 0 | 212° | 100° |
| 1000 | 210° | 99° |
| 2000 | 208° | 98° |
| 3000 | 207° | 97° |
| 4000 | 205° | 96° |
| 5000 | 203° | 95° |
| 10,000 | 194° | 90° |

In our previously cited example, the Denver cook has to boil the food longer because the temperature of the boiling water is only about 203°F, even though its bubbling appearance resembles that of water boiling in Miami at 212°F.

Simmering is a different matter. Here, the Denver cook has a speed advantage, albeit ever so slight. Assume that both cooks simmer at the identical temperature, say 195°F. The water in the Denver pot will be circulating more vigorously and, therefore, the effect of convection will be more pronounced. Of course, if both cooks use vague visual clues such as "when bubbles first break the surface," as opposed to a thermometer reading, to ascertain the simmer point, then the Denver denizen would have to cook the food longer.

### Does weather affect the boiling temperature of water?

As one of our local television weather forecasters keeps reminding his viewers, "Storms and low atmospheric pressure go hand in hand, while clear, sunny days take place during high atmospheric pressure conditions."

If he is right — and he is — then the boiling point of water is a degree or two lower on stormy, as opposed to fair, weather days. Consequently, boiled food will take longer to cook on a stormy day.

**Will a given volume of water boil at a higher temperature in a tall, narrow pot than in a short, wide one?**

Yes. Since the tall, narrow pot has a greater depth, its bottom-lying water is under greater pressure from the water above it than is the water at the bottom of the short, wide pot. And as previously stated, the greater the pressure, the higher the boiling point. The difference is approximately 1°F.

**What causes a lid to stick to a pot?**

Remember when your carrots were done before the rest of your meal, so you turned off the heat, only to discover that in ten minutes you could not remove the lid from the pot? Charles's Law and Boyle's Law, taken together, explain that kitchen phenomenon. In simplified terms, the combined law would read:

> At a constant volume, the pressure of a gas is proportional to its temperature.

Of course, if you cover a partially filled pot of liquid and bring it to the boiling point, the air space inside the pot experiences little increase in pressure because the built-up pressure created by the heat lifts the lid, allowing most of the expanding gas to escape.

However, once you turn off the heat source, the pressure inside the pot will gradually decrease — along with the temperature. If the lid and pot are precision-matched (as a quality brand should be), the outside air has less than an open invitation to squirm inside. Water molecules, forming an airtight seal, assist in keeping outside air molecules from entering. Within five minutes or so, the difference between the two pressures becomes so pronounced that it creates a "suction," making the separation of the lid and pot a herculean task.

Some novice cooks try to pry open the lid with a tool, a tactic that usually damages the pot, lid, and ego. Other neophytes — under the impression that if the food inside cools, the lid will promptly loosen — place the pot in cold water. This last method runs contrary to the laws of Boyle and Charles, and therefore is exactly the opposite of what the cook should do.

When you encounter an unyielding lid, place the pot over moderate heat for a short time. The temperature of the air inside the pot will soon rise, and in accordance with the laws of physics, so will its pressure. When the pressure nearly equals that of the outside, the lid and pot easily part.

### At what temperature does water simmer?

Few cooking terms have been defined more arbitrarily or vaguely than "simmer." Yet precision in the use of the word "simmer" is critical because there is a real difference in required cooking time when you raise or lower the temperature of the water by just a few degrees.

In an attempt to fashion a universal benchmark, we scrutinized a number of respected cookbooks to gather a consensus. The normal simmer at sea level, at normal atmospheric pressure, is about 195°F; a high simmer, about 210°F; a low simmer, about 180°F. Unless your cookbook advises you otherwise, use these guidelines.

Frequently used phrases such as "when the first bubbles appear" do not accurately describe the moment when water reaches 195°F (or 210°F, or 180°F) because visual data at a specific temperature vary according to a pot's size, depth, width, material, condition, cleanliness (or greasiness), and water volume. When you add other variables, such as personal interpretation, altitude, or water hardness, the lack of reliability of sight measurement magnifies.

### If steam is a degree or two hotter than boiling water, why does a food take longer to steam than to boil?

Even more important than a cooking medium's temperature is its ability to transfer heat to the food. Steam is a poorer heat conductor than water and, as a result, gives up its heat to the cooking food less readily.

## Is braising best done in the oven or on top of the stove?

Braising consists of browning a food in hot fat, then simmering it in scant liquid in a covered pan. In most circumstances, the oven is preferable for this operation. First of all, top-of-the-stove braising has an inherent drawback. If the liquid in the pot boils, the food's texture and flavor will likely suffer. If the fluid medium is kept below the boiling point, then the part of the food resting in the liquid will cook significantly faster than the portion projecting above it. This uneven cooking occurs because insufficient steam is generated in the pot.

In contrast, the heat of an oven more uniformly engulfs the pot. And because the need to generate steam is not as crucial, you can cook the food at a slower pace and lower temperature, two conditions that are essential for braising a tough piece of meat. Oven braising has yet another advantage: It requires less pot watching.

## Why is it undesirable to roast meat in a covered pan?

If you want meat that is roasted rather than braised, there is every reason not to use a cover. Uncovered, the meat is cooked by dry heat. Covered, the meat is cooked, in part, by moist heat generated by the steam trapped inside the covered pan. The meat's surface will tend to be mushy rather than crisp — and pale brown, rather than the deep brown normally associated with a well-roasted piece of meat.

For cooks who cover their roasting meat to prevent it from drying out, there is a practical alternative: Baste the meat often (every fifteen to thirty minutes) and do not overcook it. If however, you insist on roasting with a cover and are following a standard cooking time/temperature table, you have to shorten the recommended time or, better yet, lower the temperature setting by about 25°F.

## Why should roasting meat be set on a rack instead of on the pan's flat surface?

As a meat roasts, it releases juices that collect at the bottom of the roasting pan. If the meat rests on the pan, its underside will cook in the liquid and therefore will be cooked by moist, rather than dry, heat. The result is unsatisfactory: The meat's underside overcooks before the rest is done because moist heat cooks faster than dry, and conduction from the pan's surface intensifies the problem. Another disappointing outcome of the non-rack roasting method is a mushy, rather than crispy, bottom.

## Why is the surface temperature of a roasting meat lower than the temperature of the oven?

One of the most obvious explanations is that the air molecules are hotter because they come in direct contact with the oven's heat source or scorching interior walls. Another significant reason is that the meat's colder interior absorbs heat from, and cools, the warmer surface. As the meat's internal temperature increases during cooking, this cooling influence diminishes in importance.

A third major factor, evaporation, is less apparent. As the meat cooks by dry heat, some of its internal juices flow to the surface and evaporate. This ongoing process produces a cooling effect. (When water evaporates, it cools the surrounding area because the change from liquid to gas requires heat calories.) Thus, for this reason — and because animal flesh is a less efficient conductor than metal — you can briefly touch a roasting meat but not the pan in which it sits.

## Why can I insert my unprotected (save for a pot holder) hand safely into a 350°F oven for a short time to retrieve a pan?

Your hand is partially cooled for a brief period by the moisture that evaporates from your skin. If you immerse that same hand in boiling water (a mere 212°F by comparison) for even a briefer time, you will badly scald yourself, because the cooling effect is lost in the water and because water is a better heat conductor than air.

By the same token, if you place a pot of water in your 350°F oven and let it boil, the steam rising from the pot will be a better heat conductor than the comparatively dry air that normally fills your oven. In addition, the steam will saturate the oven's air, and few of the water molecules on your skin will evaporate into the air quickly enough to cool your hand and give it brief respite from the hot air and scalding steam. Consequently, you could burn yourself if you inserted your unprotected hand into such an oven.

## What is the difference between oven-roasting and baking?

From the standpoint of method, there is no difference, since both techniques cook foods by dry heat in an oven. To a lexicographer or recipe writer, distinctions exist. If the food you are cooking is a whole bird or a piece of meat (other than a ham or a minced-meat preparation) that will later be divided for serving, then — in virtually all cases — you are roasting. With all other foods — hams; fish; single-serving portions of meat; pâtés, including meat loaf (a pâté is nothing more than a glorified meat loaf); casseroles; baked goods, including breads and cakes; fruits and vegetables — you are, with rare exception, baking.

So if friends are having you over for a dinner of "baked leg of lamb followed by a roasted cake," it may be that they lack verbal, rather than cooking, skills.

## Can I broil at less than 550°F?

Yes, but only if you have an electric broiler that has variable temperature settings or an atypical gas broiler that has a variable flame. These broilers maintain a specific temperature by varying their heat intensity and are therefore versatile enough to properly broil some dishes — such as whole fish — that are better prepared in the 400° to 500°F zone.

Unfortunately, most gas broilers offer only one temperature

setting — 550°F. This limitation occurs because such units use the same heat intensity for, say, 350° or 550°F. An automatic device periodically turns the heat source on and off to maintain temperatures below 550°F. The setting must read BROIL in order to assure a constant flame.

### How far should I place a food from the broiler's heat source?

Most foods are cooked between three and six inches from the broiler (measured from the flame or electric coil to the highest point of the food).

Generally, the thinner the food, the closer to the broiler you can place it. If you place a food too close to the broiler in relation to its thickness, it will be dry or overcooked on the outside before the inside is properly cooked. If you place a food at too great a distance from the broiler, the exterior will not develop the sought-after deep color and somewhat crusty texture by the time the center of the food is cooked.

Your preference about degree of doneness should also play a part in determining the distance between the broiler and food. The rarer the meat is to be cooked, the closer you can place it to the heat source, because cooking time will not be long enough to overcook the food's exterior.

### If heat travels upward, how can an overhead broiling element cook foods with such intense heat?

Although some conduction and convection cooking occurs within the broiler, it's mainly radiant heat that cooks the food. This heat emanates from the broiling element and, to a lesser extent, from the metal walls, which have absorbed some of the heat. Whereas convection heat by nature rises, radiant heat travels in any direction. It moves in a straight line until it is absorbed by an object or is reflected. In the latter case, it begins another linear journey, this time prescribed by the laws of angular reflection.

**Why do some cooks leave the broiler door ajar when broiling meat?**

They want to improve the flavor and crusty texture of the meat by maximizing the broiling and minimizing the roasting aspect of cooking. (Pure broiling incorporates only radiant thermal heat, while roasting encompasses radiant, conduction, and convection thermal heats.) With the door ajar, the pan and air inside the broiling unit don't become as hot as they normally would. This cooler temperature reduces the effects of conduction and convection cooking in the broiler. It does not reduce the intensity of the radiant heat emanating directly from the broiling element. Professional cooks use this open-door technique more than do home cooks because they tend to have better exhaust systems.

# 3

## M·E·A·T·S

W hy is a "bloody red steak" not really bloody?

This colorful and popular expression is a misnomer. Blood contributes little to the redness of a steak because most of that liquid is bled out of the meat at the slaughterhouse or butcher shop. The confusion is easy to understand because myoglobin, the principal pigment in raw meat, shares certain characteristics, including color, with hemoglobin (the red pigment in blood). However, myoglobin is distinct from blood; it is found in muscles, not arteries.

### What determines a meat's myoglobin content and, therefore, its color?

The quantity of myoglobin in flesh varies by animal species — beef has more of it than pork, for example. Myoglobin content and depth of color can also differ noticeably according to anatomical location — a turkey's drumstick, for instance, is much darker than its breast meat. The color of the meat you serve also depends on how it was stored and cooked, as well as on the animal's age and feed.

**What is "anemic veal"?**

A strictly milk-fed calf has a pink-tinged creamy white flesh because milk almost totally lacks certain minerals (particularly iron) that are necessary building blocks for the body's production of the red myoglobin.

As soon as the calf starts to eat foods like grass and grain, which contain iron, its flesh tone starts to redden. By the time the weaned calf is a few months old, the flesh is pinkish red. Before it reaches the half-year mark, the color is rosy red. At baby beefhood (between six and twelve months old), the meat is cherry-red. At the animal's maturity, the color is dark red and continues to deepen with time and exercise.

In the past two decades, the premium veal industry has increased profits by putting into large-scale operation a technique that prevents a weaned calf from developing myoglobin. The chosen animal, which spends the last part of its short life in indoor stalls with limited opportunity for exercise, is fed a special formula of water infused with dry milk solids, fats, and other nutrients. Like cow's milk, the liquid is virtually iron-free; unlike cow's milk, it is relatively cheap and contains none of the butter fat that helps give veal its sublime flavor. Leaving nothing to chance, the calf engineers keep metal objects like pails and pipes well beyond reach of a calf's licking tongue, lest the wrong minerals enter the digestive system. In effect, premium veal brands are typically products of animals raised by man to be anemic. Thus, the expression "anemic veal."

Another drawback of veal from a typical "special formula" calf is an inappropriately coarse texture. A calf's flesh at birth is fine-grained to a fault, but as the animal ages, it coarsens. When the calf is three months old, the texture of the muscle grain is ideal — neither too fine nor too coarse. At four months, the texture becomes too coarse to merit epicurean raves. Moreover, the sought-after veal flavor is better from a three-month-old calf than from a four-month-old. Normal milk-fed calves are traditionally slaughtered at the age of about three months; "special formula" calves at about four months. The additional month — a 33 percent increase in lifespan — does make a profound difference. Why do the special-formula calf raisers wait the extra month? More growing time means more meat per animal and therefore larger profits.

### Why is a fresh cut of raw meat red on its surface and brown inside?

Contrary to what some shoppers suspect, the outside of the meat is not redder than the inside because the butcher treated it with a chemical spray. Mother Nature, not the meat monger, is responsible. When an animal dies, its heart stops pumping oxygen-rich blood to the various muscles. Denied that oxygen, the myoglobin protein in the muscles loses its bright red pigmentation and acquires a purplish, and then brownish, tinge.

Another color change starts to occur when the meat is butchered into retail cuts and wrapped in porous plastic film, giving the meat's newly exposed surfaces access to the oxygen in the air. As the meat sits in the refrigerated display case, oxidation finishes turning the myoglobin on the meat's exposed surfaces bright red. (Butchers refer to this color development as "bloom.") So, though the outside of the meat is the shade of red that consumers are taught to look for, the inside remains brown simply because the unexposed myoglobin lacks enough oxygen. If you cut open the meat and give it time to aerate, the new surfaces should become bright red.

### If oxygen intensifies the red color of a raw meat's exposed surfaces, then why does the meat eventually turn brown?

Curiously, too much oxygen has the same effect on meat as too little oxygen — both conditions can give it a brownish tinge. When myoglobin overoxidizes, it is transformed into a brown pigment called metmyoglobin. Therefore, a raw, red meat will turn brown if it is exposed long enough to the air. This color change can occur even if meat is wrapped in plastic or paper, because both allow air to pass through. However, refrigeration does slow the browning process.

**Why does the color of cooked beef indicate its degree of doneness?**

The red pigment in rare meat, myoglobin, undergoes chemical changes as its temperature rises. When the meat's degree of doneness is rare (an internal temperature of approximately 135°F), the myoglobin in the interior still retains most of its red color. When the meat is medium-rare (approximately 145°F), the myoglobin is pink. At medium (approximately 155°F), just a trace of the pink remains. By the time the steak is well done (160°F), all myoglobin in the meat has turned drab brown. (Note: These figures are after-the-rest, not remove-from-the-oven temperatures. This topic is discussed later in this chapter.)

**Why doesn't ham become grayish brown when cooked?**

A cured ham contains nitrite salt, which reacts chemically with myoglobin to create nitrosomyoglobin, a substance that stays rosy red even when exposed to high temperatures.

**Why does the inside of shish kebab cubes lose its red hue so quickly?**

The acid in the marinade (we are assuming that you marinate your shish kebab meat) lowers the temperature level at which myoglobin turns from red to drab brown.

**What makes one cut of raw meat naturally tougher than another?**

Connective tissue is the key determinant. The greater the proportion or the firmness of connective tissue in raw meat, the tougher that flesh will likely be.

## What is connective tissue?

A steer's muscle is approximately 75 percent water, 20 percent protein, and, collectively, 5 percent fat, carbohydrates, and minerals. If you allow us to simplify a complicated biological structure, such a muscle consists mainly of bundles of microscopic muscle fibers bound together — much like a coaxial cable — inside tiny, semitransparent tubes of connective tissue. Without this tissue, the meat would be a flaccid mass.

The quantity and firmness of connective tissue in a raw piece of meat are determined by three factors: the anatomical location of the cut of meat, the animal's activity, and the animal's age.

## How does the anatomical location relate to toughness?

An animal uses certain muscles more than others. Muscles in the legs, belly, and neck of a four-legged animal do more work than those located along the mid-backbone.

The accompanying illustration shows the nine primal cuts of beef. The least exercised, and therefore the most tender, primal is the short loin, followed by the sirloin and rib primal cuts. Degree of toughness even varies within each primal: As a general rule, the closer the meat is to a hoof or horn, the tougher it will be. Therefore, the portion of the chuck (or round) that lies closest to the mid-carcass will be more tender than the part situated near the head (or rear leg) of the animal.

It follows that not all cuts of beef marketed under the same primal designation possess equal tenderness. The sirloin primal is a good case in point. Certainly, the sirloin steak that is cut from next to the short loin is much more tender than one taken from the area bordering the round. In order of their proximity to the short loin, the three basic steaks of the sirloin primal are the pin bone, flat bone, and wedge bone. They derive their names from the cross section configuration of the one bone they all share: the hip bone.

Unfortunately, most stores market sirloin steaks simply as "sirloin steaks" rather than subclassifying them. Should your

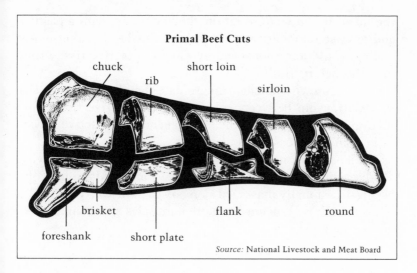

**Primal Beef Cuts**

chuck · rib · short loin · sirloin · brisket · flank · round · foreshank · short plate

*Source:* National Livestock and Meat Board

butcher not give you complete information, look for the shape of the hip bone. If the hip bone cross section is circular and on one side is noticeably bigger in diameter than the other, you are holding a pin bone sirloin steak. If the cross section is flat like a bar, the steak is a flat bone sirloin. If the cross section is triangular, you have a wedge bone steak.

Sometimes the difference between the pin bone and wedge bone isn't obvious. When confronted with that situation, remember that the steak will be a pin bone sirloin if the overall piece of meat has a configuration slightly resembling that of a porterhouse steak, the cut that lies immediately next to the pin bone sirloin. The difference between these two cuts is the thickness of a sharp butcher knife.

### How does an animal's activity affect meat's toughness?

The more an animal exercises, the greater the connective tissue development, and the more connective tissue, the tougher the meat. If you were to let one bovine freely roam a pasture and to raise its identical twin in a confined space, the roving sibling would have considerably more connective tissue running through its flesh.

One reason why ranchers emasculate their bovine charges is the relationship between exercise and connective tissue formation. A steer (desexed male) is generally less active physically than his uncastrated brethren.

The Japanese minimize connective tissue development with soothing hands. A steer that is raised for their famous Kobe beef is occasionally massaged along its back to keep the animal relaxed, because tension would flex muscles and therefore exercise them.

### What relation is there between an animal's age and the toughness of its meat?

The longer the animal lives, the more opportunity it has to exercise its muscles — and connective muscle development is usually cumulative. The aging process itself also helps firm connective tissue, making the meat tougher.

### What is the cutoff age for veal?

The United States Department of Agriculture does not have any standard based on a specific bovine age. Instead, its grading inspectors define a meat as veal, "calf," or beef, using criteria — such as deepness of flesh color and hardness of bone — that reflect an animal's age. Based on the agency's standards, veal becomes "calf" meat when the animal is about three months old and beef on about its ninth birthmonth. The National Livestock and Meat Board agrees that the animal's three-month birthday is generally when the meat should no longer be considered veal. Many butchers ignore, or are ignorant of this authoritative consensus because they sell calf meat ("baby beef") as veal and, even worse, charge the higher veal prices for it.

**If meat from an older animal is tougher, why is it usually the most desirable selection for braising and stewing?**

Slow moist-heat cooking methods like braising and stewing tenderize even a somewhat tough meat by breaking down most of its connective tissue. Thus, the original toughness of the raw meat is not a major factor when using such methods. The difference in the flavor of meat from an older animal, however, can be decisive. Since it is generally more flavorful, it should normally be your first choice for moist cooking.

**How can I counteract the natural toughness of connective tissue?**

One approach is to use the most tender primals of U.S. Prime Grade meat. Other methods include cooking meat that has been aged, marinated, sprinkled with a commercial meat tenderizer, ground, scored, or pounded. Each of these techniques, as well as the procedures of carving across the grain and slow cooking with moist heat, will be discussed in subsequent Q&A's.

**How does slow moist-heat cooking soften connective tissue?**

The prime component of connective tissue is the protein collagen. That name derives from the Greek words *kolla* (glue) and *gen* (a word appendix signifying "production of"). In everyday English, collagen produces glue or, in this case, gelatin.

In a hot, moist environment (boiling water, for instance), collagen can be partially transformed, over a period of time, into gelatin. When this metamorphosis occurs, connective tissue softens and dissolves, making the meat more tender.

The second major constituent of connective tissue is elastin. Unlike the more predominant whitish collagen, the yellow-tinged elastin protein does not soften — or at least, not perceptibly — in the dual presence of heat and water.

**If slow, moist heat softens the collagen in connective tissue, why does it sometimes leave meat tough?**

Heat and prolonged cooking have opposite effects on the two main solid components of meat: Both soften connective tissue, but at the same time they harden muscle fibers. Fortunately for the cook, the tenderizing of the connective tissue more than compensates for the hardening of the muscle fibers — that is, if the meat is cooked properly.

Granted, you can moist-cook meat slowly for several hours with a liquid at 140°F without unduly toughening the muscle fibers. However, these time-temperature coordinates scarcely soften the connective tissue. To accomplish that mission with a 140°F temperature, you need to cook the meat for at least six hours, a period that will likely toughen the muscle fibers and create a bacterial-engendered health risk.

At the other extreme, you can moist-cook meat at, say, 212°F. Within an hour or so at that comparatively high temperature, much of the collagen will have gelatinized. Unfortunately, much of the muscle fiber will have coagulated too much and toughened.

Our experiments indicate that in most situations, two or three hours of slow moist cooking at 180°F strikes a balance between softening the connective tissue and not hardening muscle fiber or risking contamination. As a bonus, less shrinkage occurs at our recommended temperature than if you were to cook the meat at a higher temperature.

**Does aging the meat make a real difference?**

If meat is stored for up to several weeks in an ideal aging environment, it undergoes an enzymatic change that softens some of the connective tissue. The optimal temperature is between 34° and 38°F; freezing would inhibit the chemical process, and too high a heat would foster excessive bacterial and mold development. U.S. Prime Grade, with its thick layer of fat that helps prevent the growth of destructive microorganisms, is the most suitable meat for aging.

The process, by the way, does more than tenderize. Aging also deepens the red flesh color and — mainly because of the 10 to 20 percent shrinkage that occurs — intensifies the meat's flavor. (Of course, all this is reflected in the price.) Finally, the longer you age meat, the quicker it will cook to any desired degree of doneness.

Not to be confused with the traditional aging method is the "Cryovac" process, which involves tightly wrapping and hermetically sealing the meat in polyethylene bags. Though this modern technique hardly tenderizes the meat, in comparison to the old-fashioned method, the mass-market meat industry favors it because less shrinkage occurs and because the so-called aging can conveniently take place as the meat is shipped across the country from the slaughterhouse to your butcher's refrigerated walk-in storage locker.

Another instant aging technique is to apply two minutes of intermittent electrical shocks to the hanging carcass.

### How does rigor mortis affect tenderness?

Rigor mortis is a chemical change that stiffens meat. This process usually begins several hours after the animal is killed and continues for another twelve to thirty-six hours until an enzymatic action makes the connective tissue even more tender than it was before rigor mortis set in.

The graph on page 50 illustrates the relationship between the post-slaughter time and the degree of tenderness for U.S. Prime Grade meat stored in a 35°F environment.

Whoever first advised thousands of years ago that one should either cook an animal immediately after killing it or, otherwise, wait at least two days knew from practical experience what modern science has confirmed.

### How does marinating tenderize meat?

The marinade's acid (be it derived from lemon juice, wine, or whatever) is the potent substance that chemically softens the

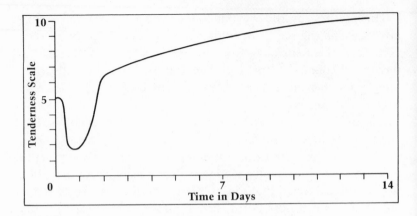

connective tissue. Acid also reduces the time required for heat to convert collagen to gelatin. To be effective, sufficient marinating time is necessary. With some dishes you can achieve adequate results in as few as several hours, though there are specialties, such as the famous German sauerbraten ("sour roast"), that call for a week-long marination.

### What other factors determine a marinade's effectiveness?

Marination is a chemical process. The lower the temperature, the more slowly the chemical reactions occur. This explains why marinating at room temperature is considerably faster than doing it in the refrigerator.

The degree to which the food is covered by the marinade also influences effectiveness. The greater the coverage, the faster the marination process occurs because liquid is a significantly superior medium than air for chemical reactivity. Unfortunately, to submerge a large piece of meat in a bowl or jar requires a large volume of marinade. For this reason, we recommend marinating in a tightly sealed plastic bag with its excess air squeezed out. This reduces the amount of marinade needed.

As a bonus, the package can be easily turned upside down periodically to coat the food's entire surface — and your hands remain clean.

The configuration, thickness, and type of meat also determine marination effectiveness. Other variables are the quantity and strength of the acid used.

## Why does marinating a roast make it less juicy?

Even though the roast absorbs some of the liquid marinade as it lies submerged in it, the cooked meat will likely be less succulent than if it were not marinated. Acid, a major component of marinades, tends to diminish a meat's moisture-retention capacity, especially during cooking. However, on balance, the marinated meat's juice loss is usually more than compensated for by a gain in tenderness and flavor.

## How do commercial meat tenderizers work?

Most of the powdered meat tenderizers sold in grocery stores use papain as the tenderizing agent. Papain is derived from unripe papayas, and works in much the same manner as the natural enzymes in meat which help soften connective tissue as the meat is aged. Both are termed proteolytic enzymes because they break down the proteins in muscle fibers and connective tissue into smaller molecules.

Commercial meat tenderizers have a number of shortcomings, though. They are virtually impotent at refrigerator temperatures, only semieffective at room temperature, and inactivated once the temperature rises above about 150°F. Because the papain seldom penetrates deep inside a cut of meat, the cooked food may end up tender (or even mushy) on the surface and tough in its interior. If you increase accessibility to the interior by deeply piercing the meat, as some papain-promoting recipes suggest, your efforts will be counterproductive. Your cooked meat will be tougher than it would be normally because you have created channels through which a lamentable share of juices escapes during the cooking process. The store-bought products also tend to be laden with salts and other additives that can impart an unwanted flavor to your finished dish.

Today, some slaughterhouses inject a papain solution into an animal shortly before it is to be killed. The papain enters directly into the animal's bloodstream, which carries the tenderizer to muscle tissue throughout the body. While the meat from this animal is cooking, the enzyme is activated (and, finally, inactivated when the temperature reaches approximately 150°F). Although it is true that this tenderizing technique produces meat that has a more uniform texture than meat sprinkled with papain, the flesh still tends to become mushy when cooked because the enzyme destroys too much of the muscle fiber firmness.

### How does carving a piece of meat across the grain and into thin slices make connective tissue more tender?

Grain defines the direction of the tubular connective tissues in meat. "To cut across the grain" means to slice the connective tissue at right angles. Obviously, the thinner the slices, the shorter the resulting connective tissue segments. The shorter the segments, the less chewy the meat, and therefore the more tender it will seem to the eater.

If you have trouble ascertaining the grain of the meat, try to remember this guideline: Typically, the grain flows in a direction from the middle of the carcass to the animal's extremities (limbs, head, and tail).

### How do grinding, scoring, and pounding tenderize meat?

As with cutting across the grain, grinding appreciably shortens the length of connective tissue. Scoring does the same thing, but only on the scored surface. Pounding with a mallet helps tenderize meat by mashing some of the connective tissue.

A dubious variation of pounding is the one depicted in the

Academy Award–winning motion picture *Rocky*. As you may recall, the pugilistic folk hero of the movie practices for his world championship fight by pummeling the beef carcasses hanging from the hooks in a refrigerated warehouse. While fist pounding tenderizes the meat to some extent, the bruising effect on the meat nullifies any gain. Sorry, Rocky.

**Why should true London broil be cooked no more than medium-rare — and why should the meat be sliced across its grain?**

London broil's creation was inspired by pragmatic considerations. Centuries, if not millennia, ago, someone discovered how to broil the naturally tough and (then) inexpensive flank steak and end up with a tasty meat crusty on the outside and tender on the inside — a gastronomic bargain. The secret is twofold. First, broil the meat quickly and briefly to keep the muscle fibers from overcoagulating and, therefore, toughening. This entails using very high heat and not cooking the meat more than medium-rare. Second, reduce the length of the many tough and chewy connective tissues by using a sharp knife to

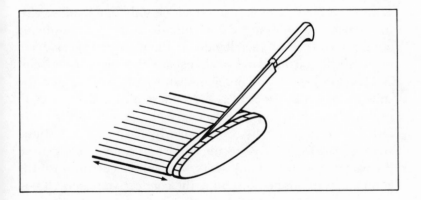

cut the meat into thin slices perpendicular to the flow of the grain. In the accompanying illustration depicting a side view of a flank steak, the double-ended arrow indicates the direction of the grain.

Most cookbooks suggest that you cut the meat on the diagonal because the resulting slices will be larger and therefore more visually appealing. Granted, geometry confirms that a slice of a given thickness will be 41 percent larger if it is cut on a 45° slant rather than at right angles to the surface (a 90° angle). On the other hand, geometry also proves that the resulting length of the connective tissue segments in the 45°-angle slice will be 41 percent longer than those in the 90° version. The issue is whether the gain in cosmetics compensates for the loss in tenderness. We do not think so.

### Why do many butchers sell round steak rather than flank steak as London broil?

Although the authentic (and best) London broil is made with flank steak, most meat labeled "London broil" in supermarkets is round steak. This switch evolved in the post–World War II years, when millions of Americans took up the fashionable backyard sport of barbecuing. London broil became one of the favorite specialties. Since each steer has only two flank steaks, its availability plummeted and the price soared. Enterprising butchers soon began merchandising the then inexpensive and relatively abundant round steak (usually the top round subcut) as "London broil." The problems with that ruse are that the substitute isn't as flavorful as the flank steak and that the grain in a round steak — in its position on a platter — runs vertically rather than horizontally. Consequently, if you cut the round steak vertically, relative to the surface of the serving platter, the way you would a flank steak, you will be cutting with the grain and will not be shortening the connective tissues. If you are to reduce the chewiness of the cooked meat, cutting the meat on a 45° bias is advisable, but even then, the resulting length of the connective tissue segments will be 41 percent longer than those in a perpendicularly sliced London broil made with flank steak.

**Why does a piece of meat get tougher as it cools on my plate?**

As the meat cools, so does its collagen-turned-gelatin. When the gelatin cools, it thickens and, therefore, the meat loses some of the tenderness it had when it was first brought to the table. This thickening is a strong argument for the use of heated dinner plates.

**Why is a well-marbled steak tastier than a leaner one?**

In addition to muscle fibers and connective tissue, muscle has tiny bits of embedded fat running through it. That fat, called marbling, is the source of much of meat's characteristic flavor and aroma. In fact, it is because the fat of each animal species has a distinctive cooking aroma that an educated nose can tell whether the meat cooking in the host's kitchen is beef, pork, or lamb. Thus, when you buy beef that contains scant marbling, you deprive yourself of the full enjoyment of a first-rate steak.

Marbling, a form of stored energy for the animal, promises you more than flavor because its presence indicates two conditions. First, a rich diet — based on foods like corn — was necessary for the animal to develop substantial fat deposits. This type of diet enhances the quality of the meat. Second, once the marbling did form, the animal must not have had cause to use it as an energy supply. Marbling, therefore, is usually a sign that the development of tough connective tissue resulting from physical exertion has been minimal. The meat from this indulged animal, if properly cooked, will almost invariably be tender.

While it is true that the "good life" leaves the tasty fat deposits intact, the meat's flavor — unlike its texture — does not benefit directly from the animal's inactivity. Exercise not only toughens the flesh, it increases the flavor of the muscles. It follows, then, that if you want a steak from the relatively unexercised rib, short loin, or sirloin primal areas to be as tasty as it is tender, the flavor boon of marbling is crucial.

Marbling performs yet another worthy function — it helps prevent the cooking meat from drying out by keeping the individual muscle fibers juicy. The fat in the adipose tissue that rims the steak, or resides in large pockets, also does this job. However, marbling does it better because it is dispersed within rather than outside the muscles.

If you are concerned about the calories and saturated fats in well-marbled meat, take into account that most of that fat melts and drains out of the meat by the time the steak is cooked. In regard to the band of fat that may surround the steak, trim it off the cooked meat and don't eat it.

### Why is ground chuck usually better than the more expensive ground sirloin for hamburgers?

Ground chuck normally has more fat than ground sirloin. That extra fat not only contributes flavor, it also helps keep the meat moist when grilling or broiling. And, since more fat and less water will ooze out of the meat into the pan during the cooking process, frying temperatures will be higher and the splatter less.

Unless your diet dictates that you stay clear of saturated fats, you need not be overly concerned about the higher fat content of ground chuck (as long as it is not excessive) because most of it will drain out of the meat as it cooks. If calories are your concern, remember that a smaller but succulent hamburger is more gastronomically rewarding than a larger hamburger of identical calorie count that is dried out.

Another advantage of ground chuck is that it comes from a more exercised, and therefore more flavorful, part of the anatomy than does ground sirloin. True, the original sirloin steak was more tender than the original chuck steak, but after the meat is tenderized by grinding, that plus becomes a big zero.

**Why is ground meat more perishable than, say, a steak?**

Grinding fosters bacterial contamination in two ways. First, the meat is subjected to spoilage-causing microorganisms that may be present on the butcher's machine or hands. Second, the surface area of the ground meat has enlarged to many times its original size, thus making the meat more vulnerable to air-borne bacteria.

**Why do some cooks prefer the blade-end chop over the loin-end chop for frying?**

The lamb, pork, and veal blade-end chops have a higher fat content and a lower water content than do their loin-end counterparts. This creates two of the benefits mentioned earlier in the Q&A on ground chuck (see p. 56). The extra fat adds extra flavor and, because the fat-to-water ratio is higher, less water will exude out of the meat into the frying pan. Better browning and less splattering result. On the other hand, the loin-end chop has its adherents because it's more tender.

**Why should the fat layer surrounding a steak be slashed at approximately three-quarter-inch intervals?**

Fat shrinks faster and more extensively than meat during cooking and, consequently, a thick, lengthy belt of fat will warp the steak as it is pan-broiled, broiled, grilled, or barbecued. When the steak curls, various points along its previously flat surfaces will cook unevenly. And a buckled steak isn't very attractive.

**What does the color of beef fat reveal?**

Yellow-tinged fat indicates that the steer was grass-fed, white fat suggests that the animal was fed (at least during its final months) corn or other cereal grain. Consequently, a steak surrounded by a pearly white layer of fat should be more tender — and expensive.

**When using a meat thermometer, why should I test the thickest part of the meat and avoid letting the thermometer's point touch a bone or pocket of fat?**

Since the center of the meat's thickest section is farthest away from the oven's heat source, it is the last part to cook. Even if the thermometer gives the desired temperature for a thinner part of the meat, the thickest segment may not be done.

Bone is a better conductor of heat than is meat. If you take your temperature reading next to a bone in the center of the meat, the reading will be higher than it would be for center flesh farther from the bone.

Fat is not as good a heat conductor as meat. Placing the thermometer point in a pocket of fat, therefore, gives a lower reading than it would for the adjacent flesh.

**How do experienced cooks tell if a meat is cooked simply by touching it?**

These cooks are testing for resiliency. As the meat cooks, its flesh becomes less flabby because it loses water and its muscle fibers contract. The more a meat cooks, the firmer and more elastic it becomes.

The skill of accurately measuring doneness of meat by its springiness cannot be taught in words. The best way to learn the technique is empirically, by testing the resiliency of the meat each time you use a thermometer. Eventually, your educated finger will relegate the thermometer to the drawer.

**Are the minutes-per-pound charts for cooking meat fallible?**

Granted, the information garnered from such charts is better than no information at all. Nonetheless, there are a host of variables that render the charts crude estimates at best.

The most significant variable is the thickness of the meat. A spherical ten-pound roast, for example, takes longer to cook than a long, narrow ten-pound roast.

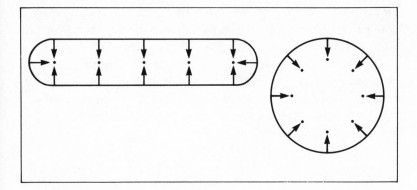

In the accompanying illustration, the arrows represent the distance heat has penetrated by conduction in a given time period. In the spherical roast, the arrows are still a long way from the meat's center, while the heat has already reached every point of the long, narrow roast.

You must also make allowances for the amount of bone and fat in the meat. All other factors being equal, a bone-in or a lean piece of meat cooks faster than a boneless or fatty one.

Other variables include the temperature of the meat when you put it in the oven and the preheated temperature of your oven. Minutes-per-pound charts and recipes usually specify these two factors, as well as figures for different degrees of doneness.

If your chart does not take into account different sizes of meat, you will have to make adjustments that reflect the fact that though larger pieces of meat take longer to cook, they require fewer minutes per pound than do smaller pieces of similar shape and composition.

There is no chart around that can take into consideration the accuracy of your oven temperature dial — chances are it is not as precise as you think. To test your oven's accuracy, buy, beg, or borrow a quality portable oven thermometer that is in good condition. Then — should you discover a discrepancy — add or subtract the variation when you set the oven dial.

If you choose to cover your roasting meat (a technique we do not recommend), you will have to alter the given figures because covered meat cooks more quickly. (You can compensate for this factor by lowering the suggested oven setting by approximately 25°F.)

### Why should a roast be brought to, or near, room temperature before cooking?

This is principally a precautionary measure against having the roast's outside overcook and dry out before the inside is properly warmed and cooked. And since a room-temperature roast cooks more quickly than its colder counterpart, you save energy.

Of course, if the roast is about six inches or more thick, its surface will undergo bacterial contamination before the center of the meat reaches room temperature. In that case, at least allow the interior of the meat to partially reach room temperature. An hour in the open should not pose a health threat except, for example, when the room is hot and humid.

When you cannot bring meat to room temperature, you should roast it at a slightly lower than usual temperature, counterbalanced with a slightly longer than usual cooking time. Less complicated but less effective is to maintain the original temperature, but to extend the cooking time; if you remove a six-inch-thick roast from the refrigerator and place it directly in a preheated 350°F oven, add about twelve to fifteen minutes to the cooking time.

If the roast is frozen, increase the original cooking time by about 50 percent. Naturally, your roast will not be as tasty and juicy, nor will its exterior be as attractive as a roast that was brought to room temperature before cooking.

**Why does it usually take twice as long to roast than to boil or steam a meat?**

One could easily conclude that roasting would be faster because it uses a higher temperature. It also employs all three types of thermal energy: conduction, convection, and radiant heat (boiling and steaming use only the first two). These advantages of roasting are more than counterbalanced, however, by the fact that liquid and steam can transfer heat to food much more efficiently than air can. Moreover, as the oven temperature increases, the air expands. The increased rarefaction lessens the ability of the air in the oven to transfer heat to the roasting meat.

**Why does the outside of a roast develop a crusty texture and dark brown pigmentation?**

As the meat cooks, some of its juices flow to the surface and evaporate, leaving behind an exposed coating of solid substances. An important chemical change called the Maillard reaction occurs to two of those substances, natural sugar and amino acids, when the meat is cooked with dry heat. The Maillard (also called browning) reaction combines sugar and amino acids on the meat's surface into new molecules.

If the cook has done a proper job, the new compounds developed by the Maillard reaction will give the meat's surface an appetizingly intense flavor, crusty texture, and dark brown pigmentation. If the Maillard reaction is excessive, the results can be gastronomically devastating, to the eye and palate. (Note: The browning reaction can take place naturally with other foods at room temperature, as it sometimes does with freshly cut fruits like peaches. It discolors their exposed flesh, giving the fruit an unappealing brown hue and off-flavor.)

Most of the new compounds created by the Maillard reaction remain on or just below the meat's surface. Some fall off the meat and coagulate on the pan's bottom, providing the flavor foundation of the esteemed pan drippings.

You can promote browning by basting the surface of the

meat with butter. Its fat content helps prevent the meat's surface from drying out while its surface molecules dutifully brown. Basting with the pan juices has the same effect.

We do not particularly recommend the dust-with-flour browning technique because it can produce a pasty texture and a floury flavor, or if overcooked, a taste of burnt toast.

**Does high heat produce a better crust on a roast than low heat?**

The higher the heat, the more the Maillard reaction (see previous Q&A) takes place. There are other variables that also determine the quality of a roast's crust. One is cooking time. The longer the joint roasts, the crustier the meat. Another is the use of a lid or foil: An uncovered meat develops a crispier, richer-colored, and more delectable crust than a covered one. Still one more factor is the fat content of the meat or basting liquid. Fat helps to keep the meat's surface from scorching and drying out, thereby retarding crust formation.

**Why does roasting beef shrink?**

You can place most of the blame for the reduction on water loss. Cooking changes the structure of proteins, decreasing their water-binding capacity. The released liquid oozes out of the meat during the cooking, resting, carving, and post-carving stages. It is not uncommon for a beef roast (which can have a moisture content of 75 percent) to lose one-third of its original size and weight when cooked at a high temperature or for too long. To minimize shrinkage, roast the meat with low heat (250° to 300°F) and cook it to no more than medium-rare.

Fat loss, another cause of shrinkage, results when fat liquefies and seeps out of the roasting meat. Well-marbled meat is especially subject to shrinkage if cooked beyond the medium-rare stage. Contracting connective tissue and coagulating muscle fiber also are major contributors to shrinkage.

# How can I tell if a smoked cut of meat has been cooked?

Knowing for sure whether a smoked cut of meat has been fully cooked by the processor is important because if you guess the answer, you may be wrong. Assume that because you mistakenly thought the meat was fully cooked, you did not cook it completely; you and your dinner guests would risk consuming pathogenic microorganisms. Your meat would lack proper flavor and texture, too. Now consider the opposite situation. The meat was fully cooked, but because you thought it wasn't, or because you wanted to play it safe, you decided to cook it for the length of time that raw meat requires. In that case, your smoked meat would become dry and tough.

Should neither the butcher nor the label provide you with the information, examine a visible bone. If it protrudes from the flesh, the meat has been cooked to at least some degree. The more the bone stands out in relief the more the meat has been cooked. This criterion is reliable, because as a cut of meat cooks, its flesh shrinks, but not its bone.

When making this observation, be sure you are looking at a bone that was exposed during the smoking process. If a smoked and fully cooked whole ham is cut in half, for instance, the newly exposed cross section of the leg bone will not reveal the desired information because it will lie flush with the surrounding flesh.

# Why should a roast be allowed to rest for about fifteen to twenty-five minutes prior to carving?

At the moment when a roast is removed from the oven, the meat near the surface contains fewer juices than the meat at the core. This disparity occurs because many of the juices that were originally in the outer meat either evaporated or were forced toward the center.

If you carve a roast immediately after cooking, when its juices are unevenly distributed, the edges of your slices will be unnecessarily dry. In addition, many of the meat's juices will seep out because the saturated muscle tissue in the interior cannot absorb and hold all the excess liquid that has collected there during cooking.

A fifteen- to twenty-five-minute respite (depending on the roast's thickness) gives much of the liquid a chance to redistribute and settle throughout the meat. This brief rest also allows the meat to become a little firmer, making it easier to carve thin slices.

## Why should I remove a roast from the oven slightly underdone?

Assume that you want to cook your roast to 140°F of doneness and you leave it in the oven until it reaches that internal temperature. Although the middle of the roast may be 140°F, the meat near the surface is probably hot enough — around 160° to 180°F — to continue cooking the colder center while you are allowing the roast to rest before carving (see preceding Q&A). By the time the temperature equalizes throughout a thin cut of meat (under three inches at its minimum diameter or point of thickness), its interior temperature will have climbed about 5°F. The center of a roast over twelve inches thick will increase in temperature approximately 15°F after the meat is removed from the oven. The center of a medium-thick roast experiences roughly a 10°F rise. These figures refer to medium-rare meats. The rise will be about 10 percent less for rare roasts, 10 percent greater for medium, and 15 percent greater for those that are well done.

## When broiling, grilling, or barbecuing, why is it unsuitable to cook a steak that is less than one inch or more than three inches thick?

The inside of a steak less than one inch thick will be disappointingly dry and tough by the time the surface is appetizingly brown. Such a steak is best pan-broiled.

The outside of a steak more than three inches thick will be overcooked before the center of the meat is properly done.

Technically, a piece of meat such as this is a roast and should be cooked as one, either by oven-roasting or pot-roasting.

### When cooking meat with dry heat, should I salt before or after the meat is cooked?

There are two antipodal, and sometimes contentious, schools of thought on this issue. The season-before-cooking faction argues that unless you sprinkle the salt on the meat before starting the cooking process, the salt will not have a chance to infuse the food and trigger a chemical flavor-enhancing reaction.

The salt-after-cooking clique asserts that presalting will draw out moisture unnecessarily from the cooking meat and will therefore make it tougher. Moreover, this group maintains, the salt does not penetrate the flesh entirely, and, accordingly, the cooked meat is unevenly seasoned. A slice from a roast that was salted before cooking verifies their point: The edges will taste more salty than the center.

The pros and cons of each argument more or less balance out, so follow whatever precept your grandmother taught you.

Salting steak that is to be cooked on a flat surface, such as a sauté pan, is another matter. If you presalt the meat, your steak will suffer. As the salt-leached juices exude from the underside of the steak, they boil or turn to steam, giving that face a mushy consistency and a surface that is a pallid grayish brown rather than an appealing rich brown. We prefer a compromise solution: Salt each side of a steak after it has been cooked and turned.

### When cooking meat with dry heat, should I pepper before or after it is cooked?

Ground pepper becomes bitter when scorched — and the heat of a hot frying or sauté pan, broiler compartment, or barbecue unit is sufficient to do the bad deed. If an oven is warmer than 325°F, the same fate probably awaits the pepper. Consequently, if you use dry heat, we recommend that you sprinkle on the pepper after the meat is cooked.

Some chefs add the pepper to a side of steak as soon as it has been cooked and turned, but unless you are careful not to scatter the pepper particles beyond the meat, your food or sauce may end up with the distasteful flavor of scorched pepper. Scattered salt is not as much of a problem because it will not scorch.

### Why is it often advantageous to sear meat?

Meat is seared by exposing its surfaces to an intense direct or indirect heat long enough to cook the outer layers of molecules, but short enough to have little effect on the meat's interior. This technique partially seals in internal meat juices and gives the surface added texture, flavor, and color. The last two qualities are also imparted to a sauce prepared from the meat drippings.

### Why is meat nearest the bone usually tastier?

In a given cut of meat, the meat closest to the bone has a distinct advantage. It is in the best position to absorb the savory flavors of the bone — the same flavors that help enrich stocks.

### Was USDA Prime beef better two decades ago?

On the average, yes. Not too many years ago, 4.5 percent of beef carcasses that were quality-inspected by the U.S. Department of Agriculture were awarded the Prime Grade. (USDA officials looked for ample marbling; white fat; bright, fresh flesh color; and firm, fine flesh texture.) When the USDA lowered its grading standards in 1976, that percentage jumped to 6.5 — which means that approximately one-third of the beef being sold today as USDA Prime would have been stamped before 1976 with the next lower grade classification, USDA Choice.

Even the USDA Choice designation isn't what it used to be. That category once encompassed 54 percent of the carcasses. Today, it includes 68 percent of them. The increase is due to the inclusion of beef that prior to 1976 would have been given the third-level grade, USDA Good.

## Is meat still safe to eat if I forget to cut off the government grade or inspection stamp?

Yes. The ink used is a harmless vegetable dye.

## Why the controversy over using hormones to stimulate animal growth?

Although it is incontrovertible that sex hormones like diethylstilbestrol (DES) can accelerate the growth of livestock, many nutritional authorities fear the effect of these natural or synthetic hormones on humans who eat the meat. Consequently, the federal government forbids giving growth hormones to some animals and limits their use with others by setting minimum periods between the day the animal last receives the hormones and the day it is slaughtered.

From a gourmet's point of view, hormone-infiltrated meat is comparatively flabby and insipid.

## What gives a slice of ham an iridescent sheen?

The glistening, greenish, somewhat rainbowlike color that sometimes emanates from the cut surface of a ham slice is a sign of oxidation and not necessarily of spoilage. When exposed to oxygen (or light), some of the nitrate-modified iron content of the meat undergoes a chemical change that alters the ham's pigmentation.

## Is a canned ham that requires refrigeration better than one that doesn't?

Generally, yes. In order to sterilize a ham so that it can be stored at room temperature on a grocery shelf the processor must heat the ham to a very high temperature. That intense heat negatively alters the ham's flavor, aroma, texture, and nutritive value. Moreover, processors seldom reserve their best hams for their need-not-refrigerate products.

**Why does the bacon of today tend to splatter more than that of yesteryear?**

In Grandpa's day, bacon was typically cured with dry salt — the slow, traditional way. In the interest of saving time and money, almost all the processors today cure their products in brine. This liquid infuses the bacon, which is the number-one cause of grease splattering out of the pan onto the top of your erstwhile clean range.

**Why is it best to fry bacon with medium heat rather than high?**

Less splatter is one answer. A more important reason concerns carcinogens. The hotter the heat, the more you convert the nitrate curing agents into nitrites, which are substances suspected of causing cancer.

**Why are so many home-barbecued chickens so black-crusted and bitter?**

The primary cause of these charred, acrid-tasting birds is the commercial barbecue sauces that the backyard chefs slosh on the chicken. High heat readily burns sugar, a major ingredient of barbecue sauces. These sauces are also liberally flavored with spices that become bitter when scorched.

Knowledgeable barbecuers will not brush on the sauce until fifteen minutes before the chicken has finished cooking. They will also use more time and less heat. If the coals are extremely hot and well packed, the barbecuer par excellence will keep the food four to six inches above the briquettes. The thicker the food, the greater the distance from the coals, and, as a direct result, the longer should be the cooking period.

**Why does chicken breast skin sometimes stick to the roasting rack?**

The skin contains collagen. When subjected to high heat, this collagen undergoes a chemical reaction, changing into a gluey gelatin. When you lift up the chicken, some of the skin adheres to the rack and peels off, diminishing the bird's table appeal. This cosmetic problem can be lessened if you grease the rack well and begin the roasting process in a preheated oven with the breast-side up for at least twenty minutes. This gives some of the newly created gelatin a chance to infuse into the fat and flesh under the skin or to ooze out into the pan. For the same reason, you should begin sautéing or broiling a bone-in chicken breast skin-side up.

**Does yellow skin indicate a quality chicken?**

Once, in most areas of the country, a yellow skin was a worthwhile (though not 100 percent reliable) clue that the chicken was imbued with extra flavor and surface fat. If the chicken had a yellow skin, chances are it grew up bathed in sun rays and enjoyed a nutritious diet, either by scratching for its subsistence around the farmhouse or by eating the right mix of foods tossed to it by its owner.

The validity of the yellow-skin criterion was undermined when, within the last two decades, some of the mass-marketing chicken farms used a ploy to take advantage of its widespread acceptance. They added marigold petals or similar sources of gold, yellow, or orange pigment to their feed formulas. Since the petals are natural, the companies are not legally forced to reveal their ruse to the shoppers.

Without the "colorful diet," the chickens would likely have ghostly bluish-white skins because they seldom, if ever, leave their cramped, sunless indoor coops. The next time you view the golden chickens in your supermarket, think flowers, not sunshine.

## Does a chicken's living environment affect its flavor?

Free-range chickens are more flavorful than supermarket chickens. Unlike the latter, which are almost always reared in crowded coops, the free-range chickens get to move around a large yard. This exercise develops more flavor in their muscles. Exercise also toughens muscles but the effect is less pronounced on a chicken than a steer. As long as you buy a young free-range chicken, there should not be an appreciable toughening effect on the meat.

The cramped and sunless living quarters of supermarket chickens also make these "shut-ins" more disease- and stress-prone. Free-range chickens live more contented lives which, research shows, results in a better quality meat and a higher flesh-to-bone ratio.

## Does the method of processing a chicken affect flavor?

Today's mass-production methods diminish a chicken's flavor. One reason is that supermarket chickens are machine- rather than hand-plucked. The mechanical plucking device removes part of the flavorful epidermis (outer skin layer) along with its feathers. Another reason is that dressed chickens are typically chilled by soaking them in water at the plant, a process that leaches out some of the built-in flavor. This loss would not occur if the chickens were chilled in air inside a refrigeration unit, as they used to be.

## Are deep-chilled chickens frozen?

Too often we've heard supermarket personnel answer a customer's honest question, "Has this chicken been frozen?" with the flippant reply, "Of course not, it's been deep-chilled." To set the record straight, just because a chicken has been deep-chilled doesn't mean it wasn't subsequently frozen and thawed.

Let's first consider what deep-chilling means. The processing plant lowers the temperature of a freshly dressed chicken to about 28°F. This makes sense because the deterioration process is slower at 28° than at 32°F, the freezing point of water. Therefore, the bird's storage life is extended. No need to worry about the chicken freezing. The 28°F temperature would freeze plain water but not the liquid in the chicken, because the natural proteins and other solids immersed in that liquid lower the liquid's freezing point. So far, so good.

Here comes the problem. Once the chicken leaves the processing plant, some shippers and supermarkets, out of greed or ignorance, store the deep-chilled chickens at a temperature below 28°F. This freezes the chicken and, accordingly, robs its flesh of some of its desirable flavor and texture.

Another way to extend shelf life is to package the chicken with plastic wrap, and to replace the oxygen inside this hermetically sealed package with nitrogen gas. This is an effective process because few pathogenic microorganisms can survive (or at least flourish) without oxygen. However, like deep-chilled chicken, a shipper can easily freeze a nitrogen-packed chicken and thaw it later without most customers being the wiser.

### How can I tell if wrapped chicken or beef in the meat display case has been frozen and then thawed?

A large pool of juices in the tray package is a telltale sign. It's usually the liquid that was once stored inside or between the cells (see pp. 239–40 for an explanation of how this liquid seeps out).

Once you cook a bird, you'll see another telltale sign. The bones will be darker than normal.

### Why does a pliable breast bone tip indicate a young bird?

As a chicken or other bird matures, the tip of its cartilaginous keel (breast bone) calcifies, becoming more ossified and brittle. This same hardening process also occurs in some of the bones of mammals. Butchers sometimes snap the lower leg bones of lamb, for instance, to ascertain the sheep's age. The younger the animal, the more easily the bone snaps and the less jagged the edges will be.

## What are the other bone tests for determining the age of birds and mammals?

Relative size is the best-known gauge. The larger a specific bone from an animal of a particular breed, the older that animal is likely to be. Another touchstone is relative color. Examine a cross section of a bone. The pinker its tone, the younger the creature. Relative porousness divulges information, too. A bone becomes denser as the animal ages.

## Why the expression "Stew an old chicken, fry a young one"?

A mature chicken, and especially an old one, has considerable connective tissue that is best tenderized with a slow moist-cooking method such as stewing. If you fried the mature fowl, you would have a tough, chewy bird.

Since the young chicken has comparatively little connective tissue, slow moist cooking is not necessary. Moreover, this method of cooking would be counterproductive because the lengthy cooking process would overcoagulate the muscle fibers. Once again, you would end up with a tough, chewy bird.

## Why is the flesh and the leg bone of a fully cooked chicken sometimes bloody?

Chicken bones contain hemoglobin, the red pigment of blood, and sometimes this protein leaches out of the bone after the bird is cooked. This leaching is particularly likely to happen if the chicken is young or has been frozen. People who put the chicken back into the oven when they observe traces of this edible hemoglobin are needlessly overcooking, toughening, and drying out the meat.

## Why is the chicken drumstick "dark meat" and the breast "white meat"?

A chicken uses its leg muscles for unhurried, long-duration movements such as roaming around the barnyard searching for insects and other food. In contrast, a chicken hardly uses its wings except for balance. When it flaps them energetically, it's usually to make a quick escape from a threat. Because the muscle requirements of the chicken leg and breast are different, the two sets of muscles evolve differently. The legs consist predominantly of slow-contraction muscle fibers, while the breast is composed chiefly of fast-contraction muscle fibers.

The slow-contraction muscle fiber is for the long-duration jobs and the fast-contraction muscle fiber for the quick-energy spurts. The fuel for the slow-contraction muscle fiber is fat and requires oxygen, which is stored in the iron-rich, red-pigmented myoglobin. Consequently, the more slow-contraction fibers in a muscle, the redder the muscle will likely be. Fast-contraction muscle fibers don't require oxygen and, therefore, myoglobin because they use glycogen (a carbohydrate) for fuel. In the absence of myoglobin, the muscles are "white."

Actually, both the chicken leg and breast contain a combination of fast- and slow-contraction muscle fibers. The leg is "dark meat" because the fast-contraction muscle fibers predominate. The opposite is true for the breast.

## Why is a duck's breast meat dark?

Unlike the chicken and turkey, the duck (and many other birds) uses its wings for more than mercurial escapes. In the wild, it flies long distances, sometimes covering thousands of miles during a migration. If its breast were made mainly of fast- rather than slow-contraction muscle fibers, the duck would exhaust its energy reserve before it could complete its journey.

# 4

## S·E·A·F·O·O·D

### What are the subclassifications of seafood?

On the facing page is a basic, somewhat simplified biological classification chart.

Fishes and shellfishes can be classified in dozens of ways, including by environment (for instance, surface- or bottom-feeding, fresh or salt water, Temperate or Tropical Zone); size; shape (round or flat); price; flavor; popularity. They can be classified as anadromous (those, such as salmon, that migrate from the sea to spawn in freshwater rivers), catadromous (those, like eels, that migrate from fresh water to spawn in the sea), or neither, if the fish spends its entire life exclusively in fresh or salt water. Last but not least, seafood is categorized by its fat content.

### Is knowing the difference between fat and lean fishes important for a weight watcher?

Yes. Because of a difference in fat content, one fish can have thrice the calories of another species. Our rankings (based on United States Department of Agriculture statistics) give calories per 100 grams (about 3.5 ounces) of raw flesh.

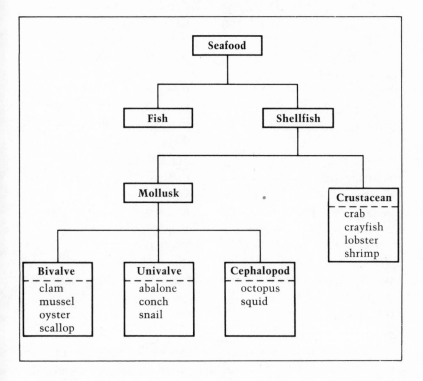

American Eel 233 calories
Chinook (or King) Salmon 222
Atlantic Salmon 217
Rainbow Trout 195
Atlantic Mackerel 191
Atlantic Herring 176
Shad 170
Butterfish (from northern waters) 169

Lake Trout 168
Pompano 166
Pacific Mackerel 159
Lake Whitefish 155
Striped Mullet 146
Bluefin Tuna 145
Pacific Coast Yellowtail 136
Yellowfin Tuna 133
Alewife 127
Weakfish 121

Pink (or Humpback) Salmon 119
Swordfish 118
Bluefish 117
Carp 115
Pacific Barracuda 113
Atlantic Sheepshead 113
Porgy and Scup 112
Striped Bass 105
Whiting 105
Freshwater Catfish 103
Brook Trout 101
Atlantic and Pacific Halibut 100
Atlantic Smelts 98
Pacific Herring 98
Rockfish 97
White Sea Bass 96
Lake Herring 96
Atlantic Croaker 96
Butterfish (from Gulf waters) 95
Pollock 95
Sturgeon 94
Red Snapper 93
Walleye Pike 93
Black Sea Bass 93
Redfish 91
Yellow Perch 91
Atlantic Ocean Perch 88
Monkfish 80
Tilefish 79
Haddock 79
Flatfishes (such as Sole) 79
Cod 78
Hake 74

Before we eliminate delicious fishes like eel or trout from our diet, we must remember that these foods have lower calorie counts than some other protein sources. T-bone steak, for instance, has 397 calories per 100 grams.

**Is the difference between a fat and lean fish important to non-dieters as well?**

Yes. Generally, the more fatty the fish, the more flavorful the fish. Vitamins and other nutrients in the flesh also tend to increase in step with a fish's fat content.

The darker the flesh color of a particular species (or a given anatomical area of a particular fish), the higher the fat content is likely to be. If you want your fish flesh to be as white as possible, lean toward lean fishes.

Fat content usually decreases in relation to the depth of a fish's living environment. At a given latitude, bottom-dwelling fishes like sole and cod are usually leaner than those, such as tuna and herring, that dwell near the surface. And any given fish will be leaner after it has spawned or experienced a food shortage.

### Why do fishes from cooler waters generally taste better?

As we mentioned in the preceding Q&A, there is often a discernible correlation between fat content and richness of flavor. Cooler-water fishes tend to have a higher fat content because, among other factors, their eco-environment contains a greater abundance of plankton at the bottom of the food chain.

Moreover, because Temperate Zone waters are colder and more turbulent than tropical ones, plankton (and mineral particles) is more likely to remain suspended in water, creating a richer food source for non-bottom-dwelling fishes. (Note: Tropical waters are clearer than Temperate Zone ones simply because they have less suspended matter.)

A good illustration of the gastronomic effect of water temperature is the comparison between the flavorful fishes hooked or netted in Georges Bank off the New England coast and the species caught in the Caribbean Sea. With rare exception (for example, the pompano), semitropical, and especially tropical, fishes are relatively bland. Shellfish from those sun-drenched shores, however, are usually gustatory delights.

### Why do river fishes generally taste better than lake fishes?

Exercise builds flavor into flesh. Since a river fish must swim against the current just to remain stationary, it obviously needs to expend more energy than a typical lake fish.

Not all river fishes oscillate their tails with equal vigor and intensity. An angler should expect less flavor in a fish that lazily wends its way along the silky bottom of a river than, say, in a trout that maneuvers its course through a cascading, cold mountain brook.

**Why do freshwater fishes have more of those small, annoying bones than marine fishes do?**

Salt water contains a greater concentration of minerals (particularly salt) than does fresh water and therefore has a higher specific density. Thus, a fish will have greater buoyancy in salt water. This added buoyancy allows a saltwater fish to have a heavier bone structure. When some of the ocean-going fishes made the switch to a freshwater home eons ago, they evolved a lighter, thinner, more delicate bone structure to compensate for the diminished buoyancy. All well and good for a fish, but what about the millions of diners who dread choking on tiny, spiny bones?

**Are farmed fishes inferior to those that live in their natural environment?**

When it comes to flavor and texture, farmed fishes (those reared in man-controlled environments like tanks and pools) are indeed inferior to those that mature in the freedom of oceans, rivers, and lakes. For instance, if you were to hatch two genetically identical trout eggs, one in the natural environment of a stream and the other in a fish farm, the difference in exercise would surely cause the farmed fish to develop a blander and less flavorful flesh.

Farmed fishes are not without their advantages to the industry and the world's food supply. As each year passes, fish farming becomes more and more profitable and productive. Nowadays, some farmers can generate more protein per acre, and at a lower feed cost, by raising fish than by rearing cows, sheep, pigs, or poultry — and the census count of these enterprising cultivators is expected to multiply rapidly within the foreseeable future.

**Why is the center cut of a fish superior to the tail cut?**

The meat from the center cut usually has a higher fat content and therefore a richer flavor. Though the tail's flesh has a more intense flavor because of the extra work it must do to propel the fish through the water, the gain in quantity of flavor does not begin to match the loss in flavor quality.

In terms of texture, the center cut is usually just right — not too flabby, nor too firm. The tail section is tough by comparison.

## How can I determine visually whether a fish steak or fillet is from the center or tail area?

Most fishes fall into one of two shape classifications: round or flat. Salmon, trout, tuna, carp, and bass are examples of the first group, and sole, flounder, and halibut are members of the second. When a round fish is cut into steaks (slices cut perpendicular to the backbone), the pieces from near the center have a slit or missing segment extending up to the backbone, giving the steak a vaguely horseshoelike appearance. That opening is the wall of the stomach cavity. A steak cut from near the tail has no slit because it was sliced from a section of the fish located behind the abdominal pocket.

A whole fillet (a boneless slice cut lengthwise from head to tail) of a round or flat fish is tapered, the narrow end being the tail portion.

## Why does the darker flesh of many fishes tend to run along their backbones and near their tails?

When a fish swims leisurely through the water, it propels itself chiefly with its back and tail muscles. These muscles consist mostly of slow-contraction muscle fiber because the work is performed with relatively slow movements over long durations. The large amount of myoglobin in the tissue around these slow-contraction fibers turns the flesh brownish red (see our discussion on slow- and fast-contraction muscle fibers in the previous chapter on meats, p. 73). The muscles in the other areas of a fish's anatomy are typically lighter hued (usually off-white) because they predominantly consist of fast-contraction fibers, which don't require the presence of the oxygen-rich myoglobin. These pale-hued muscles are generally reserved for quick movements, such as for chasing a prey or escaping a predator.

### Why is fish flesh lighter-hued than land animal flesh?

A fish expends less energy than a land animal when it moves from one point to another at a relaxed pace. Unlike the land animal, a fish doesn't have to support its own weight — its body is suspended in a virtual state of neutral buoyancy in its natural habitat, the surrounding water. Consequently, the fish needs less slow-contraction ("long haul") muscle tissue than its land counterpart. At the same time, because water is significantly denser than air, a fish needs more fast-contraction ("quick escape") muscle fiber than does a land animal. Although the fish has the buoyancy advantage, that factor is far outweighed by the water resistance the fish will experience when quick-accelerating through the denser medium. To achieve the same acceleration rate, the fish will have to expend more energy than the land animal, so it's to a fish's advantage to have as much fast-contraction fiber as possible.

Unlike most fishes, the whale has dark-hued flesh, for good reason. It seldom needs to escape predators and travels for extended periods. Moreover, its muscles contain an unusually large quantity of the red-hued myoglobin because the whale must store as much oxygen as possible in its body for sustained dives (a mammal, the whale cannot breathe under water).

Frogs, with their light-hued leg flesh, are on the other end of the spectrum. They seldom move their legs except to flee a threat, so their legs don't need that many slow-contraction muscle fibers. What they require, and indeed have, is a predominance of the fast-contraction muscle fibers.

Incidentally, the flesh of a salmon is pink for more reasons than myoglobin. Diet is a major influence. Salmon eat generous quantities of crustaceans and other creatures that contain a carotenoid pigment that "stains" the salmon's muscle tissue.

**Which is better gastronomically, the darker or lighter flesh?**

The dark areas (which are sometimes individual muscles) often have a higher fat content than the predominant lighter-colored flesh and therefore have more flavor.

On the negative side, the flavor of the dark-hued flesh can be too pronounced and oily for some tastes. Moreover, since this flesh is high in myoglobin, which turns brown when heated or overexposed to oxygen, it can detract from the lily-white appearance of the rest of the fish. The high proportion of fat normally associated with these dark areas also shortens storage life. On these grounds, the consumer sometimes chooses to remove the dark areas.

**What are the tiny dark red spots I sometimes see on fish fillets?**

Typically, they are bruise marks and indicate that the fish was handled roughly. This could happen if, for example, the fisherman hurled the fish into the boat's storage bin or the fishmonger filleted the fish in a hasty, slipshod manner. The fillet could also have become battered if the fish store clerk flung, rather than gently returned, it to the display case after showing it to a customer (one way to judge a fishmonger is to notice how tenderly he handles fish).

The bruises do more than ruin the fillet's aesthetic appeal. These defects can also affect the flavor of the fish, especially if they are numerous or if they were created more than several hours beforehand because they accelerate the deterioration of the surrounding flesh.

**What causes a raw fillet to turn yellow along its edges?**

In most instances, it is over the hill. As the fillet lies in storage, it gradually loses acidity and, unavoidably, the normally white flavone pigment in the fish flesh picks up a yellowish tint. Oxidation also plays a role in the yellowing process.

## Do gills provide a clue to freshness?

One of the best, yet often overlooked, tests for freshness of a whole fish is the condition of the gills, the respiratory organs located underneath the earlike flaps behind the eye. When a fish is alive, blood is pumped through the gills and absorbs oxygen from the water. During that absorption process, the blood's hemoglobin undergoes a chemical process and turns bright red.

If the fish is properly stored after it dies, the oxygen in the air will help keep the gills bright red for a few hours. Then, overoxidation gradually changes the hemoglobin from bright red to pink to brownish red and finally to grayish brown.

Because gills are more perishable than the flesh of the fish, they will develop an off-odor before the flesh starts to acquire the telltale scent. Consider the gills an early warning system.

## What causes a fish to develop a fish odor?

A just caught fish smells like a fresh sea breeze — not "fishy." A fish develops the foul odor (a sign of crescendoing spoilage) chiefly because attacking bacteria release trimethylamine from some of the fat in the flesh. These trimethylamine molecules, along with other substances created by the decomposition process, waft through the air, filling your nasal passages with odors reeking of ammonia. Sulfur, too, is generated by the deteriorating flesh.

Not to be confused with the "fishy" scent is the equally nauseating oil-and-kerosene odor that often emanates from fish that swam in bustling harbors.

## What are the other major freshness tests for a whole fish?

Eyes should be bright, clear, and bulging and should look alive rather than dull, cloudy, or sunken. Scales, if they exist, should be securely attached. If scaled, the skin should be shining (not slimy), and resilient when pressed with the tip of the finger. If the fish is gutted (as it should be if dead for more than an hour), the stomach cavity should be free of excess residue. Any exposed flesh should be firm and lustrous, not flabby or dull, and should cling tenaciously to any bone. When the fish is held horizontally by head and tail, the midsection should not sag appreciably.

## Why does seafood in fish stores sometimes look slimy?

This sheen is usually caused by bacterial decay, but not always. The chemical additive tripolyphosphate (nicknamed "tripoly" in the trade) is sometimes the culprit, especially when it's used excessively by overzealous fishermen and seafood processors.

The method is simple: The seafood is soaked for several hours in a tripoly solution. A resulting chemical reaction retards the water loss that occurs naturally in protein tissue when a life-form dies. Protein tissue loses water during the post-death stage because its molecular structure contracts, decreasing its water-retention ability. Tripoly raises the tissue's pH factor, causing the protein's molecular structure to unfold, thereby increasing its ability to bind water.

Money is the obvious reason why the fish industry wants to curtail water loss. If a product weighed 10 percent more when the merchants caught or bought it than when they sold it, a lot of potential profits go down the drain, literally.

The less obvious reason is also money-related. Tripoly not only does its job in eliminating water loss, it gives the industry a generous bonus. The chemical actually increases the net amount of water in the seafood by about 5 to 10 percent. The tripoly user can therefore increase the amount of seafood he has to sell without catching or buying more seafood. In essence, the seafood merchants are selling water. (Note: The seafood industry is not the only trade using this weight-building stratagem. Look in your local supermarket's display case and you'll see hams labeled "10 percent water added." However, unlike the ham processors, the seafood ones are not required to inform you that they are selling less meat than you might think.)

Seafood advertisers argue that the tripoly process makes frozen seafood more succulent than it would otherwise be. That's true, to some degree. What they don't tell you is that the tripoly treatment can give shrimp a mushy texture, soapy flavor, and — as mentioned earlier — a slimy coating when overused.

The use of these additives has raised at least two health questions. Sodium watchers are concerned because tripoly sometimes comes in forms like sodium tripolyphosphate. Moreover, phosphates can decrease the ability of bones to acquire essential calcium, a condition that can lead to osteoporosis.

### Why can't I store fish as long as other animal meat?

After an animal dies, some of its digestive enzymes erode the alimentary canal walls and invade the flesh. The flesh of an ungutted fish will spoil faster under this assault than will that of a land animal, partially because a fish's digestive enzymes are generally more efficacious. Remember, those biological catalysts that labor in the fish's digestive tract must chemically break down swallowed whole fish, bones and all. Compounding the disintegrating effect of the fish's potent digestive enzymes is the fact that fish flesh is easier to digest than terrestrial animal meat.

Glycogen also plays a role in storage. Fish (and other animals) store this carbohydrate in their muscle tissue as an energy source. At the animal's death, this supply is converted to lactic acid, an effective preservative. Unfortunately, the amount of lactic acid in the flesh of a dead fish is usually scant because a fish burns up most of its glycogen store struggling to escape from the fisherman's net or hook.

Another problem is that the potentially pathogenic bacteria that lie in wait on the outside of the fish or in its digestive tract are, unlike those of land animals, psychrophilic. That term means that these microorganisms can thrive in relatively low temperatures. At one degree above the freezing point, the bacteria that typically attack fish can thrive, whereas the action of those that normally assault beef, for instance, is retarded. Even at temperatures below 32°F, the bacteria in fish are more active than those in beef.

Freezing the fish at an exceedingly low temperature ( – 100°F, for instance) is not a flawless solution because, though the bacterial growth may be impeded at such hypo-Siberian thermometer readings, freezing ruins the fish's texture, and more so than it does the cell structure of red meat. Even dried fish does not store as well as dried red meat. Using any preservative method, fish is more perishable than meat from warm-blooded vertebrates.

Unsaturated fatty acids are more apt to oxidize than saturated ones. Since the ratio of unsaturated to saturated fatty acids is higher for fish than it is for mammals, it follows that they will oxidize, and therefore become rancid, more quickly than beef, pork, or lamb.

## Can the provenance of a fish affect its wholesomeness?

Most fishermen know that it's risky to eat fish caught in rivers and lakes polluted by industrial wastes. Few realize that it's risky to eat fish caught off one of the most popular fishing spots, a bridge. Auto exhaust fumes and the rubbish people dump in the middle of the night can pollute the waters near a bridge.

Fish caught in coastal waters (particularly if near an urban center) are exposed to far more contaminants than deep-water denizens. This is why the flesh of a deep-water, three-hundred-pound tuna is less likely to be contaminated than that of a shore-hugging, eight-ounce porgy.

A large fish (and the people who eat it) may not be as fortunate if it lives near an industrial metropolis. Its flesh will likely have a higher concentration of toxic mercury than that of smaller fishes. Here's why. Bottom-dwelling shellfish ingest mercury waste that settles to the ocean floor. The mercury in these crustaceans is transferred to fishes that devour them, which in turn is transferred to the fishes that eat them. Eventually, some of the mercury reaches the top of the food chain, fishes such as tuna, sharks, and swordfish. Because these large fishes live longer than smaller fishes, they eat more flesh in a lifetime. Because mercury is difficult to expel from the body, a large fish living in coastal waters may become a repository of an unsafe quantity of mercury before it's caught.

**Is it safe to eat sushi, the famous Japanese raw fish specialty?**

Flesh of healthy fish living in unpolluted ocean water is free of pathogenic bacterial contamination. If such flesh comes from a nonpoisonous fish, is properly stored for not more than a half a day or so, and is correctly cleaned and prepared, eating sushi poses no more threat to your health than consuming a wholesome raw oyster or clam gathered from uncontaminated waters.

Unfortunately, most of the Japanese sushi bars in America (and some in Japan) serve less than perfectly fresh fish, and the seafood is not always hygienically handled. Our recommendation is to enjoy sushi only at a quality Japanese restaurant that has a conscientious sushi chef with impeccable standards. One clue to questionable quality is when the Japanese restaurant seems to have installed a sushi bar as an afterthought. If a restaurant's sushi bar does not teem with customers during peak hours, then chances are the chef doesn't replenish his inventory on a daily basis.

**Why doesn't fish have to be cooked to tenderize it?**

Unlike red animal meat, the flesh of fish (and shellfish) has meager connective tissue, the muscle component that can make raw red meat tough and dry. The small amount of connective tissue in the flesh of a fish is more easily gelatinized by moist heat than the kind found in the flesh of landlubbers. Excess cooking (and it doesn't take much) is inappropriate because it toughens the muscle fibers unnecessarily without tendering any meaningful payment in return.

### Then why is fish cooked?

Cooking helps destroy any existing pathogenic microorganisms and — if not excessive — develops and distributes flavor, as well as coagulating the protein muscle fibers, a chemical process that gives the flesh pleasing firmness and opaque color. This coagulation can be accomplished with nonheat methods, too. Tahitians and Peruvians, for example, have for centuries marinated freshly caught and dressed fish in lemon or lime juice, calling their cooked specialties, respectively, *l'ota* and *ceviche*. French Polynesians also call their version of the first dish *poisson cru* (literally "raw fish").

### Does it make a difference to a cook whether the flesh of a fish is fat or lean?

Yes, very much so. A fat-fleshed fish is better suited for grilling or roasting because of the extra oil it contains. A lean-fleshed fish generally should be cooked in an oil or liquid; if grilled or roasted, it tends to dry out unless the flesh is frequently basted.

### Is the flesh juicier and more flavorful if a fish is cooked with its head and tail on?

Without a doubt. Decapitation and tail removal allow the juices in the flesh in the main part of the body to leak out during cooking. The head and tail also add flavor and nutrients to the cooking flesh, as well as to the developing sauce or stock. Serving the whole fish with head and tail intact also is prudent because the fish stays warmer on the serving platter, loses fewer juices, and makes a more dramatic presentation.

### Is a fillet less flavorful than an unboned piece of fish?

Yes. Bones impart a rich flavor to the surrounding flesh.

**Should I sever the gills before cooking a whole fish?**

Your decision should largely depend on the freshness of your fish. If yours is freshly killed, don't go to the bother of removing them. If it is more than a day old, extricate them, because, as we pointed out earlier, the gills spoil more quickly than the flesh and may imbue the cooking flesh with an off-flavor.

**When poaching fish, is it necessary to add wine, lemon juice, or other acidic ingredient to the liquid?**

Without acid as a counterbalance, the alkali that is probably in the pot's contents would chemically react with the flavone pigment in the flesh, giving the pigment, and therefore the flesh, an unattractive, yellowish, off-white hue.

If just enough acid is added, the pH factor of the contents of the pot will be 7.0 (that number denotes the neutralization of the opposing effects of the acid and alkali). If yet more acid is mixed in with the poaching liquid, the pH factor will fall below 7.0 (signifying acidic ascendancy). When that happens, the flavone pigment becomes even whiter than it was when you procured the fish.

**Why shouldn't broiling fish fillets be turned?**

For openers, they do not usually need to be turned. Since each fillet is usually thin, the under half will be cooked by a combination of heat penetrating through the upper half of the fish and heat emanating from the hot pan below.

A fillet is also delicate, and the act of turning it is likely to break it apart, particularly if the flesh adheres to the grate or pan. To minimize the sticking tendency that can make removing the cooked fish difficult, butter or grease the cooking surface before placing the fish on it.

**How long and at how high a temperature should a fish be cooked?**

Time and temperature are two inversely related variables of the cooking equation.

Temperature should be about 180°F if you are poaching the fish; in the low-moderate range (300° to 350°F) if pan-broiling, pan-frying, or baking; 375°F if you are deep-frying; and about 450°F if you are broiling. Lower temperatures than our suggested guidelines would prolong the cooking time too much, which would in turn needlessly sap some of the fish's delicate flavor. Higher temperatures than our recommended figures would develop more flavor, but that gain would not compensate for the resulting dryness and toughness of the flesh.

The second coordinate — time — should be as short as the cooking method allows, just long enough to coagulate the protein. Prolonged cooking — even if you use the right temperature — will rob flavor and toughen the protein, and the flesh will fall apart at the slightest provocation.

Most American cooks, be they the restaurant or home variety, nearly always overcook their fish. The element of error is usually in the time, rather than the temperature.

**What are the tests for doneness?**

In most instances, as soon as the translucent flesh turns opaque, the protein has adequately coagulated. Another test is to probe the thickest portion of the flesh with a fork. As soon as it flakes, the fish is properly cooked. Flaking occurs after heat has gelatinized the collagen in the myocommata, a type of connective tissue that holds the thin, parallel sheets of muscle fiber together. These separated sheets give the properly cooked fish flesh a flaky texture.

**Why does fish suffer more than red meat from a delay in serving?**

Cooked fish flesh loses its flavor, aroma, and texture more quickly than warm-blooded animal meat principally because these three qualities in fish are more delicate and subtle to begin with. Procrastination when serving meat is a misdemeanor; when serving fish, a felony.

**Why do crustaceans taste sweeter than fish?**

Crustaceans like lobsters have a higher proportion of glycogen, a polysaccharide that converts into the simple sugar, glucose. Glycogen is aptly named; it is derived from the Greek words *glukus* (sweet) and *gen* (a suffix meaning "capable of bringing forth"). Other substances, including the amino acid glycine, influence sweetness intensity, too.

Among the three most widely eaten crustaceans, lobster is the sweetest, followed by crab and shrimp in that order. Fish flesh, though less sweet than crustacean meat, is sweeter than land animal muscles. Whatever the flesh, sweetness starts to diminish noticeably after a day or two of storage time.

**Are lobster claws secured with wooden plugs or rubber bands for reasons other than the benefit of the cook's fingers?**

Lobsters are cannibals, and unless their claws are disabled, these crustaceans will devour each other while they are held in captivity in lobster tanks or shipping crates.

**How can lobsters stay alive out of water?**

Unlike fish, they can extract oxygen from the moisture that clings to their gills. For optimum out-of-the-water storage, the environment should be about 50°F and damp. Surrounding the lobster in wet seaweed helps.

## Why is it preferable for a lobster to still be alive at the time it is cooked, or to have expired only shortly before?

The enzymes in a lobster's (or crab's) digestive tract are quite potent and can quickly start decomposing the flesh once the creature dies. Unlike the digestive system of fishes, mammals, or birds, that of lobsters (or crabs) is difficult to remove before they are cooked.

Another reason for a cook to insist on a living lobster is that live crustaceans are far more likely to harbor pathogenic microorganisms (such as hepatitis-carrying viruses) than are live fish. And when they do, the microbe count in the lobster will also likely be much higher. Those disease-causing agents, given a head start, will multiply at a much faster pace in a crustacean. Your best defense, therefore, is absolute freshness.

Even if you could safely cook and eat a lobster that has been dead for twenty-four hours, there is seldom a way to ascertain beyond a shadow of a doubt that the uncooked lobster displayed in your local fish store has died a recent death. You can, on the other hand, determine that it is definitely not fit for purchase. Pick it up by its back. Unless the tail curls under the body, the lobster is dead or close to it.

## What is the best way to kill a lobster?

Plunging a lobster (or crab) headlong into a pot of boiling water is not one of the best options because it is not exactly a humane method. Witnessing the doomed lobster's one- or two-second-long spasm should prove this point to any doubting Thomas. The shock of this convulsive death does more than inflict pain on the lobster. It toughens its muscles and therefore your meal.

A more compassionate alternative is to sever the lobster's spinal cord, and therefore deaden its sense of pain, by thrusting the tip of a knife downward into the natural breach where the head and front abdomen shells converge.

Should a cook be too faint-hearted to perform this bit of culinary surgery before boiling the lobster, the very least one can do is to place it in a pot or basin in a sink and turn on both the hot and cold taps. When the container is filled, gradually turn off the cold water, while increasing the flow of hot water until the water is as hot as the pipes allow. As the water temperature rises, the lobster becomes increasingly insensate. It also becomes rather inactive — so this is also a good plan if a cook wants to sever the spinal cord but is apprehensive over the thought of scuffling with an energetic lobster.

We know of some cooks who submerge the lobster (or crab) in a container of beer or wine. The crustacean becomes inebriated, relaxes its muscles, and reacts less spasmodically when dumped live into the seething cauldron of water. This method has validity, but today's wine and beer prices place it beyond the budget of most people. A lobster costs enough as it is.

### Why does a lobster turn red when cooked?

Heat liberates a yellowish-red carotenelike pigment in the shell. This chemical reaction changes the color of the lobster's carapace from (typically) bluish seaweed-green to ruddy red. Cooked shrimp shells also turn red. Even the surface of crustacean meat acquires a pinkish-red hue, though not as pervasive or intense as that of the shell.

### Are there left-handed lobsters?

Yes — and there are right-handed lobsters as well. Unlike humans and most other creatures, the "Maine" (or more properly, Northern or American Lobster, *Homarus americanus*) lobster is not symmetrical — that is, its left and right sides are not mirror images of each other. A close examination of any whole Maine lobster will reveal that its two claws are different in both size and function. The larger claw has coarse teeth for the heavy-duty crushing jobs, whereas the small claw has fine teeth for lighter ripping and tearing tasks. A lobster is left-handed or right-handed depending on which side has the larger claw.

Which lobster tastes better, a right- or left-handed one? Both are equal in this department, despite what some lobster snobs aver. Which claw tastes better? The flesh from the smaller claw is sweeter and more tender and therefore superior, but the large claw contains more meat and provides a taste contrast — so we are lucky that Mother Nature designed lobsters with one of each.

## Why the rule "Never cook a clam that refuses to close its shell before it is cooked"?

It is quite natural for a healthy clam (or mussel or oyster) to open its shell if it feels relaxed as it rests on a bed of ice or in a bucket of cold water. However, it is unnatural for one of these bivalves not to clamp its twin shells tightly shut if you frighten it, say, by giving it a firm flick with your finger. Closing its shell in response to such an external stimulus is the shellfish's only meaningful defense. Should your threat not evoke the safety mechanisms designed by nature, the bivalve is dead or dying and may therefore be contaminated with pathogenic microorganisms or toxins.

## Why the rule "Never eat a cooked clam whose shells don't part upon cooking"?

When a healthy clam, mussel, or oyster expires, so does the holding power of the muscle that keeps the two shells tightly closed. If the shells do not open after the bivalve is cooked (and hence killed), it wasn't alive in the first place. Something other than the abductor muscle — perhaps an oily mass of mud — was keeping the shells closed.

## How does a scallop differ from a clam, oyster, or mussel?

Unlike the other popular mollusks, which do not travel through the water during their adulthood, a mature scallop jet-propels itself through its briny environment by rapidly snapping together its twin shells. To perform this feat, the scallop has a comparatively sizeable and powerful abductor muscle, the only part of this mollusk that we normally buy and eat. In contrast, one consumes everything inside the shell of a clam, oyster, or mussel, intestines and all.

## Why are scallops not sold in the shell?

A clam, oyster, or mussel can remain alive and healthy for days, and sometimes a week or two, out of its natural seawater environment because it can tightly clamp its shell. By doing so, the mollusk maintains its own liquid eco-environment within its protective case. A scallop, on the other hand, cannot snugly shut its two shells. Once pulled from the water, its juices run out and the coming of the three Ds — death, desiccation, and disease agents — is imminent. Professional scallop gatherers, therefore, usually shuck the bivalve on the boat, discarding the quick-spoiling viscera.

## Can a crab (or lobster) regenerate a claw?

Yes. In Florida, a mini-industry that was once threatened by depletion has revived by taking advantage of a crab's regenerative capability. Formerly, gatherers of stone crabs killed the crustacean to obtain its two claws, its only marketable body parts. To save the diminishing crab population, and hence their own enterprises, the crab hunters adopted the practice of breaking off only one of the stone crab's two claws and tossing the creature back into the sea. With one claw left to defend itself and forage for food, the crab survives, grows a new appendage, and — if unlucky — suffers through the ordeal again.

## What is a soft-shell crab?

It is not an individual species, as some believe. In order to grow, a crab (or lobster) must periodically shed its shell and grow a new, larger one. Immediately after undergoing this process (called "molting"), the crab has a soft exterior. It takes days, or longer, for the crab's exposed surface area to ossify. Till it does, the crab is highly vulnerable to predators (including two-legged diners) and is known as a soft-shell crab. The nonpareil soft-shell crab, from a seafood buff's perspective, is a young blue crab that has molted within the hour.

## Are the prawns served in restaurants really shrimp?

In all probability, yes. A true prawn is biologically different from a shrimp; the prawn has lobsterlike pincer claws. The best eating species are the Dublin Bay prawns of Ireland and the scampi of the northern Adriatic Sea. Both are larger than an average-sized shrimp but smaller than a lobster. When a restaurant serves you prawns or scampi in America, odds are a thousand to one that you are eating jumbo shrimp, a cheaper and less succulent substitute.

## Why do some shrimp taste less of iodine than others?

A marine shrimp caught near the mouth of a river will smack less of iodine than one caught in unadulterated seawater, because the seawater has a higher iodine content. Even marine shrimp that live far away from rivers can differ in flavor because iodine content in seawater and the food shrimp eat vary geographically. Shrimp acquire an iodine flavor when they eat algae (these plants are iodine-rich because they concentrate within their cells the iodine in seawater). In addition, shrimp get iodine by eating sea creatures such as sand-dwelling worms that also eat the algae. Once digested, a fair portion of the iodine remains in the shrimp's bodies.

Sometimes the iodine flavor is intensified when processors use the additive sodium bisulfite. This chemical can amplify the iodine's effect on your taste buds. Although its use to prolong the storage life of shrimp is prohibited in the United States, it is no secret that some foreign processors surreptitiously taint their shrimp with it before exporting them to America.

**Is the rule "Oysters are unsafe to eat in any month that does not contain the letter _R_" obsolete?**

From a medical authority's viewpoint, this advice is archaic for oysters harvested along the Atlantic and Caribbean coasts. It was, however, sound decades ago when the lack of refrigerated trucks and trains made the shipment of any type of oyster hygienically precarious during the warm weather, no-_R_ months, May, June, July, and August. Even so, the rule wasn't quite accurate because September is normally warmer than May.

From a discriminating palate's perspective, the _R_-less month dictum still has meaning. Oysters tend to be more watery and less meaty during the summer months when they spawn.

# 5

## D·A·I·R·Y  P·R·O·D·U·C·T·S

**W**hen and why must you scald milk for use in a recipe?

To scald milk means heating it to just below the boiling point. Use a thick-bottomed saucepan or a double boiler to prevent scorching the milk.

Scalding has two primary purposes: to kill pathogenic micro-organisms and to destroy certain enzymes that would keep emulsifying agents in the milk from doing their thickening job. Since those two goals are accomplished when milk is pasteurized at the dairy, scalding need only be done when you use raw (unpasteurized) milk. Many cookbook writers do not know this fact and therefore direct their readers to scald the milk even though it is usually unnecessary today.

### What causes milk to stick to a pan?

Any one of the following, or a combination of them, can scorch milk and cause it to stick: heating milk at too high a temperature; heating for too long; infrequent and incomplete stirring; heating in a thin-bottomed pan. And the staler your milk, the more likely it will scorch. Scorched milk gives preparations a burnt off-flavor and human dishwashers a time-consuming chore. What burns and tenaciously sticks are the milk's protein and lactose (milk sugar). When lactose caramelizes, it imparts an unwanted flavor and color to your heated milk.

## What is the film that forms on the surface of milk while it is being heated?

The film is milk protein that has been coagulated by the heat. Its existence is undesirable because it gives your final preparation a lumpy texture and (even if you remove and discard the film) a burnt taste. This film can also create another problem (see next Q&A).

## What causes this film to rise so suddenly (and overflow the pot)?

Normally, as steam bubbles emerge from the milk, they quickly burst, well below the pot's rim. However, if a film forms, the milk bubbles are trapped between this skin and the milk. As these bubbles grow in number, they push the skin upward until, eventually, the skin and some of the bubbles may overflow the pot.

The first rule of avoiding a time-consuming cleanup chore is never turn your back on the pot for even a short duration — the trapped steam can suddenly begin expanding. And, don't forget to stir the milk frequently and thoroughly, particularly if you are heating it above 140°F, the approximate temperature at which some of the milk protein begins to coagulate. Unless you have a good reason not to do so, keep the milk comfortably below the simmer point.

Even better, use a microwave to heat your milk because it reduces the cleanup chore. Milk can easily scorch in a pot set upon the range; even if the burner is set to low, the pot's bottom can reach 300°F or higher. Milk is less likely to scorch in a microwave because no portion of the milk gets hotter than the boiling point and the container never gets hotter than the milk. (Tip: The best container for heating milk in a microwave is a Pyrex-style cup because it lets you monitor the liquid and is easy to transport and clean.)

**Why doesn't homogenized milk separate?**

Dairies use high-pressure equipment to force the milk through fine openings. This breaks up the milk fat into tiny, well-dispersed globules that cannot recombine into larger fat globules because of their minute size and the movement of the water molecules in the milk. This anticombining action is furthered by the milk's casein protein, an emulsifying agent. If the fat globules were allowed to combine, they would float upward to form a distinct layer over the fat-free milk.

**How and why is milk pasteurized?**

The dairy heats the milk to either 145°F for at least thirty minutes or, more often, to 161°F for at least fifteen seconds. Either temperature-time combination kills pathogenic bacteria in the milk. Pasteurization (as well as homogenization) also makes milk more digestible.

Pasteurization accomplishes another mission. Whether or not milk is pasteurized, it will eventually spoil when nonpathogenic bacteria multiply sufficiently. The heat treatment stalls this inevitable process by significantly reducing the original number of nonpathogenic bacteria in the milk.

Contrary to statements by the dairy industry, pasteurization does give milk a slight cooked flavor. However, this flavor shortcoming is noticeable only to educated palates and is more than compensated for by the fact that pasteurized milk is, on balance, much safer to drink than raw (unpasteurized) milk, a potential source of diseases, among them tuberculosis. If you do drink raw milk, be certain that the product came to you from a reliable dairy, distributor, and merchant. If your source is a healthy pet cow in the pasture within view of your window, all the better.

**What is lactose intolerance?**

A baby produces the enzyme lactase, which helps break down the otherwise hard-to-digest lactose (milk sugar).

If children or adults stop drinking milk for an extended period of time, they may lose the ability to produce lactase in sufficient quantities. Such people are lactose-intolerant and will suffer from intestinal discomfort and other ill-effects if they consume very much milk. The symptoms usually occur because the afflicted person's small intestine does not produce enough lactase to digest the lactose. The person feels bloated because the undigested milk sugars pull extra water into the stomach. He is also apt to suffer from diarrhea and flatulence because the undigested lactose passes into the large intestine where bacteria convert it into acids and gases.

By gradually reintroducing his body to milk, a lactose intolerant will eventually be able to produce more lactase, but never in the quantity that was possible before he went on the "milk wagon." (Incidentally, a non-Caucasian is more apt to develop lactose intolerance.)

Most lactose-intolerant people can eat cultured-milk foods (cheese or yogurt, for instance) or drink cultured milk, such as buttermilk. Lactose is virtually nonexistent in those products because as bacteria transform the milk into a cultured product, they digest the lactose, turning it into lactic acid. Lactic acid plays a large part in giving cultured-milk products their characteristic sourness.

Sweet acidophilus milk, a low-fat milk product infused with lactic acidophilus bacteria, was once widely touted to lactose intolerants who wanted to drink milk. Today, few experts recommend this product because some tests indicate that the acidophilus bacteria don't digest the lactose in significant amounts. Lactose intolerants are not out of luck, however. A new commercially sold enzyme, Lactaid, is effective and is readily available in drug stores. This nonprescription product is also sold in supermarkets, premixed into milk.

### Why is cow's milk often diluted with water and sweetened with sugar before it is fed to a baby?

The percentage of casein protein in cow's milk is much higher than that in human milk because a calf has greater nutritional needs than a human baby — its growth rate is about twice that of its human counterpart. Because its casein content is higher, cow's milk is harder to digest than human milk. If the milk weren't stretched with water and the baby's intake of the milk (and its casein) thereby reduced, it would put a strain on the baby's delicate digestive system.

Sugar is added to the cow's milk to make the infant's formula taste more like human milk, which is naturally sweeter. Speaking of sugar, a parent should not let a baby get into the habit of falling asleep with a milk bottle. This beverage (as well as sugary fruit juices) is laden with bacteria that can cause tooth decay. If a parent feels the child needs a nightcap, the bottle crutch should contain plain water.

### Is adding chocolate to milk a good way to entice children to drink milk?

Though the chocolate flavoring is often an enticement, it is unsound from a nutritional standpoint. The oxalic acid in chocolate inhibits the digestive system's ability to absorb the milk's calcium. The oxalic acid chemically reacts with the calcium, producing a new compound, calcium oxalate. The intestines cannot absorb this calcium oxalate because it is insoluble. This loss of the essential mineral calcium is nutritionally detrimental, especially for growing children.

### What is the difference between 96.5 percent fat-free and whole milk?

There is none. The phrase "99 percent fat-free" on skim milk containers has misled many a shopper into thinking that whole milk is 0 percent fat-free. Most of the whole milk sold in the United States is 96 to 97 percent fat-free. Here is a breakdown of typical whole milk from a cow, stated in percentages.

| | |
|---|---|
| Fat | 3.5 |
| Nonfat components | |
| *Water* | 87.3 |
| *Carbohydrates* | 5.0 |
| *Protein* | 3.5 |
| *Minerals, etc.* | 0.7 |
| *Subtotal* | 96.5 |
| TOTAL | 100.0 |

Figures for a typical 99 percent fat-free skim milk or buttermilk are as follows:

| | |
|---|---|
| Fat | 1.0 |
| Nonfat components | |
| *Water* | 89.6 |
| *Carbohydrates* | 5.1 |
| *Protein* | 3.6 |
| *Minerals, etc.* | 0.7 |
| *Subtotal* | 99.0 |
| TOTAL | 100.0 |

### How does sweet milk become sour milk?

About 5 percent of fresh milk's content is lactose, a milk sugar that gives the liquid a slight but noticeable sweet taste. As the milk ages, certain bacteria devour some of the lactose, converting it into lactic acid. Result: The milk sours.

### Why doesn't today's buttermilk taste like yesteryear's?

Virtually all the buttermilk marketed today is artificially soured skim milk and, thus, not authentic buttermilk. True buttermilk is made from whole milk and is the direct by-product of butter making. One of the traditional processes begins by allowing whole milk to sour in order to make it easier for the butter to coagulate. When sufficiently sour, the milk is churned to separate the butter from the nonfat components, which become the buttermilk. The yellow specks you see suspended in the buttermilk are bits of butter that were too small to be removed. (The butter produced this way is not excessively sour because the sour flavor comes from the lactic acid, most of which is in the nonfat portion of the milk.)

Real buttermilk is preferable for cooking and drinking because it has a richer taste, fuller body, and higher nutritive value than the imitation. Nowadays, you almost have to live within a short haul of a dairy to find the real McCoy, and even then, there is no guarantee that your search will be successful.

Incidentally, buttermilk has a longer shelf life than whole milk for several reasons. It becomes rancid less rapidly because it has a lower fat content. Buttermilk's higher acid content helps inhibit the growth of most spoilage-causing bacteria. Some dairies prolong the shelf life of buttermilk even more by adding salt.

## Why do canned milks have an unpleasant taste?

Evaporated milk is heated in its can to a temperature well above 200°F in order to sterilize the milk. A cooked or burnt flavor is the outcome. The metal of the can also imparts an off-flavor.

Another canned product, condensed milk, does not have to be sterilized because its high (over 40 percent) sugar content serves as a preservative by hindering bacterial growth. Of course, that much sugar does not make condensed milk all that appealing, either.

## Why should nonfat dry milk be reconstituted the day before it is to be used?

Nonfat dry milk is whole milk minus its fat and water. About 35 percent of the dried powder is protein (mainly casein), and about 50 percent is carbohydrate in the form of lactose, a milk sugar. Although sucrose (the common table sugar derived from sugar beets or cane sugar) dissolves rapidly, lactose does not. Unless you give your reconstituted dry milk a rest in the refrigerator, it is apt to taste grainy. The instant dry-milk powders eliminate most, but not all, of the solubility problem.

### Is heavy cream heavier than light cream?

Contrary to what the senses in our mouths tell us, heavy cream is actually lighter than light cream. And light cream is lighter than whole milk, which is lighter than skim milk. Skeptical? As proof, consider that cream invariably rises to the top of nonhomogenized milk. This phenomenon can be easily explained because fat has a lower specific density than water. Now, consider that the fat and water percentages for cream are, respectively, about 40 percent and 55 percent, whereas those for milk are, respectively, about 4 percent and 87 percent. The figures for skim milk are about 1 percent and 90 percent.

What fools our senses is primarily the fact that fat has a higher viscosity than water. Having been taught at a very early age the misleading phrases "heavy cream" and "light cream" biases our interpretations, too.

### Why does homemade cream of tomato soup sometimes curdle?

Acid can curdle cream (or milk). The tendency to curdle increases as the ratio of acid to cream, the heat of the mixture, or the salt quantity increases. Since three of the star ingredients of cream of tomato soup are cream, acid-rich tomatoes, and salt, the threat of curdling lurks in your kitchen whenever you prepare the soup.

To thwart the curdling tendency, heat the liquefied tomato mixture and cream separately, then slowly add the acidic liquid to the cream near the end of the cooking process. Once mixed, do not heat the cream of tomato soup for very long or at a temperature above 180°F. Add the salt just before serving.

Another pointer is to use the freshest cream possible. The more a cream ages, the more susceptible it becomes to curdling because its lactic acid content increases.

## Why does cream sometimes curdle when poured into a cup of coffee?

Again, acid is the troublemaker. Chances are the cream was not as fresh as it should have been. As a cream ages, its lactic acid content increases. Your coffee, too, has acid — and the stronger your brew or the more acidic the beans, the more acid-rich your cup of java. Any acid in sufficient quantity, and especially with the help of the coffee's heat, will curdle cream.

## What determines how well a cream will whip?

Fat content has a lot to do with how well your cream whips. When you whip cream, you incorporate air into the mixture in the form of tiny bubbles. These air pockets are what give the whipped cream its light, fluffy texture. Whipped cream, an emulsion, is a delicate structure: The watery nonfat portion of the cream that encloses the bubbles is supported by the fat. The more fat in your cream (up to a point), the more effectively the encased bubbles will be supported.

Heavy whipping cream (about 40 percent fat content) increases more in volume than medium or all-purpose cream (about 30 percent fat), which in turn whips to a greater volume than light cream (about 20 percent fat). Buying heavy whipping cream is no assurance that you are buying the ideal ingredient: Some brands have a higher fat content than others.

The temperature of the fat is almost as critical as its quantity. You want it to be cold enough to be firm. If you wish to whip cream to its maximum volume, store it for at least several hours in your refrigerator. For best results, also chill your whipping bowl and beater for thirty minutes in the freezer compartment because, used at room temperature, these utensils can raise the cream's temperature by 5 degrees to 10°F. If your beater is electric, chill only the detachable metal beaters. (Interestingly, egg whites reach their greatest volume when they are whipped at room temperature, rather than straight from the refrigerator.)

As cream ages, certain bacteria transform lactose (milk sugar) into lactic acid. Since excess acid can disrupt emulsification, the cream should be as fresh as possible.

Ultrapasteurized cream has a longer storage life because it is pasteurized at a higher temperature than the standard store-bought cream. A cook pays for this convenience in ways other than money: Ultrapasteurized cream has poorer whipping qualities. One reason is that the higher pasteurization temperature denatures the proteins to the point where their jelling capabilities are reduced. (Other drawbacks are that ultrapasteurized cream has a more pronounced cooked flavor and is a less effective thickener for sauces, soups, and the like.)

If you are flavoring your whipped cream with sugar or vanilla, incorporate these ingredients near the end of the whipping process. Adding them too early hinders the bubble development. If you mix them into the cream after it has reached maximum volume, you will have to overwhip the cream in order to disperse the sugar and vanilla uniformly. Overwhipping is an irreversible culinary blunder. You are, in effect, churning the cream. Before your very eyes, some of the whipped cream will metamorphose into butter.

## Why are aerated creams poor substitutes for homemade whipped cream?

An aerated cream has a cooked flavor because it was heated to a temperature high enough to sterilize it. Natural flavor is further altered by preservatives, and texture is too foamy and unstable. Even worse than aerated creams are the pseudo–whipped creams that are marketed under banners such as dessert topping. These fakes smack of their nondairy ingredients: hydrogenated vegetable oils, artificial flavoring, and preservatives.

## What is the composition of butter?

Despite the efforts of the American dairy industry to standardize butter, its composition can differ from batch to batch because of factors such as the cow's breed and feed, season, local legislation, and dairy policy. If we take an across-the-board average, the composition by weight percentages is as follows:

|          | SWEET BUTTER | SALTED BUTTER |
|----------|:---:|:---:|
| Fat      | 81  | 81  |
| Moisture | 18  | 16  |
| Salt     | 0   | 2   |
| Other    | 1   | 1   |

"Other" comprises, in descending order of weight, protein (mainly casein), carbohydrate (mainly the milk sugar lactose), and minerals other than salt. Butter is rich in vitamin A. Its calorie count is approximately 100 per tablespoon.

## Is butter color a reliable indicator of quality?

Natural butter can vary from the palest of yellows to a deep yellow, depending on the cow's breed and feed. Certain breeds, such as those from the Channel Islands (Jersey and Guernsey) produce deeper yellow butters. All cows produce their deepest-colored butter in the springtime and early summer when the grass they eat is particularly rich in orange-yellow carotene. When winter comes, so does a paler butter.

Because the average American consumer wants consistency, butter manufacturers try to give their products year-round uniformity by using dyes such as annatto seed extract or carotene. A butter made with winter or Holstein cow milk, for instance, can therefore be made just as rich in color as one from springtime or Jersey cow milk.

Color is a quality indicator, however, when it comes to uniformity in a particular sample. White streaks or multiple shades of yellow are not positive signs.

### Why is salted butter a bane to cooks?

The salt content of salted butter can vary from brand to brand, from region to region. One batch of butter may have 1½ percent salt and another twice as much.

Even if you stick with one brand and know its exact salt content, it is a headache to calculate the amount of salt you must subtract from a recipe that calls for a given quantity of sweet (unsalted) butter. Since the recipes from virtually all serious cookbooks are based on the use of sweet butter, people who cook with salted butter create an extra complication for themselves (unless, of course, one's religious code dictates its use).

### Why is standard stick butter better for cooking than whipped butter?

Whipped butter is merely standard butter inflated with air. A disadvantage of whipped butter is that almost all recipes are based upon standard butter measurements. You must increase the volume of butter called for by one-third if you use whipped butter, because that product is approximately 25 percent air. The situation becomes even more complicated because units of tub butter cannot be measured as easily and exactly as units of stick butter.

Whipped butter's advantages lie beyond the stove. Because it is airier, whipped butter spreads more readily on bread and melts more quickly when used as a topping for warm foods like waffles.

### How do I keep butter from scorching?

Butter begins to scorch when the heat changes the character of the protein. One way to help prevent or minimize this problem is to use clarified butter, from which the protein has been removed. Another is to use a fifty-fifty mixture of butter and vegetable oil, which has a higher smoke point than pure butter. Whether you employ the clarified butter or the fifty-fifty method, do not expect your cooked foods to pick up the full, rich flavor of whole butter.

## Why does butter go rancid?

Oxygen is the chief culprit. Off-tasting and -smelling compounds are formed when oxygen comes in contact with the unsaturated fats in butter. You can slow down this chemical reaction by lowering the temperature (frozen butter lasts longer than refrigerated butter, which lasts longer than room-temperature butter) and by tightly wrapping the butter (to minimize surface exposure to air). Another method for fighting rancidity is to change the butter into clarified butter (see pp. 110–12).

Just because a butter goes rancid doesn't necessarily mean it has become unwholesome. In fact, butter's vulnerability to bacterial spoilage is lower than most people think because butter is a water-in-oil emulsion. Consequently, each water particle is sealed in an envelope of fat. This means that the bacteria dispersed in the water and in the butter cannot spread freely.

## What are the advantages of clarified butter?

Clarified butter is superior to regular butter in two salient ways. You can fry with it at a higher temperature and you can store it longer. These benefits are not won without a sacrifice: Clarified butter lacks most of the characteristic buttery flavor that mainly comes from one of the removed substances, the protein casein.

You can fry with clarified butter at a higher temperature because you raise its smoke point from about 250°F to 350°F when you remove the butter's protein, which is the component that scorches first.

Clarified butter has a longer storage life because it is primarily the protein in the butter that makes butter vulnerable to spoilage. If it is superclarified, as is the fabled *ghee* of India, you can store clarified butter at room temperature for months without ill-effects.

### What are the principles of clarifying butter?

To clarify butter, you must separate the fat from the nonfat ingredients. The more completely you remove the nonfats, the more suited your clarified butter will be for frying and storing. Many otherwise intelligently written cookbooks detail unnecessarily burdensome procedures for doing this. Our method is less complicated. Moreover, it eliminates the risk of scorching even one molecule of butter, a threat posed by the often recommended technique of melting it in a pan over a flame.

When butter melts, its emulsion breaks down. The butter then begins to separate into three distinct strata: a thin, whitish upper layer of foam; a thick, yellow middle layer of fat (your clarified butter); a medium-thin, whitish bottom layer of water infused with carbohydrates and, especially, proteins, casein being the most important.

The protein-carbohydrate water solution that makes up the bottom layer contains no fat because the fat, having a lower specific density than the material below, follows the immutable law of nature by rising. (Or you could say with equal logic that the solution sinks.)

The foamy upper layer is often erroneously referred to as an impurity-based scum. This layer is principally made up of water, proteins, and carbohydrates, and is thus similar to the bottom layer. It is prevented from dropping through the fat layer because the trapped air in the frothy structure literally keeps these particular nonfats floating on top of the fat layer. By the time the bubbles burst, the fat layer will have solidified, preventing the denser upper layer from settling to its natural level.

The air bubbles form chiefly because, as the butter melts, bacteria attack some of the carbohydrate lactose, fermenting that milk sugar and thereby producing carbon dioxide gas (as well as some alcohol). Another source of the gas in the bubbles is the air content of the butter (most American unsalted butters are about 4 percent air by volume).

When your melted de-emulsified butter is refrigerated, the fat layer solidifies. Refrigerator temperature is not cold enough to firm the watery bottom layer.

## Clarified Butter

Before diving into this procedure, read the preceding principles on page 110.

STEPS
*Tips and Insights in italic*

1. Cut up a stick (¼ pound) of unsalted butter into small chunks.

   *The smaller the chunks, the more quickly the butter melts.*

2. Place the chunks in a cup-sized bowl.

   *An ovenproof glass bowl is best because it allows you to monitor the clarifying process.*

3. Cover the bowl and place it on the warm spot over your stove's pilot-light area. In this step and in Step 4, do not stir the butter.

   *Alternatively, place the covered bowl in an oven set at its lowest possible heat.*

4. When the butter has completely melted (30 to 60 minutes), store the covered bowl in the refrigerator for at least 1 hour.

   *Do not disturb the bowl until the middle (fat) layer has solidified.*

*(Continued)*

5. Lift out the solidified fat disk. Scrape off as much of the foam and slimy bottom layer as you can without damaging the disk. Finish the cleaning step by quickly rinsing the disk under cold running tap water. Pat it dry with a paper towel.

*If kept covered and in the refrigerator, clarified butter of this sort can be stored for weeks, and often longer.*

**To Make a Superclarified Butter:**

Keep repeating Steps 3 through 5 until no traces of the nonfats remain. Ideally, you will end up with 100 percent butter fat (technically, milk fat).

**Should I buy a cheese that has an ammonia scent?**

Many a cheesemonger has convinced uninformed customers that the ammonia scent of a surface-ripened cheese such as Camembert indicates that it has reached its peak of maturity and that French gourmets love eating their cheese in this condition. Not so. Once you can smell more than a trace of ammonia, the cheese is over the hill because it is sensory confirmation that certain enzymes are attacking countless amino acids, a process that spoils the cheese.

**Why is it impossible to buy a perfect Brie cheese in America?**

If a Brie is to reach perfection, it must be made with unpasteurized milk. Unfortunately for lovers of surface-ripened cheeses, our government does not permit any cheese made with unpasteurized milk to be imported unless it has been aged for sixty days. If a natural Brie were stored for that period, it would become malodorously overripe, and even if an importer smuggled in authentic Brie, the normal trans-Atlantic shipping time would have taken its toll. So the French cheesemakers have only two alternatives if they wish to make a Brie for the American market. They can preserve the cheese in a can (a horrible product) or make it with pasteurized milk (which negatively changes the flavor and ripening qualities of a Brie).

A made-for-America French Brie is customized in yet another way: Its fat content is usually at least 50 percent. The version made for Gallic consumption has a fat content of only around 40 percent.

## Why can I store a hard cheese longer than a soft cheese?

A hard cheese has a lower water content. Since water is a medium conducive to the growth of spoilage-causing bacteria and mold, a hard cheese like Cheddar (about 37 percent water content) will last much longer than cottage cheese (between 70 and 80 percent water content).

Once any cheese is opened, however, you want it to retain moisture for the sake of texture. To minimize moisture loss, keep it tightly wrapped in your refrigerator. This shield also helps keep the cheese and its storage mates from exchanging odors.

Ping-Ponging a cheese back and forth from refrigerator to dining room table robs it of moisture, as well as hastening decay. If you have a piece of cheese too large to eat all at once, cut off and bring to room temperature only what you plan to eat and leave the remainder tightly wrapped in the refrigerator.

## Why does a cheese sometimes refuse to melt in a sauce?

Chances are the cook heated the cheese at too high a temperature or for too long. Such treatment separates the protein from the fat and makes it tough, rubbery, and stringy. A cook who continues to heat the sauce in the hope of melting the unsightly protein lumps is pursuing an impossible dream. Once the damage has been done, further cooking only makes matters worse.

A cook's two primary goals, therefore, are to minimize the level of heat and length of time that will be necessary to melt a particular cheese. The first goal is reached by keeping the heat source at a low setting and, for even heat distribution, using a thick-bottomed pan or double boiler. To achieve the second goal, bring the cheese to room temperature and cut it into small pieces. If the cheese is dry — as, for instance, a Parmesan — it should be finely grated. Add the cheese just before you have finished cooking the sauce, stirring all the time.

Different types of cheeses have different melting characteristics. Processed cheeses like American cheese melt more quickly and easily than most natural cheeses because they have low melting points. Among the natural cheeses, the driest ones — if finely grated — tend to melt better than their moist counterparts because their protein is less likely to separate from the emulsion and coagulate into tough, chewy strands that diminish the appearance and texture of the dish. This is why knowledgeable cooks prefer to use "cooking cheeses" like Parmigiano-Reggiano (authentic Parmesan) for preparations like sauces, where the cheese must become well integrated. The longer this cheese has been aged, the better its cooking qualities.

For some culinary specialties, a cheese's tendency to become stringy is a sought-after quality. A case in point is mozzarella, a protein-rich cheese. Can you imagine eating an Italian-American–style pizza without having to bite off those strands of melted cheese that stretch between your mouth and the slice?

**Why can you make yogurt, crème fraîche, and other cultured milk products at room temperature without fear of harmful bacterial development?**

Lactic acid inhibits the growth of certain bacteria that assault the highly perishable protein in the milk. As the milk sours, its lactic acid content increases. Thus, the developing yogurt, for instance, can be safely kept in a 110°F environment for a half day or so. However, if left too long at that temperature, certain molds will feed on the lactic acid, thereby eliminating the yogurt's defense against spoilage-causing bacteria.

## Why does commercial fruit-flavored yogurt have so much sugar?

As makers of fruit preserves, jams, and jellies know, if enough sugar is used, it helps preserve fruits. Yogurt manufacturers also take advantage of this storage-extending ability. Often, though, even more sugar than needed is added to satisfy the sweet tooth of the typical customer.

It is a sad fact that many lovers of fruit-flavored yogurt think they are eating a particularly healthful food. If you offer the same people bread smothered with jam, they probably wouldn't give it too high a nutritive rating. Yet, fruit-flavored yogurt is essentially yogurt with jam or preserves.

What tricks people into thinking that they are consuming a healthful product is the phrase "100 percent natural" printed on the container. Sugar is an empty calorie food. It has virtually no nutritive value and can harm teeth and other parts of the body, yet the manufacturer can use the phrase because the sugar is "100 percent natural" by definition. So is a rotten apple.

If you enjoy yogurt (as we do), eat it plain or add your own fresh fruit. Unless you plan to store your yogurt mixture for a few days, there is no need to add sugar to preserve the fruit.

## Why does ice cream contain so much sugar?

The coldness of the ice cream numbs our taste buds, diminishing their sensitivity. In order to make the ice cream taste sweet, the producer must use twice as much sugar as it would if the ice cream were meant to be served at room temperature.

Sugar serves another purpose: It lowers the freezing point of the ice-cream mixture and therefore decreases the possibility that ice crystals will form.

### Why do ice crystals form in ice cream?

If the ice cream journeys unhurriedly from store to home freezer, makes too many trips in and out of the home freezer, or is kept in a typical home refrigerator frozen-food compartment (which is not cold enough), some of the ice cream's water content, in the form of minute ice crystals, will separate from the fat content and eventually reform into larger ice crystals. These new crystals give the ice cream an icy, and therefore grainy, texture. As long as the water remains in an emulsion with the fat, the original ice crystals will not change their form or the ice cream's texture, unless the ice cream is stored for a prolonged period or at a temperature well below 0°F.

### Is there a way to judge the relative quality of an unknown brand of ice cream before buying and opening the container?

"Overrun" is the measurement of the volume of air that is whipped into a given volume of ice-cream mix (cream, sugar, flavoring agents, etc.). If the air is equal to one-half the mix, the overrun is 50 percent. If it is equal to the volume of the mix, the overrun is 100 percent. If it is 1½ times the volume of the mix, the overrun is 150 percent.

Quality ice creams have lower overruns than those of low quality (roughly 80 percent, versus 100 percent or more) and therefore justifiably cost more than the substandard products, which — quite literally — are a lot of cold air.

Now, how does understanding the concept of overrun help one judge the relative quality of ice cream in a supermarket when the producer does not print the data on the container? If your store has a scale for customer use, you can roughly gauge the ice cream's overrun. Weigh the unknown brand and also a known high-quality brand of equal volume and similar container. The less (or more) the unknown brand weighs, the more (or less) overrun it has.

There is another way to judge overrun before taking the first bite, but this necessitates purchasing the ice cream and taking it home. Place a small sample in a bowl at room temperature. The more quickly it melts in comparison to a high-quality ice cream, the higher its relative overrun is likely to be. A good ice cream takes its time to melt and will not as readily run down the side of a cone on a hot summer day.

Many producers use stabilizers like gelatin to help retard the melting speed of high-overrun ice creams. If the stabilizers are used with abandon, the ice cream may melt even more slowly than quality ice cream, though that sight will not hoodwink aficionados. They will spot telltale signs such as the tiny air bubbles that emerge on the surface as the ice cream melts and the chalkiness or gumminess of its texture.

**Should I scoop ice cream with a circular, horizontal motion, as many ice cream parlors do?**

Not if you want to retard melting, which is usually a must when serving the product at home meals. Many ice cream parlors use the circular motion because slow melting is not their top priority. Profits are. An employee would get fewer servings per tub if he pressed the scoop downward into the ice cream than if he dragged the scoop in an arc on the ice cream's surface. With the first method, the ice cream compacts, creating a denser, slower-melting scoop. With the second method, the ice cream curls, creating air spaces. The customer ends up with a faster melting, poorer-value product.

# 6

# E·G·G·S

Why are refrigerated eggs easier to separate than room temperature ones?

The viscosity of the egg white (albumen) and the surface tension of the yolk membrane are noticeably greater at refrigerator temperature than at room temperature. This means that the albumen will more readily slide away from the yolk — and that the yolk membrane will less likely rupture during the separation process when the cook moves the egg back and forth between the halves of the egg shell.

### At what temperature should egg whites be whipped?

Although egg whites separate from yolks better at refrigerator temperature (see previous Q&A), they whip to their maximum volume at room temperature. One reason is that the surface tension of the albumen is lower at room than at refrigerator temperature. Thus, small air pockets can be more easily incorporated into the albumen to form a foam.

A foam is a superstructure of bubbles. Each bubble comprises a pocket of gas trapped inside a spherical film of liquid. Typically, the gas is air (as is the case with soap bubbles and beaten egg white) or carbon dioxide (think of a beer head). The liquid cannot be pure water because its surface tension is so great that it's difficult to disperse pockets of gas within the water. Not so with albumen. Although it consists chiefly of water, it has enough other substances dissolved into it that its surface tension is sufficiently low to allow foaming.

**Do egg whites whip better in a copper bowl?**

Yes, a copper bowl reduces the time and energy needed to whip egg whites (the precise reason why this phenomenon occurs is still being debated by scientists). Though this advantage is a welcome relief when you are using the arm-tiring, old-fashioned whisk method, it is of slight value with a manual or electric mixer. These efficient modern contraptions do their whipping chores almost as well in a stainless steel, enamel, or glass bowl.

A copper bowl also helps stabilize the beaten egg whites. If you are using a noncopper bowl, a pinch of cream of tartar whipped with the egg whites will stabilize your creation (see p. 120).

Next to copper, stainless steel should be your first choice. Aluminum grays the eggs. Plastic is too porous, and fat can easily lodge in it (see next Q&A). Porcelain and glass have relatively slick surfaces that can slow down the whipping process because the egg whites tend to slip down the walls of the bowl with too much ease.

Whatever the bowl's material, it should be round-bottomed. This increases the likelihood that all the albumen will get its fair share of time in contact with the mixing blades. If you use an electric rotary mixer, be sure its blade moves around the bowl, at least to some degree. Fixed rotary blade mixers whip foam unevenly.

**Why does even a speck of yolk make it difficult to whip egg whites?**

Egg whites cannot be whipped to their maximum volume if they come in contact with any fat beyond the trace amount they already contain. Even a speck of yolk will cause a problem because one-third of a yolk's composition is fat. So separate your eggs diligently, and if a speck of yolk happens to taint the egg whites, remove that yellow villain with one of the sharp, jagged edges of an empty egg shell. Yolk, however, is not the only potential source of volume-reducing fat. Grease in the whipping bowl or on the whipping instrument is just as bad.

## Why should egg whites be beaten slowly at the beginning of the whipping process?

Vigorous beating at the start tends to create air bubbles that are too large. Large bubbles are less stable than the small ones that form when you begin by whipping the liquid for a few minutes at a low-to-medium speed. Once the egg whites (or cream) are half whipped, a medium-to-fast speed is appropriate.

## When whipping egg whites, why should I wait to add ingredients like sugar or cream of tartar until midway in the preparation?

While salt and sugar lend flavor, cream of tartar and other acids help stabilize the foam. However, if you add these substances at the beginning of the whipping process, your beaten egg whites will take longer to whip and will never achieve their maximum volume. If you add the extra ingredients near the end, you would not have enough time to incorporate them uniformly into the egg whites before the stiffened mixture starts to become unstable from overwhipping. Not only would the foam begin to collapse, it would become increasingly drier because protein molecules would begin to lose their ability to bind with water molecules.

## When making a meringue, which sugar is preferable: confectioners' or granulated?

Confectioners' sugar more thoroughly distributes itself through the beaten egg whites. Moreover, when heated, the granulated sugar particles tend to tunnel through the beaten egg whites, popping some of the essential air bubbles in the process. They can also give a meringue an undesirable gritty texture.

### How can I tell if an unopened egg is raw or cooked?

Spin the egg on its side on a flat surface. If your egg rotates smoothly, with effortless grace, it is hard-cooked. If your egg wobbles noticeably, it is uncooked. The wobbling occurs because centrifugal force continuously changes the raw yolk's position inside the egg and so keeps altering the egg's center of gravity.

### Why do simmered or boiled eggs sometimes crack?

Once an egg is laid, its yolk and albumen (egg white) cool and, as a result, contract. This shrinkage creates an air pocket at the egg's larger (nontapered) end. Our illustration indicates that space with crosshatching.

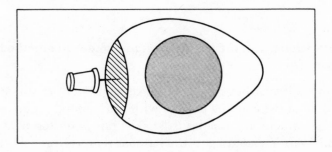

The air in the pocket can cause the shell to crack when you place the egg in simmering water (or, if the cook insists, in boiling water). The reason is that the heat of the water expands the trapped gas (air) in the pocket, creating an atmospheric pressure many times greater than exists in either the water or your kitchen. This built-up pressure easily cracks the fragile shell, releasing the trapped gas and, unfortunately, allowing some of the albumen to ooze into the water.

The problem can be overcome simply by piercing the egg's big end with a standard pushpin (available in most stationery stores or, perhaps, from a friend who works in an office). Its metal pinpoint is short enough not to rupture the membrane that separates the trapped air from the albumen but is thick enough to make a convenient hole for the air to escape through as it expands while being heated in the simmering water. Result: no cracked shell.

So from now on, remove your egg(s) from the refrigerator, pierce it, and gently ease the cold egg into a waiting pot of boiling water. (Adjust heat and simmer for five to seven minutes for soft-cooked eggs and twelve to fifteen minutes for hard-cooked eggs, depending on preference. However, always use the fifteen-minute timing if you plan to slice the eggs for use as a garnish.) If you do not have a pushpin or other suitable piercing device, then you must bring your eggs to room temperature before adding them to the hot water. This technique is not as foolproof as the pushpin method, but it is more reliable than the begin-in-cold-water method (see next Q&A).

**What's wrong with the popular begin-in-cold-water method for boiling eggs?**

Timing is iffy, at best. You cannot get consistent results even if you time the cooking process with split-second accuracy — several influential variables exist. The tap water temperature usually varies according to the outdoor temperature and time of day by as much as 15°F. Even if you use the same pan, the quantity of water you put in it will vary daily unless you measure the volume carefully. Finally, your range probably doesn't have the precision controls that would allow you to set the same exact cooking temperature each day.

**How can I prevent the yolk of a hard-cooked egg from becoming green-tinged?**

That unsightly surface color is produced when extreme heat or prolonged cooking chemically combines the sulfur in the egg with the iron in the yolk to form a harmless substance called ferrous sulfide. You can eliminate the problem by following three rules. First, use fresh eggs (ferrous sulfide develops more readily in older eggs). Second, never cook the eggs longer than fifteen minutes. Third, once cooked, bring a halt to further cooking by quickly cooling the eggs in cold water.

**Why is a hot hard-cooked egg easier to peel than a cold one?**

As the cooked egg white cools, it begins to stick to the shell's innermost membrane. Two other egg-peeling tips are to start at the larger end (the one with the air pocket) and, if the shell is giving you a difficult time, to remove it under cold running tap water.

If you want to slice the egg, chill the whole peeled egg in the refrigerator for at least fifteen minutes. By so doing, the yolk is less likely to crumble or break away from the white.

**Why should eggs be poached in vinegar-spiked water?**

Vinegar helps give your poached eggs a more compact shape because its acid content lowers the cooking liquid's pH factor. This precipitates the setting of the egg whites before they have had a chance to spread too far in the simmering water. Vinegar also blanches the egg whites, enhancing their snowy luster. These benefits are overshadowed, however, when the cook uses other than a quality vinegar or pours the vinegar into the pan with a heavy hand, a bad habit common among short-order chefs. A proper ratio is about one teaspoon of vinegar (or one-half teaspoon of lemon juice) per quart of water.

Salt also helps speed the coagulation process, but like vinegar, you must use a sparing amount lest you overpower the egg's flavor. A pinch or two of salt per quart of water should suffice.

## Why are the whites of some fried eggs too rubbery?

Chances are that the cook allowed the protein in the albumen (egg white) to set beyond the ideal point of being firm but tender. Solidification occurs when the cook uses too high a heat or fries the egg for too long — this lessens the ability of the egg white's protein molecules to bind water molecules. If you want a perfect fried egg, we advise cooking it over as low a heat, and as slowly, as possible.

Technically, it is impossible to fry an egg in the classic sense and simultaneously have a perfectly cooked egg white and a firm yolk. If you cook the yolk to its coagulation temperature (about 156°F), you will overcook the egg white (which begins setting at about 145°F).

People who do not like runny yolks should turn the eggs "over easy" rather than wait for the yolks to firm as they cook "sunny side up." Another solution is to baste the tops of the yolks with the pan fat or oil. Or, you could braise the eggs by covering the pan with a lid — the trapped steam hastens the cooking of the yolk tops.

The hue of a "sunny-side up" yolk is a bright orange-yellow. However, a thin milky-white layer appears on the top of the yolk if you use any of the three egg-cooking methods mentioned in the previous paragraph. What you see is a thin layer of albumen that naturally coats the egg yolk membrane. You don't notice it at the beginning of the cooking process because, at that stage, it is transparent.

## Why does the portion of the egg white that lies nearest the egg yolk set more slowly than the outer portion?

An obvious reason is that it is thicker. Another one is that it doesn't come in direct contact with the pan — the portion of the egg white that lies nearest the egg yolk sits on top of the second type of albumen, the one that comprises the entire bottom layer of the cooking egg. A third reason is less known. The inner albumen layer coagulates at a temperature of about 5°F higher than does the second type of albumen.

## Why do I add a liquid to scrambled eggs?

Your cooked scrambled eggs will be fluffier and more tender if you beat into the raw eggs approximately one or two teaspoons of water per egg. This liquid steams as your egg mixture cooks, giving the scrambled eggs a lighter texture. The eggs will also be moister because the cooked protein molecules can bind more water molecules than can uncooked ones.

Milk produces the same effect as water and has the extra advantage of enriching your preparation. For even better results, use cream.

## Are grade AA eggs worth their premium price?

Grade AA eggs cost more than Grade A eggs, which cost more than Grade B eggs, primarily because the higher the grade, the plumper the yolk and the thicker the egg white. These two qualities are desirable for frying or poaching because the cooked eggs will be more compact and visually pleasing. Since there is only slight difference in flavor (and even less difference in nutritive value) among the AA, A, and B grades, for most cooks it would be a waste of money to use any egg but a Grade B for recipes that call for beating eggs, as is also the case when making baked goods. Your priority for those recipes should be freshness, not the grade given by the United States Department of Agriculture.

## Are brown eggs more nutritious and flavorful than white eggs?

No. Though some chickens that lay brown eggs produce more nutritious and flavorful eggs than the breeds that lay white eggs, the opposite is true just as often. Therefore, shell color is not an indicator of quality.

Eggshell color marketplace preference is regional: In Boston, the brown egg is more popular, whereas in most other areas of our country, the white is the top choice.

### Are fertilized eggs more nutritious than unfertilized eggs?

Many health food stores make this claim. However, the chicken's embryo in a fertilized egg is so small that the amount of extra nutritional value it offers is inconsequential.

### Why do some egg yolks have blood spots?

A yolk membrane can pick up blood spots as it travels down the hen's reproductive tract before the surrounding albumen (egg white) and shell have been formed. If the tract is bleeding, some of the blood can attach itself to the yolk. The blood spots are harmless blemishes and, contrary to some food books, do not indicate fertilization.

### Which is better, a week-old or a fresh-from-the-coop egg?

It depends. A week-old egg (if pierced with a pushpin, as described earlier) is preferable for preparing a hard-cooked egg because the shell is easier to peel.

An egg fresh from the coop has more flavor and nutritional value. It is also the first choice when frying or poaching because the fresher egg will have a thicker egg white and firmer yolk, qualities that increase the eventual compactness and attractiveness of the cooked egg. It is also superior when you use the yolk to leaven, thicken, or emulsify a preparation. Finally, the recently laid egg is easier to separate because as an egg ages, the membrane of its yolk weakens.

For the record, the egg nestled in a box in the supermarket display case is, typically, three to seven days old, though two- or three-week-old eggs are not rare in municipalities that do not require open dating. Some firms extend the storage life of their eggs to six months by coating the shells with a light mineral oil that helps keep harmful bacteria out, beneficial moisture and carbon dioxide in. Another method of giving whole eggs superlongevity is storing them in carbon dioxide chambers.

## Can I tell if a raw egg is fresh without breaking it?

Yes. Place the suspect egg in at least several inches of water in a bowl or pot. If your egg sinks and lies on its side, you have a fresh egg. If it sinks but stands partially or fully erect on its tapered end, your egg is over the hill, though technically still edible. If it floats, you are looking at a rotten egg, more suitable for a garbage heap than a stomach. An egg acquires buoyancy as it ages because, while its yolk and albumen (egg white) are gradually losing moisture to the outside world through the porous shell, the size of its air pocket is increasing.

Of course, fresh does not necessarily mean wholesome. Though rare, it is possible for a salmonella-carrying hen to transfer salmonella bacteria into the egg during the egg-forming process.

## Should raw eggs be frozen in their shells?

No. Always shell the eggs first because freezing expands the contents of the eggs more than the shells' capacity. Result: cracked eggs. You can freeze the yolks and whites separately or together. The relatively high fat content (32 percent) of yolks gives them a shorter freezer life than whites. Since freezing deteriorates texture and flavor, freeze eggs only when necessary.

## Why are most refrigerator models designed with the egg storage compartment on the swinging door?

Accessibility, rather than storage life, is the prime reason for the egg compartment's traditional location. We believe that the door is one of the least sensible locations because the eggs are jarred each time you open and shut the door. Moreover, the eggs are repeatedly exposed to temperatures well above the ideal. That perfect temperature, by the way, is about 30°F, just above an egg's 29°F freezing point.

A wiser storage strategy is to keep eggs in their original carton (if it's clean) at the rear of the coldest shelf. Not only does this technique minimize jarring and temperature fluctuation, it saves you the transferring chore — and helps shield eggs from refrigerator odors.

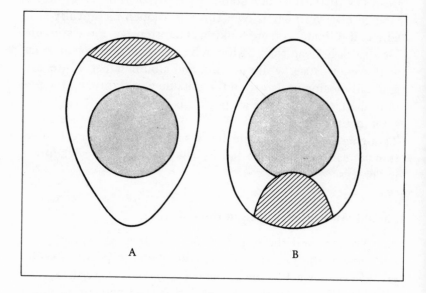

A                    B

### Why should eggs be stored upright?

"Upright," in egg-storing terminology, means with the larger end up (tapered end down), as shown by egg A in the illustration above.

Upright storage helps retard spoilage because it maximizes the distance between the yolk and the egg's natural air pocket. That gaseous space is potentially the egg's most prolific breeding environment for airborne pathogenic bacteria, and the yolk is more perishable than the albumen (egg white). It stands to reason, therefore, that you must keep the yolk as far away as possible from the air pocket.

The separation between the yolk and air pocket is greater in egg A for two reasons. First, although Mother Nature built in a complicated design system, in the form of two chalazas, to keep the yolk anchored in the center of the egg, the yolk does have some freedom of movement — just enough to make a difference in the relative positions of the yolks in eggs A and B. The one in egg B is closer to the air pocket because the pocket arches upward (as does any air bubble rising through a liquid), whereas the pocket in egg A is flatter because it is already above the liquid's surface.

# 7

# F·R·U·I·T·S  A·N·D
# V·E·G·E·T·A·B·L·E·S

## What is the difference between a fruit and a vegetable?

From the botanist's viewpoint, a fruit is the ovary of the plant — that is, the section of the plant that houses the seeds. By that definition, tomatoes, eggplants, cucumbers, and pumpkins are fruits. Except for seeds and spices, the other edible parts of the plant are classified as vegetables.

In the lingo of cooks, greengrocers, and officials of the United States Department of Agriculture, a plant food is a vegetable if you usually eat it as part of a meal's main course, and a fruit if you normally enjoy it as a dessert or as a sweet between-meal snack. By these guidelines, tomatoes, eggplants, cucumbers, and pumpkins are vegetables. But unless you are a botanist, we suggest you either opt for the common usage or call the foods in question "fruit-vegetables."

## Why do most raw, unprocessed fruits and vegetables tend to deteriorate so quickly?

Attack by microorganisms is one obvious answer. Deterioration also occurs because of enzymatic action within the fruit or vegetable. In addition, the decomposition process generates heat, which accelerates the rate of microbial and enzymatic damage, and moisture loss withers the food.

## Why are fruits and vegetables like apples and cucumbers sometimes coated with wax?

The food industry does it for its own sake, not yours. A coating of wax helps seal in moisture and therefore extends storage life, as well as minimizing costly weight loss. It also gives the fruit or vegetable a sheen, which in the eyes of some customers is a sign of quality. Informed shoppers, however, know that it is an impossible chore to wash off all the wax. Even if food industry spokespersons are correct in their claim that the wax is safe to eat, it does give food an off-flavor. It also thwarts your efforts to scrub off pesticides that may have been sprayed on the fruit before it was waxed. The list of fruits and vegetables that are falling victim to the wax treatment is lengthy, and growing: Apples, cucumbers, oranges, lemons, grapefruit, bell peppers, pears, cantaloupes, plums, and yams are among the casualties.

## How important is cellulose content in determining how long to cook a vegetable?

Cellulose, a complex carbohydrate, is the chief constituent of the cell walls of vegetables (and fruits). The higher its proportion in the cells, the firmer the raw vegetable will likely be. To tenderize the cellulose, and therefore the vegetable, the cook generally uses a combination of heat and moisture.

Some foods present a special problem. Consider broccoli and asparagus. The stems have a higher cellulose content than the tips and will therefore still be undercooked by the time the tops are tender unless remedial action is taken. Suitable solutions include cooking the stems and tips separately or cooking them together but giving the stems a head start. You can also shorten the cooking time required for the stems by paring them (a significant percentage of the cellulose resides on or near the surface) or by cutting the stem into smaller pieces.

Difference in cellulose content is the principal reason why brown rice has to be cooked approximately twice as long as white rice to make it palatable and digestible. Unlike white rice, brown rice still retains the outer bran layer, which has a high cellulose content (the endosperm — the white inside part of the cereal grain — has far less cellulose).

Apples like Red or Golden Delicious are unsuitable for cooking because, lacking sufficient cellulose, they become mushy and lose their shape. In addition, they do not contain enough acid to balance the sugar often added by the cook. York Imperial, Rome Beauty, and crab apples are among those that cook well.

### How necessary is moisture for the softening of cellulose?

The need for moisture can be demonstrated by trying to cook a beet with dry heat (baking, for instance), rather than with moist heat (simmering, for example). The beet does not contain enough moisture to soften its high cellulose content. Near the other end of the cellulose-and-moisture spectrum is a tomato. In fact, the tomato has so little cellulose and so much moisture, its structure will collapse if overbaked.

### What other roles do heat and moisture play in tenderizing vegetables?

Heat destroys the osmotic capability of the cells and therefore diminishes the food's structural firmness. Heat in conjunction with moisture also tenderizes by dissolving some of the pectic substances that help glue the individual cell walls tightly together.

### Does acid affect the cooking time of vegetables?

Acid slows down the cooking process, which helps explain why beans cooked in a casserole made with tomatoes require

10 to 20 percent more cooking time than a nonacidic baked bean dish. Alkali has the opposite effect of acid; it shortens cooking time.

## What other factors determine the cooking time of vegetables?

Dozens of other variables enter the equation, including individual preference, piece size, cooking method, degree of heat, and atmospheric pressure — factors that we discuss elsewhere in this book.

## Is it advisable to cook vegetables in as little water as possible?

Water can leach water-soluble vitamins (B and C) out of food. The less water you use, the fewer vitamins you lose. Many leafy vegetables, including spinach, need no water because the moisture that clings to the leaves after you have washed them is ample for the first minute of cooking. As the leaves cook, they contribute enough water of their own for the pot. However, cooking in a generous pot of water is called for when you want to reduce the strong flavors of some vegetables.

## Does prolonged cooking bring out the flavor of either cabbage or turnips?

Too many homes reek unnecessarily with objectionable odors because the cook has been misled by a recipe or by grandmotherly advice into believing vegetables like cabbage and turnips should be cooked for a long time. For your nose's sake, and for the sake of texture, don't overcook such vegetables.

Another way to avoid the disagreeable qualities sometimes associated with cabbages and turnips is to buy them young and fresh. As these vegetables mature or spend time in storage, their flavor and odor strengthen. If you are forced to use some that are overmature or have been stored for a while, you can still minimize the potent taste and smell. Cut them into small pieces and cook them in an uncovered pot with plenty of water.

Each of these three steps encourages the leaching out of unwanted flavor and odor compounds into the water.

Interestingly, cooking onions and their cousins for prolonged periods (just as long as you don't burn them) has an opposite effect. Long-simmered garlic, for instance, is surprisingly mild. Of course, one of the prices you pay for extended cooking times for members of the onion family is loss of texture.

### Is it better to boil or simmer a vegetable covered or uncovered?

Whether or not you use a cover depends on your priorities. When you cover a pot, you reduce the number of nutrients that dissipate into the air. A covered pot also cooks at a higher temperature than a lidless one, so the vegetable cooks more quickly, and nutrients have less time to leach out of the food. Without a lid, the vegetables better retain their vivid green (see the next Q&A).

### What causes a green vegetable to turn muddy green when cooked?

Acid, coupled with heat, is the villain. In combination, they denature chlorophyll, the chemical compound responsible for giving green fruits and vegetables (as well as the leaves of the forest) their characteristic pigmentation.

By cooking without a lid, you can minimize the discoloration caused by acid (which is generally volatile and dissipates into the air). Or you can shorten the cooking time, or add an alkali to neutralize the acid (see the next Q&A).

### Why do green vegetables cooked with baking soda have a brighter color?

Baking soda helps maintain the vivid green because it is an alkali and therefore neutralizes the discoloring acid in the vegetable and cooking water. However, we strongly advise against using baking soda for this purpose. It destroys vitamins (particularly vitamin C and thiamin), and by softening the hemicelluloses of the vegetable's cell walls, gives the food a mushy texture.

## What causes red cabbage to turn bluish purple when cooked?

The principal pigment in red cabbage is the chemical compound anthocyanin. Acid turns it red; alkali, a bluish purple. The cabbage is red to begin with because of its high acid content. When it is cooked for more than a brief period, much of its acid escapes into the air with the steam. When enough of the acid has dissipated, the alkali in the pot becomes predominant and turns the cabbage bluish purple. The harder the water, the greater its alkalinity, and therefore the more the cabbage discolors.

Now you know why the traditional Middle European dish of red cabbage and acid-rich apples evolved. If you do not have tart apples, use another acidic food or flavoring agent, such as citrus fruit. Whatever you do, do not overcook, lest the acid soar toward your kitchen ceiling.

## What gives carrots and other yellow-orange fruits and vegetables their color?

Carotene. Besides adding a colorful excitement to foods, this chemical compound — unlike the other major fruit and vegetable pigments — is a valuable nutrient. Because it is a provitamin A, it can be converted by your body into vitamin A.

If you've ever seen a vegetarian with a yellow skin tone, he may be suffering from hypercarotenum. It is often caused by eating or drinking vast amounts of carrots or carrot juice. Some of the carotene overdose is deposited in the fatty tissue beneath the skin.

## Why does lemon juice prevent discoloration of avocado and potato slices?

The discoloration of the exposed flesh is largely caused by oxidation, and ascorbic acid in the lemon juice slows down that process. Another technique is to cook the food, because heat inactivates the enzymes in the food that would otherwise bring about discoloration in the presence of oxygen. (However, don't cook avocados, for the reason we explain in the next Q&A.)

### Why should I not cook avocados?

When heated, avocados undergo a chemical reaction that produces unwanted, bitter-tasting compounds. That's why you seldom see hot avocado dishes on menus or canned avocado products on supermarket shelves.

### Can a mushroom be too white?

The common supermarket-variety mushroom is bright white when harvested. By the time it reaches the produce bin or salad bar table, it will have developed a slight brown discoloration. This is natural. What is not natural is for the mushroom to have a bright lily-white hue at this stage. That would indicate that the mushroom was treated with a chemical like sodium bisulfite to retard discoloration. This type of preserving agent can cause allergic reactions.

### What causes boiled white onions or potatoes to turn yellow?

The whiteness of these vegetables, as well as that of salsify and cauliflower, is due to the pigment flavone. When this chemical compound is subjected to prolonged heat or alkali, a brownish-yellow tint develops.

Several countermeasures can help keep your vegetables white. First and foremost, do not overcook them. Also, buy young, fresh vegetables in good condition. If your pipes carry hard water, try adding a touch of cream of tartar or lemon juice to help neutralize its alkalinity. The more of these acids you add, the whiter your vegetables will cook, but do not add so much that the flavor of the whitener becomes obvious.

**Why is the onion family so widely used in cooking?**

Onions, scallions, shallots, and other clan members do more than add flavor of their own. Just as their volatile oils can irritate your eyes, they can irritate your taste buds and olfacto-receptors — a plus if kept within bounds because when slightly teased, these organs tend to be more sensitive to flavors and scents of foods.

**Why are onions cooked in butter more flavorful than those cooked in water?**

The butter not only contributes its own distinct flavor, but it lets you cook at a temperature higher than 212°F. This increase helps expel some of the raw onion vapors. It also chemically converts some of the onion molecules into new, sweet-tasting ones. Butter, being a fat, also captures more of the desirable onion essences that would otherwise dissipate into the air.

**When a recipe calls for sautéing both onions and garlic, why is it essential to add the garlic near the end of the sautéing process?**

If you sauté the garlic for as long as is required for the onions, you will certainly burn the garlic, producing a bitter flavor. If you shorten the sautéing time of the onions to accommodate the garlic, your onions will be insufficiently cooked, giving your dish a raw, unsweet, oniony flavor.

**What brings tears to my eyes when I chop onions?**

When you chop or slice an onion, you release a gas, the lachrymator agent propanethiol S-oxide. It wafts upward and chemically reacts with the water in your eyes to form sulfuric acid. Your body reacts defensively: Tears are produced to expel the irritant.

Some people are innately more susceptible to the tear-producing chemical reaction than others. However, the more frequently one cuts onions, the greater his tolerance. That's why the "crier" is more apt to be a person who cuts onions only occasionally.

Over the years, we have heard hundreds of suggestions for averting the rivers of tears that run down the cook's cheeks and into the food. A few work, but most are — in a word — ridiculous. Should your eyes be extremely sensitive to the onion's volatile oils, wear safety goggles (available in most hardware stores for a few dollars), or — if you own one — a scuba-diving mask. Skier's goggles will not serve your purpose because their ventilation holes allow the tear-producing fumes to penetrate the goggles and reach your eyes.

### Why does the inside of a whole onion sometimes pop out when I boil it?

The force that pushes the inside section of the onion out through one of the polar openings is pent-up steam. To avoid this, give the steam one or more extra escape routes by piercing the onion with a thin skewer before you add it to the water or stew. Another popular countermeasure is to make a quarter-inch-deep X-shaped incision into the root end. Whatever technique you employ, simmer the onion, because boiling increases the chances of onion-pop by bouncing the bulb around the pot.

### Should green-tinged potatoes be left in the greengrocer's bin?

Yes. The green surface blemishes are caused by overexposure to light. The tainted areas will taste bitter and contain at least some level of toxic solanine — not enough to kill you, but enough to make you think twice about eating one of these tainted taters. Potato sprouts contain this same chemical — avoid them.

### Why shouldn't a raw whole potato be stored in the refrigerator?

The cold environment of the refrigerator encourages excessive conversion of the potato's starch into sugar. This chemical process makes the tuber uncharacteristically sweet — if you want a "sweet potato," buy a sweet potato.

**Why are the McDonald's and Burger King french fried potatoes thinner than the norm?**

More than consumer preference is involved. Since the raw, pre-cut potatoes are shipped and stored frozen, much of the starch in the vegetables converts to sugar. That extra sugar means that the french fries brown faster when cooked. If fast-food establishments served normal-sized American french fries, their product would either be too brown on the outside or under-cooked on the inside.

**Why are new potatoes better than Idaho and other mature potatoes for making potato salad?**

Because new potatoes have more moisture and a lower starch content, they will absorb less of the cooking water, as well as less of the mayonnaise or vinaigrette dressing. Therefore, new potatoes will be less likely to break when the salad is mixed and served. Just as important, because it is not so thoroughly absorbed, the sauce has not as much opportunity to overpower the more delicate flavor of the potatoes. When less of the sauce is absorbed, we consume fewer calories.

**Why are Idaho and other mature potatoes better than new potatoes for baking and frying?**

Mature potatoes are drier, starchier, and mealier than new potatoes, so they will become fluffier and lighter-textured when baked. And since mature potatoes contain less water, there will be less splatter when they are fried in hot oil.

**Why should potatoes be pierced before they are baked?**

A pierced baked potato will have a better texture — mealy rather than soggy — because more of its moisture can escape.

Even people who prefer soggy-textured baked potatoes should pierce the potato deeply at least in one spot. Otherwise, the trapped steam can explode the potato.

## Why is it imperative not to overcook or overwork mashed potatoes?

Both excesses rupture many of the potato's cell walls, allowing many starch granules to escape from their cellular prison. These granules, which have become gummy during the cooking process, give your finished mashed potatoes a pasty, rather than a fluffy, consistency. Your potatoes will be airier if you mash them in a vertical rather than stirring motion — and if you don't perform that task until just before serving time.

Whatever you do, don't try to mash potatoes in a food processor. Its sharp and fast blades can rupture the cell walls so quickly and effectively that you'll end up with gluey potatoes in practically no time.

## Why are leftover potatoes better than fresh ones for making pan-fried potatoes?

You can't cook raw potatoes at as high a temperature as you can previously cooked potatoes. If you did, the outside of the potato pieces would be burnt before the interior was properly cooked. This problem doesn't exist for leftover potatoes because their interiors don't need cooking. The advantage of pan-frying potatoes at a fairly high heat is to minimize the development of a sticky film of starch on the surface of the potatoes. This substance can cause the individual potato pieces to stick to the pan and break apart when you try to dislodge them.

## Why should I soak potatoes before french frying them?

If the surfaces of the cut potatoes are too dry, a sticky layer of gelatinized starch will develop on the exposed flesh soon after the potatoes are put in the hot oil. This can cause the potatoes to stick to each other and the pan. For best results, soak the freshly cut potatoes for several minutes in ice-cold water. Rinse them briefly under a fast stream of cold tap water and drain them in a sieve or colander. This step removes some of the surface starch. Pat them dry with paper toweling — you don't want any water droplets clinging to the potato surface lest the hot oil splatter when you lower the pieces into the pan. Promptly add the potatoes to the preheated oil before their surfaces lose their remaining moisture.

### Why should corn be eaten as soon as possible after it is picked?

A chemical reaction converts the sugar in the corn into starch — and the longer the corn is off the stalk, the greater the conversion. Corn connoisseurs can detect the drop in sweetness within an hour after harvesting, which explains the rationale for this seemingly snobbish recipe: Don't pick the corn until a pot of water (not more than a minute's run from the cornfield) is boiling.

Heat also affects the conversion process. The higher the temperature of the ear, the faster the chemical reaction occurs. For this reason, unless you intend to cook the corn immediately, refrigerate it as soon as it enters your kitchen.

### Why shouldn't I boil corn in salted water?

Table salt is not pure sodium chloride. It contains traces of other substances, including calcium, an element that can toughen the skin of corn kernels during cooking (as well as that of legumes like peas and lima beans). That is why it's generally a good idea to let your guests salt their corn on the cob at the table. Not only can they suit their individual preferences, but the corn will be more tender.

In any event, the toughening effect of table salt is not as pronounced today as in decades gone by. Modern salt-processing techniques remove much of the calcium before the product reaches the supermarket shelf.

**Why does popcorn pop?**

As the popcorn kernel is heated, its internal moisture converts to steam. The steam pressure increases gradually until the kernel's structure is no longer capable of restraining the pent-up steam. At that split second, the kernel explodes, forming the characteristic fluffy morsel. Ordinary corn doesn't explode like popcorn because it has a lower internal moisture content and, because it has a weaker structure, the steam pressure cannot build up as much.

For obvious reasons, popcorn must be popped in an enclosed container. However, once the corn is popped, the lid should be removed or the popcorn bag opened promptly lest the popcorn reabsorb some of the released steam trapped in the chamber. If this happens, the popcorn will lose some of its crisp texture.

Another rule for successful popcorn is to store the unpopped popcorn in an airtight container. Otherwise, the kernels will lose internal moisture and, hence, popping power.

**Why do cookbooks recommend soaking carrot and celery sticks in ice water?**

If these vegetables are less than fresh, they may have lost some of their crispness. Soaking them in ice water returns some of this crispness because the food cells regain some of their lost water through osmosis. The water absorption reswells the individual cells, causing them to press against each other and once again make the entire structure of the food more rigid and therefore crisper. The fact that its temperature is lowered by the ice water also helps crisp the tired vegetable, but to a much lesser extent than osmosis.

If the vegetables are fresh — as they should be — soaking will have the opposite effect: They will lose a bit of their crispness because of water build-up between the walls of the already plump cells. For some relatively dry vegetables like carrots, however, that scant loss is more than compensated for by the pleasant texture imparted by the extra moisture.

## Why do beans cause flatulence?

Beans contain certain sugars named oligosaccharides that the enzymes in the small intestine cannot fully digest. Consequently, these sugars pass undigested into the next gastro-intestinal-tract chamber, the large intestine, where bacteria ferment them. This chemical process produces the unwanted hydrogen, methane, and carbon dioxide gases. One way to minimize bean-induced flatulence is to discard the water in which the beans were soaked.

Beans, of course, are not the only source of flatulence. Vegetables such as broccoli, brussels sprouts, cabbage, and spinach create flatus, too, as do fibrous foods like cereal bran and fruit. Sometimes food isn't to blame — swallowing air by gulping water, wolfing food down the gullet, or chewing gum are major causes for many people.

## Why does bean curd produce less gas than plain soybeans?

Bean curd (tofu) is made by grinding soaked soybeans, extracting the liquid (called bean curd milk) and then coagulating that liquid with an agent like calcium sulfate. Much of the soybeans' oligosaccharides (see previous Q&A) are removed during this process.

## What is textured vegetable protein?

TVP, as it is known, is a meat substitute. More often than not, the product is manufactured from soybeans because this Asian staple — unlike the other popular legumes — contains all eight essential amino acids and can be easily molded into any desired shape.

Compared to meat, TVP has fewer calories and less saturated fat. On the negative side of the coin, the color and flavor additives in TVP-based products like artificial bacon bits and meat extenders can produce unpleasant tastes, smells, and textures. Soybean-based TVP can also foster flatulence.

**Why are young cucumbers, eggplants, zucchini, and other fruit-vegetables better than those that are larger and more mature?**

Most fruit-vegetables reach the first stage of maturity before they have completed their growth. If harvested then, they are more tender than if allowed to grow to their maximum potential size. Because of changes that occur in cellular structure as the cell walls begin to thicken, the food toughens appreciably. At the same time, the woody cellular substance, lignin, which cannot be softened by cooking, becomes more abundant. Fully mature fruit-vegetables have another undesirable quality: more seeds.

Despite the superiority of young mature fruit-vegetables, greengrocers usually stock the fully grown ones. Profit is the motive. On a pound-per-pound basis, it costs less to grow the biggies because of labor savings. The fully grown specimens sell better, too, because most American shoppers associate largeness with quality.

**Why do most of the mass-marketed tomatoes have inferior flavor and texture?**

These tomatoes have a relatively bland flavor and a cottony texture because commercial growers harvest their produce prematurely, and so the tomatoes are still very green, immature, and unripe when picked. This practice reduces spoilage losses because the tomatoes are less fragile and are therefore better shippers — and being less perishable, they are marketable longer.

The tomatoes are red when they reach the store because the food industry artificially turns them red by gassing them with ethylene. If they had been left on the vine to ripen naturally, they would have generated their own ethylene gas in time enough to trigger the color change. Though both artificially ripened and vine-ripened tomatoes are red, those that are reddened by nature have significantly better flavor, aroma, and texture.

**How can I use the ripening effect of ethylene gas to my own advantage at home?**

Sometimes your greengrocer's entire supply of fruits such as apples, avocados, and peaches is unripe. This is not an intolerable problem as long as the fruit is not more than slightly unripe and you give it time to ripen further. The additional ripening will make the fruit taste sweeter because some of the starches will be chemically converted into sugar. In addition, the fruit will likely lose acidity, making it taste comparatively sweeter. But if you let these fruits finish their ripening process at home, you run the risk of having them spoil before they become fully ripe. Your best solution is to hasten the ripening process by harnessing the ethylene gas that the fruit naturally generates. Rather than letting the gas dissipate into your kitchen air, trap it by placing the fruit in a paper bag. The ethylene gas becomes concentrated and therefore accelerates ripening.

Be sure to pierce the bag with a half dozen or so well-distributed pencil-sized holes, for in order to stay sound, your fruits — like you — need to "breathe." Like animals, they take in oxygen and expel carbon dioxide (though the nonfruit part of the plants does the exact opposite).

**Why shouldn't you serve cold tomatoes?**

They won't be as aromatic and savory because cold hinders the conversion of the vegetable's linolenic acid to Z-3 hexenel, the compound that accounts for much of the desirable ripe-tomato scent and taste. Cold also reduces the volatility of molecules and therefore the number of Z-3 hexenel molecules that will reach our olfactory receptors. Make it a point to bring refrigerated tomatoes to room temperature before serving.

Another way to foster Z-3 hexenel development is to ripen store-bought tomatoes at room temperature for several days. Break the habit of tossing them in the refrigerator when you return home from the market.

### Do apple seeds contain poison?

Apple seeds do contain cyanide, the deadly poison used by executioners and spies. But this shouldn't stop you from enjoying apples, because the quantity of cyanide in the seeds is minute. Even if you were to swallow hundreds of seeds, the cyanide would pass through your digestive tract intact because it is encased by the seed's hard shell, which is impervious to the effects of both normal cooking and gastric juices.

Certain other seeds, including those of apricots and peaches, also contain traces of cyanide in their kernels. Since these seeds do occasionally split open, the eater is often exposed to the cyanide. The quantity of poison in one split seed, however, isn't a serious threat to a healthy person.

### Is one end of a fruit sweeter than the other?

The blossom end is generally sweeter than the stem end because it usually develops more sugar. Prove this phenomenon to yourself: Cross-taste opposite ends of an orange segment.

### Are people fantasizing when they claim they can tell the sex of a tomato or an eggplant?

We have met many shoppers who brag that, by examining the size of the scar on the blossom end of the fruit, they can tell the "boys" from the "girls" and therefore determine which tomatoes and eggplants have more seeds. Though there tends to be a positive correlation between the smallness of the scar and successful seed development within these fruit-vegetables, the scar size cannot have anything to do with their sex because these foods are botanically perfect. The term "perfect" signifies a life-form that can self-pollinate. Scar size can relate to the number of seeds in the food because when self-pollination occurs under less than optimum circumstances, seed development is below par and the scar size is larger than usual. A few fruit and vegetable buyers also erroneously claim that they can ascertain the sex of other perfect plants such as pineapples.

Some fruits and vegetables, however, are either male or female — the asparagus is an example. Nonetheless, the difference is not readily apparent to the naked eye at the marketplace because the telltale sexual characteristic (pistil, as opposed to stamen, development) is not conspicuous at the stage of the food's maturity when it is harvested.

# 8

# S·A·U·C·E·S   A·N·D
# T·H·I·C·K·E·N·E·R·S

**How are sauces and other liquids thickened?**

You can thicken them by raising the ratio of solids to liquid, by using a thickening agent, or by employing a combination of these alternatives.

Increasing the solids can be accomplished in several ways. One procedure, which chefs call "reduction," is to boil the liquid for a period of time so that some of it evaporates. Many recipes, especially those of the classic French cuisine, advise the cook to reduce the liquid to one-half or less of its original volume, because reduction does more than thicken. It concentrates flavor. Moreover, it does not give the sauce a floury taste and grainy texture, shortcomings that are sometimes detected in starch-thickened sauces.

Another popular technique for thickening a sauce is to introduce a quantity of minute solids, such as puréed vegetables, into the preparation; the more water-absorbent these food particles are, the thicker your sauce becomes.

Still another method for thickening a sauce is to cool it. An increase in viscosity occurs because, as a liquid cools, its water molecules lose kinetic energy and become less mobile. If you freeze the liquid (at 32°F or 0°C, for pure water), the molecules cease frolicking about altogether, transforming your preparation from a liquid to a solid.

Thickening agents are many. The list includes emulsifying agents that, for instance, make hollandaise sauce possible; egg protein that helps set custard; starches like wheat flour; gelatin extracted from bones and seaweed; pectin from fruits. Each of these categories is discussed in ensuing sections.

Blood, cream, and those two favorites of Cajun cookery, filé powder and okra, are thickening agents, too. Cheesemakers and pudding manufacturers coagulate milk with rennin, an enzyme from the stomach lining of certain young animals, notably calves. Gum arabic and gum tragacanth are but two of numerous other widely used thickening agents, though they are more likely to be found in commercial food-processing plants than in home kitchens.

### What is an emulsified sauce?

In the simplest terms, an emulsion is a stable mixture of two liquids — such as oil and water — that normally separate from each other. Emulsions can be temporary (measured in seconds or minutes), semipermanent (hours), or relatively permanent (days, months, and sometimes years).

Mayonnaise is the best-known and most widely consumed emulsified sauce. Basically, it is an emulsion comprising oil, egg yolks, and either lemon juice or vinegar. Related sauces include chantilly (mayonnaise mixed with whipped cream), gribiche (a piquant mayonnaise made with hard-boiled yolks), and rémoulade (mayonnaise plus chopped pickles, mustard, and other flavoring agents).

Hollandaise is the most celebrated emulsified sauce. It is an emulsion consisting of butter, egg yolks, and lemon juice combined with a little water, salt, and cayenne pepper. You will find its recipe at the end of this series of Q&A's on emulsions. Well-known derivatives include béarnaise (hollandaise enlivened with shallots, tarragon, and vinegar), choron (flavored with tomato), maltaise (infused with orange), and mousseline (combined with whipped cream). Other world-renowned emulsified sauces include beurre blanc and sabayon (zabaglione).

Sauces are not the only emulsions. Whole milk, for example, is one, too. If milk fresh from the cow is left to stand, the emulsion breaks down and the cream (butterfat) rises to the top. Homogenization, a process that creates a relatively stable emulsion, prevents this separation.

### How and why does a sauce emulsify?

To understand the emulsifying process, we must first accept the scientific principle that oil and water do not naturally mix. Quite literally, they find each other's presence repulsive. A good illustration of this aversion is homemade oil-and-vinegar salad dressing.

When you shake or beat your salad dressing, you do more than disperse the oil throughout the vinegar: You also break down the oil into droplets minute enough to remain temporarily suspended in the vinegar (which from now on we will call water, because that tart condiment is, in effect, mainly water). The second you stop agitating the dressing, the oil droplets start to combine into units too large to be suspended in the water, and thus slither their way upward, separating from the water in the process. The oil rises to the top and the water sinks because oil has a lower specific density than water.

If you want a stable emulsion, you need an emulsifying agent, which prevents the oil droplets from combining into larger units. Emulsifying agents occur naturally in many animal substances, including egg yolks, milk, and blood.

An emulsifying agent helps to keep the oil particles from combining in three basic ways. First, the agent coats the oil, serving as a physical barrier between the droplets. Second, it reduces the water's surface tension, which, in turn, reduces the water's ability to repulse oil. Third, the agent gives the surfaces of the oil droplets identical electrical charges; since like charges repel each other, the droplets repulse each other.

The stability of an emulsion is undermined when the sauce is subjected to one of the following:

- Temperature extremes. Mayonnaise separates when frozen, and hollandaise curdles when heated close to 190°F, for example.
- Excess agitation. Overbeating destabilizes both mayonnaise and hollandaise sauce.
- An opposite electrical charge. A hollandaise sauce or mayonnaise sometimes does not properly emulsify during a thunderstorm, a phenomenon of nature replete with positive and negative electrical charges that neutralize some of the emulsifying electrical charges in the sauce.

### Are eggs essential for making hollandaise?

Lecithin, the emulsifying agent in egg yolks, is not the only emulsifier that can be used with butterfat. You can substitute the milk protein casein, for instance, if emulsion is your only goal. (In fact, the small quantity of casein in regular butter does, to a slight degree, help emulsify your homemade hollandaise sauce.)

Hollandaise sauce, however, needs egg yolks because they perform other functions. They contribute flavor, color, and nutrients. They provide some water; if they did not, you would have to increase the amount of tap water called for in the recipe. Yolks supply a little fat, which supplements the butterfat.

Finally, some of the ingredients in the yolk work as a team to enhance the stability of the sauce by increasing the sauce's viscosity.

### Why should unheated raw egg yolks never be added to a hot sauce?

The sudden change in temperature will curdle the egg yolks. This curdling does more than ruin the visual and tactile appeal of your sauce. It also prevents the beaten yolks from becoming uniformly distributed throughout the sauce, an essential for optimal thickening. Solution: Before adding the beaten yolks to your sauce, gradually raise their temperature by quickly blending into them small amounts of the heated sauce. Now you can add the yolks to the heated sauce without repercussions.

### What are other ways to stabilize an emulsion?

Acid (if used sparingly) is one of the most effective emulsion stabilizers. It is principally for this reason, and not because of flavor, that you add lemon juice (or vinegar) to your hollandaise sauce and mayonnaise. Think of lemon juice's tart taste as a delightful bonus. Other natural emulsifiers/stabilizers include mustard, cayenne pepper, and onions, which explains why they are common ingredients in vinaigrette sauces.

At the expense of flavor and texture, commercial sauce manufacturers give their products hyperstability by throwing into their mixing vats such stabilizers as monoglyceride and diglyceride. Many restaurant chefs also scuttle flavor and texture by indiscriminately adding gelatin, or starches such as arrowroot.

### Can I make an emulsified sauce in a blender or food processor?

Our answer is a guarded yes for mayonnaise and "not recommended" for hollandaise sauce.

Although blender mayonnaise cannot rival the hand-whisked variety, it is nonetheless good, if properly made. Blenders are slightly superior to food processors for making sauces like mayonnaise because their thinner, sharper blades produce a smoother texture and incorporate more air into the developing sauce.

Some cookbooks have recipes for blender or food processor hollandaise sauce. If you follow these recipes, the egg yolk will be insufficiently cooked and the sauce's texture will lack the silkiness of authentic hollandaise. Why go to all the bother of preparing a pseudohollandaise sauce in a blender or food processor when our recipe for the real McCoy is almost as easy and yields markedly superior results?

## Hollandaise Sauce

(1 cup: 4 to 8 servings)

No other sauce has created more fear among cooks than hollandaise. Based on their sad but true experiences, they envision this emulsion curdling or separating as their guests gather around the dinner table.

Consistently preparing the perfect hollandaise sauce is not as difficult as most cooks imagine. If you understand the principles of emulsification and faithfully follow the steps and tips in our recipe, the task will be a snap — unless a thunderstorm is at hand.

Buttery and rich, hollandaise sauce has an affinity for fish, vegetables (particularly artichokes, asparagus, and broccoli), and eggs, the classic example being Eggs Benedict.

**3 yolks of large eggs**
**½ cup unsalted butter**
**1 tablespoon fresh lemon juice**
**¼ teaspoon salt, or to taste**
**pinch of cayenne pepper**
**1 tablespoon water**

STEPS
*Tips and Insights in italic*

1. Bring eggs to room temperature.

*You may want to include an extra egg in case your sauce curdles. (This remedial action is described later.)*

(Continued)

2. Cut up ½ cup (1 stick) of butter. Put in glass measuring cup, and place over pilot-light area or in pan of hot water. When melted (roughly 30 to 45 minutes), stir to blend.

*Melt butter slowly. If butter becomes too hot, allow to cool to lukewarm before using.*

3. Premix lemon juice, salt, and cayenne in small bowl. Reserve for Step 8.
4. Prepare an improvised double boiler. The bottom part is a large, thick-bottomed skillet (or sauté pan) in which ½ inch of water is brought to a near simmer (170°F). The upper part is a small, thick-bottomed saucepan.

*You can use a standard double boiler, but our improvised boiler is superior because, if necessary, you can more quickly determine the heat level and then regulate it.*

5. Into the upper part of the improvised double boiler, put egg yolks and 1 tablespoon of water. Beat ingredients together till just blended.

*Use a stainless steel, tin-lined copper, or heatproof glass saucepan. (The lemon juice reacts chemically with aluminum, carbon steel, and iron, creating an off-flavor and -color.) A stainless steel whisk is a more efficient beater than a wooden spoon.*

6. Place saucepan in skillet. Constantly beat egg-water mixture with moderate strokes until it thickens slightly to a batterlike consistency (approximately 1 to 2 minutes).

*The skillet water must be hot, but not so hot that the sauce curdles. The ideal temperature for this step and Step 7 is about 170°F (or 160°F, if your* saucepan is not thick-bottomed). If water starts to become too hot, quickly lift saucepan, stir mixture, and adjust temperature setting. Beating the mixture too energetically or too long in this step will impair the yolks' ability to emulsify.

7. Slowly pour lukewarm butter into saucepan. Start with about 1 tablespoon (½ liquid ounce) of the butter, then — when thoroughly blended — add 2 more tablespoons and blend. Gradually add increasing quantities until all the butter has been incorporated. This step takes several minutes.

In order to break the butter into tiny droplets that can be coated with the yolks' emulsifying agent, you must beat the sauce constantly and somewhat vigorously. Consistently scrape all surfaces, so that no part of the sauce overcooks or becomes lumpy.

8. The sauce is cooked when it can fall off your whisk or spoon in thick drops. At this point, remove saucepan from skillet water and promptly beat in the premixed lemon juice, salt, and cayenne.

Should the sauce prove to be too thin, return to heat and continue to beat. If you overcook the sauce, it might thicken (or worse, curdle). If it becomes too thick, beat in approximately 1 tablespoon of hot water. If you do not have cayenne, substitute finely ground black, or preferably white, peppercorns.

9. Serve immediately, while warm (not hot).

The sauce may curdle if served on top of an extremely hot food, such as one just removed from the broiler or deep fryer.

(Continued)

## If Your Sauce Curdles or Separates

A hollandaise sauce has a mean streak: If you give it an opportunity to curdle or separate, it will.

If the sauce is just beginning to curdle, remove the saucepan from the skillet water and quickly lower the temperature of the sauce by swirling in an ice cube, which you have kept handy for such an emergency. After several seconds, discard the ice cube and vigorously beat the sauce.

If this remedy fails, you must begin the emulsification process again, In a clean saucepan, lightly beat one egg yolk with 1 tablespoon of water, as you did in Step 5. When thickened as in Step 6, gradually add to the new egg-water mixture the curdled sauce, as in Step 7.

Of course, because you have altered the balance of ingredients, your resurrected sauce will not be as stable an emulsion as one made with the basic recipe.

If you cannot save the hollandaise sauce, go ahead and serve the curdled version. Just name it after your favorite aunt, particularly if she has a French-sounding name — Sauce Georgette, for example, sounds impressive. As long as your guests do not know that your botched creation was supposed to be a hollandaise sauce, they will probably enjoy it, because, despite its curdled state, it will still have a pleasing taste.

## If Serving Must Be Delayed

You can keep the sauce lukewarm (110° to 120°F) for approximately 1 hour by placing it in a covered container within a larger container of hot water (about 150°F). Fluff with whisk or spoon before serving.

If it is necessary to store the sauce for more than an hour, cover it and refrigerate, then bring to room temperature before reheating to 110° to 120°F. The sauce should not be stored this way longer than two days.

Hollandaise does not freeze well; the emulsion is partially destroyed because the oil freezes more slowly and thaws more quickly than the other ingredients.

## Why do homemade vinaigrette sauces sometimes sink to the bottom of the salad bowl?

As most cooks know, salad dressing tends to slide off wet leaves — the water barrier decreases adherence. However, even if the cook dries the leaves properly, the dressing may still end up in the bottom of the salad bowl because few home cooks know how to make a true vinaigrette sauce.

A genuine vinaigrette sauce is an emulsion. If the cook merely stirs the oil and vinegar together with a few fork strokes, he has formed an oil-and-vinegar sauce, not an emulsion. Even if the cook does a good job drying the leaves, their surfaces will retain their natural water content. Since oil and water repel each other, the water on the leaves' surfaces will "push away" the oil, diminishing the oil's chances of sticking to the leaves.

In contrast, the oil in an emulsified sauce will not be repelled by the water on the leaves because the oil in this sauce doesn't come in direct contact with the leaves. Rather, the oil exists as minute droplets sheltered within the vinegar. Each droplet is separated from the other droplets by the surrounding water. Think of thousands of discrete, evenly scattered beads of oil in a glass of water.

Two basic types of emulsions exist: oil-in-water and water-in-oil. A vinaigrette sauce is the oil-in-water variety (we use the term water because vinegar is about 95 percent water). Its oil is dispersed in the form of tiny droplets in the water. Milk and mayonnaise are also examples of an oil-in-water emulsion. Butter, in contrast, is an example of a water-in-oil emulsion. Its water is dispersed as tiny droplets in the oil.

To see firsthand how a true and so-called vinaigrette sauce differ, try the Vinaigrette Sauce recipe that follows.

PRINCIPLE-ILLUSTRATING RECIPE

## Vinaigrette Sauce

(¼ cup)

This salad dressing recipe produces a genuine vinaigrette sauce, one that is emulsified. To see the striking difference between the emulsified and nonemulsified sauces, prepare one of each, then compare them side by side. Begin by making the nonemulsified version. Put all the ingredients in a small glass bowl, then lightly mix them with a few swirls of the fork, as most home cooks do. Next, make the emulsified sauce using the same ingredient list, but this time, follow the recipe steps.

Visually analyze the two sauces — look for dissimilarities in color, consistency, and so on. Then, sample the sauces — notice that the emulsified sauce tastes less oily. Now, dribble some of each sauce on dried lettuce leaves — observe how much better the emulsified version clings.

**¼ cup olive oil**
**2 tablespoons red wine vinegar**
**½ teaspoon finely minced onion**
**⅛ teaspoon mustard**
**pinch of dried thyme**
**pinch of cayenne pepper**
**pinch of ground peppercorns**
**pinch of salt (to taste)**

STEPS
*Tips and Insights in italic*

1. Put all the ingredients in a small jar.

*Oil and pure water won't emulsify — you need an emulsifying agent to create a negative electrical charge around the tiny oil droplets that you create in Step 2. Since like charges repel, the rate at which the oil droplets recombine into larger units will be slowed down. This recipe has a number of emulsifying agents, including onions, mustard, and the acid in the vinegar.*

2. Vigorously shake the jar vertically for 5 seconds.

*You are creating an emulsion by breaking the oil pools into minuscule droplets. A vertical shaking motion works best. You know you've been successful when the oil and vinegar appear to be a single substance — and when the mixture thickens and becomes opaque.*

**Serving Tips**

1. A homemade vinaigrette sauce is unstable. It will soon begin to de-emulsify. This underscores the wis-

*(Continued)*

dom of waiting to make your vinaigrette sauce until just before you're ready to dress and serve the salad.
2. The higher the temperature, the less stable the emulsion. So, for a longer lasting emulsion, consider pre-chilling the oil, vinegar, and especially, the salad leaves and salad bowl.
3. Our recipe calls for a 4 to 1 oil-to-vinegar ratio. You could increase the emulsion's stability by lowering the ratio to 3 to 1, if you don't mind increasing the dressing's tartness. A 2 to 1 ratio would increase the stability even more, but the resulting dressing would be too acidy for most sophisticated palates.

**Variations**

1. You can also emulsify the sauce using a whisk and a round-bottom bowl. Cooks with quick wrist movements can even use a fork. However, you may have to incorporate the oil gradually to create the emulsion.
2. Experiment by substituting ingredients — a vinaigrette sauce is a creative cook's dream. Remember, though, that the sauce will be only as good as the quality of the individual ingredients.
3. We specify red vinegar so that you can easily distinguish the vinegar from the oil in the nonemulsified mixture. For your regular vinaigrette sauce, use white vinegar, if you prefer.
4. There is no one perfect oil for a vinaigrette sauce, but a delicate one like walnut oil is more suitable for a salad dressing than a richer, fuller-flavored one.

# Why do eggs thicken a custard?

When heated, the protein in egg whites, and more particularly in the yolks, cooks and solidifies. Ideally, the solidifying protein simultaneously thickens the liquid (for example, milk) in which it is suspended.

Under ideal conditions, which are discussed both in this section and in the Maltese Falcon Custard recipe that follows, there is an optimal proportion of egg protein to other ingredients. For the standard milk-based custard, use one large egg for every two-thirds of a cup of milk. If the egg size is small, medium, extra large, or jumbo, adjust the ratio accordingly. Since egg white also contains protein, you can use the whole egg, counting each egg white as about the equal of one egg yolk (your finished custard, however, will not be as rich and smooth-textured as one thickened strictly with yolks).

Milk itself contains proteins that thicken, so if you substitute a liquid such as water in a recipe, you will need to increase the number of eggs.

Extra egg is also necessary if you add sugar, and even more so if you add acid, because these ingredients reduce the thickening ability of protein. A good illustration of this principle is zabaglione sauce: The required ratio of yolks to liquid is ten times higher than for custard, in part because of the effect of the acid in the Marsala wine. In the opposite vein, you can reduce the eggs required for a custard when you incorporate starchy ingredients such as rice, because starch is a natural thickener.

If the milk is raw, you must scald it to destroy the enzymes that interfere with the thickening power of the protein in the eggs and milk. Scalding pasteurized milk is unnecessary because the dairy has already subjected it to a high, enzyme-destroying temperature.

For the sake of simplicity, we and other writers generally speak of protein in the singular. Technically, however, there are many types of protein. Since each type solidifies at a different temperature in a zone ranging from slightly below 140°F to slightly below 180°F, we must temporarily switch to the plural to draw attention to their different properties. Your custard mixture reaches its full glory when it is heated to slightly below 180°F, the temperature at which all the proteins have finally coagulated. Above 185°F, some of the proteins lose their coagulating effectiveness and your custard starts to "weep," either in the kitchen or eventually on the dessert plate in front of your dinner guest. Prolonged cooking, even below 180°F, does the same damage.

---

## Maltese Falcon Custard

(4 servings)

Maltese Falcon is a fitting name for this special custard. In culinary parlance, Maltese usually implies the presence of oranges. The image of a soaring falcon suggests the heights this dish can reach if prepared properly.

We feature this rather than the standard, somewhat unexciting egg-and-milk custard recipe found in most cookbooks because Maltese Falcon Custard is considerably richer and more delicate. Granted, our selected recipe requires a bit more skill and effort to prepare than the standard custard, but we think you will find that the gustatory gain more than compensates. Our recipe is also a better learning device for you because it better illustrates the relationship between eggs and other ingredients, such as acidic foods, that you might add to your mixture.

Once you have successfully prepared Maltese Falcon Custard and mastered the principles on which it is based, you will be in a good position to create at

---

will thousands of other interesting custards made with fruits, vegetables, liqueurs, or what have you.

**6 egg yolks**
**1¼ cups whole milk**
**½ cup heavy cream**
**¼ cup orange juice**
**3 tablespoons sugar**
**½ teaspoon vanilla**
**1 teaspoon finely minced orange rind**
**pinch of cinnamon**
**pinch of nutmeg**

STEPS
*Tips and Insights in italic*

1. Bring eggs to room temperature.

*Our recipe calls for twice the normal proportion of yolks to liquid, primarily because the orange juice, which we substituted for part of the milk content, contains significantly more acid and less protein than does milk.*

2. Preheat oven to 325°F. Bring pot of water to a near simmer and reserve for Step 6.

3. In saucepan, mix milk, cream, and orange juice. Slowly heat to about 150°F.

*Do not let mixture simmer, or the acid in the orange juice may curdle the cream. (If using raw milk, scald first.)*

4. In mixing bowl, lightly beat yolks, then blend in remaining five ingredients.

*If orange is waxed, scrub it well. Use only the outermost (orange-colored) layer of the rind, as the subsurface white rind is objectionably bitter.*

*(Continued)*

5. Gradually stir the heated liquid into the egg mixture.

*The yolks may curdle if the liquid is much hotter than 150°F or if you add the liquid all at once.*

6. Pour mixture into a 1-quart soufflé or other suitable ovenproof dish. Place this dish in a wider, high-rimmed pan. Fill the pan with approximately 1 inch of hot water, prepared in Step 2. Place entire unit in preheated oven. Bake for about 50 to 60 minutes, or until a sharp-pointed knife inserted into the custard comes out dry and clean.

*Do not open the oven door prematurely — this will lower the oven temperature, delaying cooking time. Because retained heat will continue to cook the middle of the custard after the dish is removed from the oven, test for doneness halfway between the center and rim of the dish. The reason this custard takes a little longer to bake than an all-milk-based one is partly due to its higher acid content. Generally, the wider the dish and the fresher the milk and eggs, the shorter the cooking time.*

7. Cool by placing dish on rack at room temperature for 30 minutes. Cover and chill before serving.

*The yolks in the custard make it vulnerable to bacteria attack, so do not leave it at room temperature longer than necessary.*

**Variations**

1. Before pouring the custard into its baking dish, coat the bottom of the dish with a layer of caramel (melted sugar). Just before serving the chilled custard, invert and unmold it onto a serving dish.

> 2. Prepare the custard in individual-sized, ovenproof dishes. Because of the smaller size of these dishes, the baking time will be cut by as much as half, and the probing test should be done in the exact center of the custard.

## How do you make a soft custard?

Unlike a standard custard, a soft custard has a loose consistency resembling that of the so-called soft custard ice cream served on cones. This supple property makes a genuine soft custard ideal for filling pastries and topping desserts.

The secret of making the preparation soft is to reduce the amount of binding that occurs between the egg protein molecules while you cook the custard. This requires stove-top (not oven) cooking because the mixture must be stirred constantly.

## How does starch thicken a sauce?

In two ways. First, the physical presence of the starch — a solid — lowers the proportion of the liquid in the sauce and, therefore, increases the sauce's viscosity.

The second way is more complex and more significant. Each of the minute starch granules traps water molecules and, in the process, reduces the proportion of free-flowing water in the sauce. When the starch is heated, the molecular structure of each granule stretches, thereby increasing water retention.

## What determines the viscosity of a starch-thickened sauce?

There are several variables that, collectively, will dictate the thickness of your finished sauce. For the sake of simplicity, we will restrict ourselves to the use of white wheat flour as the starch in the ensuing discussion. (See the next Q&A for details on different types of starch.)

### Quantity of Flour

This variable is the most significant and can be easily determined by a formula, as the following examples indicate. The standard equation for a medium-thick sauce is 2 tablespoons each of butter and flour per cup of liquid. If you want a thin sauce, decrease the butter and flour to 1 tablespoon each. For a thick sauce, use 3 tablespoons each. To make an extra thick sauce for purposes such as coating food for deep frying, use 4 tablespoons each. Any higher ratio of flour to the liquid produces a goo more suitable for mending broken crockery than satisfying empty stomachs. Butter quantity, incidentally, can be varied with some flexibility. If you want to make the sauce richer, use more butter. If you want to do the opposite, use less.

### Quantity and Type of Other Ingredients

If you add other solids, such as cheese, to a sauce, your mixture will become thicker because the solids lower relative water content. Ingredients like dry rice or pasta not only take up space but if used in sufficient quantity, may even absorb most or all of the liquid. You will need to use slightly more starch if you are adding sugar, or an acid such as wine or lemon juice, since these ingredients chemically alter a starch's thickening power. One solution is to add part of the sugar or acid near the end of the sauce making. The type of liquid matters, too. Cream produces a sauce of denser consistency than an equivalent volume of milk, which in turn yields a thicker product than does stock.

### How the Flour Is Incorporated into the Sauce

You have three basic alternatives. You can add the flour in the form of a slurry (typically, cold water and flour), *beurre manié* (small balls of softened butter blended with flour), or *roux* (a cooked, heated mixture of butter and flour). Of the three alternatives, the *roux* is best in terms of dependability, smoothness of texture, and maximum viscosity with minimum use of flour.

### Types of Roux

*Roux* are classified traditionally by their color: white, blond, brown, or black. The color is a function of cooking time — the longer you cook a *roux*, the darker and more flavorful it becomes. These are desirable attributes for some dishes, but there's a trade-off. The more you cook a *roux* beyond the white stage, the weaker the thickening power of its starch molecules. Thus, you need to use more blond than white, more brown than blond, and more black than brown *roux* to thicken a given quantity of sauce.

### How the Roux Is Cooked

One of the prime purposes of the *roux* step is to separate the individual flour granules. If the granules were allowed to combine, they would form lumps, dry inside and surrounded by a water-resistant membrane that would eventually hinder water absorption and therefore thickening capacity. This lumping would also lessen the appeal of your finished sauce. Another purpose of the *roux* step is to begin stretching the molecular structure of the individual flour granules. You must cook the *roux* at least 3 to 5 minutes if you want to achieve optimal granule separation and to induce the stretching process. Also, you must stir the *roux* frequently and cook it with low heat because scorched flour thickens poorly and scorched butter tastes abominable.

### How Long the Sauce Is Cooked

As mentioned earlier, you need to cook the flour granules in order to increase their capacity to retain water. However, there is a point of diminishing returns. If cooked too long or quickly, the viscosity and stability of the sauce diminishes because the starch's molecular structure stretches too much, allowing the trapped water molecules to escape. The exact critical point varies according to a host of factors, including the type of starch used.

### Serving Temperature

Starch-thickened sauces increase in viscosity as they cool. Take this factor into account when you prepare your sauce. If you thicken your sauce to the desired viscosity on your stove, it will likely become an unappetizing, gummy mass when it cools in the dining room.

### Length of Storage

The longer you store a starch-thickened sauce, the thicker it tends to become. Reason: moisture loss.

## Will substituting a different kind of starch affect the finished sauce?

Very much so. Viscosity, stability, texture, and translucency are all affected because the molecular structure differs with each type of starch, be it derived from wheat, corn, rice, rye, oats, millet, barley, or other cereal grain; from cassava, potato, or other root or tuber; from soybeans, peanuts, or other legumes; or from almonds or other nuts.

For example, if you substitute cornstarch for white wheat flour, you will have to alter the formulas given earlier. Use half the quantity of cornstarch because it has twice the thickening power of white wheat flour. If you substitute arrowroot, use slightly less than half the quantity because arrowroot has slightly more than double the thickening power of white wheat flour.

Whole wheat flour is less practical as a thickener than white wheat flour because the refined product has a higher starch content. Our experiments indicate that cake or pastry white wheat flour is more suitable than its all-purpose counterpart, which in turn is better than baker's flour. The last type produces a grainy sauce reminiscent of the pastes we used in elementary school. Specially processed instant wheat flours, such as the Wondra brand, can be sprinkled directly into sauces but direly lack stability.

Regular white wheat flour is superior to cornstarch and arrowroot in stability; a sauce made with it is less likely to sep-arate and break down when subjected to prolonged heat.

Both cornstarch and arrowroot produce a sauce that is smoother and more transparent, qualities desired for many so-phisticated dishes. Those two starches are generally incorpo-rated into a sauce by means of using slurry (a fluid blend of flour and a liquid such as water), rather than the *roux* or *beurre manié* method, and this addition is usually done near the end, rather than at the beginning, of the sauce-making process.

### Why does an instant flour dissolve more easily than a regular flour?

Regular flour does not readily dissolve in water because it tends to lump. The outer flour molecules gelatinize soon after they come in contact with the hot water, forming a membrane-envelope that effectively blocks the water's access to the flour molecules contained within. Result: The inside of each lump remains dry, giving your mixture a grainy texture.

Flour firms have developed instant products designed to minimize obstinate lumping and therefore dissolve more eas-ily. Typically, the instant product consists of small granules that have been chemically or mechanically processed into ir-regular shapes. When these granules do adhere to each other, spaces are left through which water can reach the middle of the lump.

PRINCIPLE-ILLUSTRATING RECIPE

## Mornay Sauce

(1½ cups: 6 to 10 servings)

Mornay sauce, a marvelous topping for green vege-tables, eggs, and fish, is named for, and reputedly

*(Continued)*

created by, Philippe de Mornay, a political and gas-tronomical crony of King Henry IV of France. This sauce is a derivative of the basic white sauce, made of butter, flour, seasonings, and a liquid such as milk, cream, or stock. There are as many descen-dants of the basic white sauce as there are stars in the firmament — Mornay sauce is one of the most celebrated.

Before following this recipe, please familiarize yourself with the preceding Q&A's on how a starch such as flour thickens a basic white sauce.

**2 tablespoons unsalted butter**
**2 tablespoons white wheat flour**
**1 cup whole milk**
**½ cup grated Gruyère cheese**
**¼ cup grated Parmesan cheese**
**½ teaspoon salt (or to taste)**
**pinch of cayenne pepper**

STEPS
*Tips and Insights in italic*

1. Slowly melt butter in saucepan.

*Use a thick-bottomed saucepan to prevent scorching butter. If you do not have one, substitute a standard or improvised double boiler (see hollandaise sauce recipe, p. 154).*

2. Blend flour into butter with whisk or wooden spoon. Cook mixture over low heat for 3 to 5 min-utes.

*Eliminate lumps by stirring frequently and scrap-ing sides and bottom thoroughly in this step and in Steps 3 and 4. Undercooking leaves a raw flour taste.*

3. Thoroughly blend 1 ounce of milk into the *roux*. Repeat the process, gradually adding a little more milk each time, until all the liquid has been incorporated. This step takes a minute or two.

*Ideally, the milk should be at room temperature, but if it is refrigerator-cold, this step will take a little longer. Adding the milk too quickly will create obstinate lumps.*

4. Continue cooking at below the simmer point for 4 to 10 minutes, depending on sauce volume.

*If the heat is too low (under 140°F), the flour will not gelatinize (swell) sufficiently to absorb the maximum quantity of water molecules. If you allow the sauce to reach the simmer point, you overstretch the flour's molecular structure, reducing its water-retaining qualities. Cooking for too long also stretches the molecular structure excessively. Your sauce is ready when you notice a marked acceleration in the thickening process, which indicates that the stretched starch molecules are absorbing the water molecules in appreciable quantities.*

5. Add the cheese. Stir until melted.

*Finely grated or ground cheese will melt more quickly and thoroughly.*

6. Season with salt and cayenne.

*The amount of salt needed varies according to the salt content of the cheeses selected. If cayenne is unavailable, substitute freshly ground black, or preferably (for appearance's sake) white, peppercorns.*

*(Continued)*

### If Your Sauce Is Too Thick or Thin

If your sauce becomes too thick, beat in a little extra milk. If too thin, blend in one or more balls of *beurre manié* (see p. 166).

### If Your Sauce Is Too Lumpy

You can smooth out the lumps in a blender or food processor. However, there is a trade-off: The agitation will disengage some of the water molecules trapped by the starch molecules, thereby thinning your sauce.

### Serving Tips

Serve immediately. If delay is unavoidable, keep sauce warm (about 140°F) and stir periodically to prevent a surface film from developing. If the delay has to be for more than approximately 45 minutes, refrigerate the sauce, though it will never be even remotely as smooth and satiny as it was originally.

For added visual appeal, glaze your Mornay-sauced foods under a preheated broiler.

### Creative Variations

Our featured Mornay sauce recipe is classic, not *de rigueur.* Once you have mastered it and have learned why the sauce thickens, be daring: Vary the ratio, quantity, and type of cheese, substitute stock or cream for part of the milk, or add other solid ingredients, such as finely minced ham.

## How does gelatin thicken a liquid?

Gelatin is a protein extracted from animal bones and connective tissue. Another rich gelatin source is seaweed. Irish moss (carrageen) is usually used whole, but most seaweed-derived thickeners are processed into products such as agar-agar.

Gelatin increases the viscosity of a liquid because when you moisten the gelatin granules, they swell up to approximately ten times their original size, trapping water molecules in the process. This phenomenon is somewhat similar to the thickening action of starches, but the final results are different. A gelatin-thickened preparation will be finer-textured and will retain its stability under a broader range of temperatures.

The firmness of a gelatin-thickened mass depends on the ratio of gelatin to liquid, the temperature of the mixture, and the presence of any other ingredients you may have added.

Too little gelatin will result in a limp product. Too much gelatin, and your creation may be capable of bouncing into your dining room on its own. The paragon mixture, when chilled and unmolded, will support its own weight, yet quiver slightly if shaken, and in kids' terminology, appear to be "nervous pudding."

Firmness varies inversely with the temperature of the preparation. Once thickened, the preparation can be changed back into a liquid simply by heating it. Rechill that liquid, and you once again have a solid. This alternating process can be done a number of times, though not indefinitely because repeated temperature extremes partially destroy the gelatin's thickening ability.

Some ingredients, including sugar in excess, inhibit gelatinization. Fresh pineapple is particularly difficult; it contains an enzyme named bromelain that severely retards thickening. If you want to include fresh pineapple in your mixture, destroy the hindering enzymes by simmering the fruit pieces for several minutes. If you use canned pineapple, you can skip the parboiling step because the enzymes have already been deactivated.

**Why are veal bones preferable to beef bones for stock making?**

Veal bones cost more per pound than beef bones but they yield a more delicate flavor. Just as important, veal bones have more collagen — thicker stocks result.

**Why shouldn't I dissolve dry, unflavored gelatin powder in hot water?**

If you pour hot water directly into the dry, unflavored gelatin, some of the granules will lump and so will not properly dissolve. This lumping diminishes the gelatin's thickening power and produces a detectable grainy texture in your prepared dish.

First blending the unflavored powder with a little cold water softens and wets the crystals. When the hot water is then added, the moist crystals readily dissolve.

If you are blending at least an equal portion of sugar into the plain dry gelatin, you can forego the cold water step because sugar counteracts the clotting effect. For best results, however, the hot water should be under 180°F.

**What causes gelatin desserts to develop a rubbery skin?**

There are several possible causes. In some cases, the surface of the prepared gelatin was exposed to air for too long (the dish should be kept covered). Sometimes the cause is age — so serve the dish the day you make it. At other times, the cook used too high a proportion of gelatin powder to liquid.

**How does pectin set a jelly?**

The essential thickening agent in jelly is pectin, a carbohydrate that occurs naturally in most fruits. If your jelly does not set, you can safely assume that either too little pectin or an incorrect proportion of other ingredients went into it, or that cooking conditions interfered with the thickener's job.

Two main factors determine a jelly's pectin content. The

first is the type of fruit used. For instance, apples, citrus fruits, cranberries, sour blackberries, and quinces have a high pectin content. The opposite is true for apricots, pineapples, sour cherries, peaches, nectarines, raspberries, and strawberries.

The second pectin-content determinant applies to all fruits: the stage of ripening. An almost ripe fruit is more appropriate for making jelly than a fully ripe or unripe one because useful pectin is at its maximum just before the fruit reaches its peak of ripeness.

To compensate for a pectin-deficient fruit, you can add a commercial pectin concentrate in liquid or powder form. Only a small quantity of this concentrate is necessary; beware of an overdose, which will give the jelly a tough, rubbery consistency, making it difficult to spread on toast — assuming someone would want to eat such an unappetizing product in the first place. The proportion of pectin can also be increased by reducing (boiling down) the fruit juice used in the jelly-making process.

Pectin alone will not set a jelly, for it requires both acid and sugar to thicken properly. Most fruits contain acid, but acid content also changes with the ripening process. Here is one more variable that makes an almost ripe fruit preferable to a fully ripe one: the higher acid content. If you are using ripe fruit and a commercial pectin, you can supply the necessary acid by adding approximately one tablespoon of lemon juice per cup of fruit juice. Since jelly recipes call for fistfuls of sugar, deficiency of it is unlikely to be the cause of any setting problems.

Heating makes the pectin in fruit water-soluble, a condition that is necessary for jelling. However, you must be careful not to destroy the pectin in your mixture by cooking it at too high a temperature or for too long.

# 9

## S·E·A·S·O·N·I·N·G·S

**W**hat effects do heat and cold have on the taste of flavoring agents?

The perceived intensity of salty, sweet, and bitter taste qualities is greatest in the 60° to 120°F zone.

Consequently, when seasoning a hot preparation that is to be served later at room temperature, such as potato salad, use less salt than your taste buds suggest during the test sampling. Do the reverse when you salt-test a room temperature food like a leftover soup that you plan to reheat. Incidentally, almost any leftover dish needs to be reseasoned with aromatic flavoring agents (herbs, for instance) because some of the essential oils of these agents are lost during the storage and reheating process.

### Do in-flight chefs face special culinary problems?

They must use more aromatic seasonings than normal because food tastes blander in an airplane than on the ground. First, the cabin pressure decreases the volatility of the odorant molecules and therefore the passenger's capability of sensing them. Second, the cabin's relatively dry atmosphere dehydrates and therefore impairs the passenger's olfactory sensory mechanism.

The cabin's low humidity also dehydrates the passenger's entire body. Consequently, the chef should not season liberally with salt because it would increase the body's need for water. Many passengers compound the dehydration problem by consuming quantities of coffee and alcohol (both diuretics), canned tomato juice (extremely salty), and soft drinks laden with thirst-producing sugar. The one liquid that would do them the most good is plain water, which they seldom imbibe on planes.

### Does being nervous alter the cook's taste perceptions?

The folk wisdom "an unpleasant experience leaves a sour taste in the mouth" is physiologically valid because tension increases acidity in the mouth. A cook who is sampling a dish to adjust the seasonings should keep that in mind if, for example, he is anxious about the meal's success or he just had a stressful argument. Foods will taste tarter than they really are.

### Does the phase of the menstrual cycle or a pregnancy affect how a cook might season a dish?

The phase of the menstrual cycle or of a pregnancy affects sensitivity to odors and, therefore, could affect how a cook adjusts seasonings. The ability of a female cook to taste-test foods is keenest during the middle of the twenty-eight-day cycle and during the first three months of pregnancy. During the last two-thirds of pregnancy, however, her sense of smell is less acute than normal.

### When sautéing, deep-frying, or broiling, why do many chefs not add spices such as cinnamon and pepper until near the end of, or after, the cooking period?

When subjected to the high temperatures of these cooking methods, most spices quickly scorch. This scorching alters the chemical composition of the spices, giving them a disagreeably bitter flavor.

### Why should herbs also be added near the completion of the cooking process?

Seasoned cooks know that an herb's most prized quality is its bouquet, not its taste, though that too is much appreciated. An herb's fragrance is ephemeral — it doesn't take long for the heat to dissipate its precious volatile oils. That's why herbs (especially fresh ones) should be added near the end of the cooking process, even when you cook at a gentle simmer.

### How does sugar affect the taste of a bitter, salty, or sour substance?

Sweetness lowers the intensity of a bitter, salty, or sour taste quality. This phenomenon partially explains why a coffee drinker adds sugar to a bitter brew, why a cook adds a pinch of sugar to an oversalted dish, and why a lemonade maker uses sugar to counteract the acidity of the lemon juice. Interestingly, the reverse is true, too. A bitter, salty, or sour substance lowers the intensity of sugar. That's why it's difficult for our taste buds to detect how much salt and sugar some processed foods contain.

### Which is better, rock or sea salt?

Most of the salt (sodium chloride) merchandised in America is rock salt. It is mined from existing salt deposits that were laid down eons ago by now extinct seas. In contrast, sea salt is harvested from extant seas by trapping the saline water in tidal basin pools — and by taking advantage of free solar power to evaporate the water until only the salt remains. It has a stronger flavor and a more interesting character than rock salt. Understandably, it is *de rigueur* for some food connoisseurs. Sea salt's alleged nutritional superiority over rock salt, however, is nonsense. The amount of the extra trace minerals it contains is too trifling to matter.

## Why is kosher salt better than regular salt for sprinkling on food like corn on the cob?

Kosher salt crystals are larger and because they have a more jagged configuration, they cling better to food surfaces. Kosher salt is so named because it was specially developed as an aid for Jews who adhere to kosher dietary laws, one of which requires that as much blood as possible be removed from meat before it is cooked; the characteristics of kosher salt make it better suited for drawing out the blood.

## What does MSG (monosodium glutamate) do?

MSG highlights the flavor of food, and especially of salt (sodium chloride). One of the several reasons serious cooks should not use MSG is that when the chemical reacts with salt, a peculiar off-flavor develops.

If you have not already identified the strange, distinct flavor created by MSG, then conduct the simple experiment that we have devised. Half fill three glasses with tap water. Using separate spoons, stir 1/8 teaspoon of MSG into glass A; 1/4 teaspoon of salt into glass B; and 1/8 teaspoon of MSG plus 1/4 teaspoon of salt into glass C. Take a sip from glass A and notice that MSG by itself is virtually tasteless. Next, after rinsing your mouth out with fresh plain water, take a sip from glass B and make a mental note of the natural taste of this briny liquid before sampling the remaining glass. Finally, take a sip from glass C. Notice how the natural salt flavor has been amplified, a direct result of the MSG-and-salt chemical reaction. But more important, note the distinct metallic taste produced by this chemical reaction.

There is some preliminary evidence that suggests that more than a slight-to-moderate consumption of MSG is unhealthy. However, the widely held belief that even small doses of

MSG produce headaches, palpitations, and other physical distresses — and that one falls victim to these by eating in inexpensive Chinese restaurants — is largely poppycock (unless one happens to be one of those rare people who has a particularly low tolerance to MSG). For example, why do so many of the victims seem to develop those symptoms only when they eat in low-priced Chinese restaurants and not when they eat in other budget eateries, such as the local corner coffee shop, which are apt to use just as much MSG as a run-of-the-mill Chinese restaurant? Therefore, unless the chef did use an MSG megadose (an infrequent occurrence), the so-called Chinese restaurant syndrome would appear to be chiefly psychosomatic.

## What is the difference between black, white, and green peppercorns?

All three are produced from the berry of the same tree (*Piper nigrum*). Their distinguishing characteristics derive from variations in harvesting time and processing methods.

The most common of the three, the wrinkle-skinned black peppercorn, is picked slightly immature and then dried whole. The relatively smooth-surfaced white peppercorn is picked at full maturity. After it is soaked to facilitate the removal of its skin, it is dried skinless. Green peppercorns are picked immature and then are preserved, skin and all, by pickling.

Some cooks prefer to use white peppercorns in pale preparations such as white sauces and cream-based sauces. If black peppercorns were used, the black specks of the ground dried skin might detract from the food's visual appeal. Other cooks prefer to take advantage of the wonderful intense flavor and fragrance that the skin of the dried pepper provides. Green peppercorns, the mildest and classiest of the three, are often cooked and served whole in dishes like braised duck.

Pink peppercorns, by the way, are not true peppercorns. They resemble the true item in size and shape but hardly in flavor.

**What is the difference between green and red chilis?**

Color indicates how ripe the fruit was when it was picked. Color has nothing to do with species. All chilis — and the world has countless varieties — are green when young. If left on the vine to ripen fully, the fruit loses much of its chlorophyll content — and the previously hidden red (or, in some cases, yellow or orange) becomes visible.

**What is the hottest part of the chili pepper?**

The white, spongy ribs contain the greatest concentration of capsaicin, the compound that makes some of us reach for the nearest fire extinguisher. The seeds are the next most potent part, partially because they cling to the ribs. If you discard the ribs and seeds, you will have eliminated over 90 percent of a chili's fire power. Parboiling the flesh reduces the chili-hotness even more.

**Why are some people less affected by chili-spiced dishes than others?**

With rare exceptions, the more frequently one eats chilis, the more immune one's sensory receptors become to the potential palate-scorching bite of these incendiary capsicums. Chances are you have already encountered chili snobs who base their gastronomical superiority on their ability to eat hotter foods than you can. Remind those braggarts that their skill stems from previous exposure to chilis and not from innate talent.

**Why are chilis generally more popular in tropical than in Temperate Zone cuisines?**

As with many questions about culinary traditions, the answer is multifaceted — there are at least six reasons.

First, chilis make living in the scorching tropics more bearable because this species of capsicum helps cool the body. Yes, that seemingly paradoxical statement is true because the consumption of the essential oils of chilis turns the body into, if you will, a walking air-conditioning unit. Chilis usually cause the diner to sweat. When the heat of the day or a dry breeze evaporates this perspiration, the diner's skin cools, because as water changes from a liquid to a gas, it absorbs a lot of heat calories from its surrounding environment.

Second, hot chilis perk up the appetite, an important consideration because tropical weather does anything but whet the desire for food. On a hot, muggy day in the tropics, you have as much appetite as you would in a steam bath.

Third, hot chilis add needed zest to a diet that would otherwise be, for the most part, comparatively bland. Though tropical fruits are ambrosial delights, vegetables and seafood in the tropics are generally much blander than in the Temperate Zone.

Fourth, chilis are a natural preservative. This makes chilis valuable to people who live in the tropics because the hotter the climate, the faster and the more likely food can spoil.

Fifth, as contemptible cooks have long known, chilis can swamp the telltale taste of spoilage.

Sixth — tourists take note — chilis tend to reduce, to at least some degree, the incidence of diarrhea and some other intestinal disorders.

Even chilly-climate cuisines can benefit from chilis. Besides providing flavor excitement for its own sake, chilis aid digestion by accelerating the flow of gastric juices.

### How much difference is there between sugar refined from sugar cane and from sugar beets?

Both are sucrose sugars. The difference between the two in taste and cooking properties is all but imperceptible to even an expert's palate. What's more, few brands specify or intimate on their labels whether the sugar was made from sugar cane or from sugar beets.

There is, however, a significant difference in sweetness between sucrose sugar and the other leading forms of sugar. Sucrose is only about two-thirds as sweet as fructose, the sugar that is derived from fruits. Sucrose is approximately twice as sweet as dextrose, a glucose sugar that is also known as corn or grape sugar. Sucrose is about thrice as sweet as maltose (malt sugar) and roughly six times sweeter than lactose (milk sugar).

## What is the essential difference between white and brown sugar?

Brown sugar contains molasses, a by-product of the cane sugar refining process. It is this dark, sticky substance that gives brown sugar its distinguishing flavor, aroma, and color. Despite the claims of some health food faddists, brown sugar is practically as low in nutritional value as white.

## Why does a vinegar-based marinade lose some of its sharpness after a food has been soaking in it?

An obvious reason is that some of the natural juices of the food seep out and dilute the marinade. A not so apparent reason is the effect of the chemical reaction that occurs when alkali and acid are combined in a liquid (this topic is covered more fully in the discussion of baking powder in Chapter 11). More often than not, at least one of the food ingredients you are marinating has an alkaline content that interacts with the acid in the vinegar (or lemon juice or wine), perceptibly diminishing the sharpness of your acidic marinating/flavoring agent.

## Why do I get inconsistent results when I try to extend my wine vinegar by adding leftover wine to it?

The most common cause of failure is that the wine vinegar has been pasteurized, as are most of the low- and medium-priced commercial varieties. Pasteurization kills the helpful mother microorganisms (more about the mother below).

Another major cause is that the wine has been infused with preservatives. This treatment is generally restricted to jug and other inexpensive wines — and since a vinegar is only as good as its ingredients, you wouldn't want to use those wines in the first place.

To make a decent vinegar, you need a starter: a floating, jelly-like film of microorganisms called "mother of vinegar." When these bacteria attack the alcohol in the wine, they convert it chemically into acetic acid, the substance that gives vinegar its characteristic acidity. You can develop your own mother from scratch by pouring several tablespoons of unpasteurized wine vinegar into a crock, exposing it to air for a half hour, adding a worthy wine, covering the opening with cheesecloth, and letting the mixture stand undisturbed in a dark, cool, dry spot. The mother should be clearly visible within a couple of weeks if the right bacterium has started working.

Once armed with the mother, gently place it on top of the wine, cover the crock with cheesecloth, and leave the mixture in peace. In a couple of weeks or so, you should be able to enjoy your own homemade vinegar.

Unfortunately, success can be elusive because, among other pitfalls, your wine could be attacked by one of the other common airborne bacteria that will produce an acetic but displeasing flavor. A much surer and easier course of action is to buy a starter from a local vinegar plant (some do sell it) or "borrow" some from a vinegar-making friend.


**Why should I avoid using the cooking wines found in supermarkets?**

A centuries-old maxim says never cook with less than a good wine because a bad one will impart its inferior qualities to your food. The flavor and bouquet of supermarket products labeled "cooking wine" are, in one word, inferior. If a cooking wine contains alcohol (not all do), the cook must contend with another negative. The manufacturer must by law make the alcoholic cooking wines undrinkable by infusing them with copious amounts of strong flavoring ingredients, such as salt or MSG. These additions throw recipes based on regular wine out of kilter.

**Why shouldn't I be too concerned about serving a slow-cooked, wine-enriched dish such a Coq au Vin to children?**

Wine normally has an alcoholic content of about 10 to 14 percent — the remaining liquid is water. When you cook with wine in an uncovered pot for more than a short time, virtually all of the alcohol dissipates into the air because alcohol has a relatively low boiling point (about 175°F at sea level, as compared with 212°F for water). The scant quantity of alcohol that remains with the water should not be cause for alarm — after all, traces of alcohol occur naturally in food; they are widespread and difficult to avoid. Children frequently consume traces of it in fermentable foods such as very ripe apples. And a teaspoon of sherry in a bowl of soup shouldn't cause alarm, either. The issue is really a matter of principle.

**Why should sherry not be added to a soup until just before serving it?**

Soup is lightly laced with sherry for the elegant fragrance that it adds. Since much of the sought-after subtle aroma of sherry dissipates into the air within minutes after the fortified wine comes in contact with the hot soup, it is essential not to add it too soon.

An even greater cooking transgression than adding the sherry too early is to compensate for the expected fragrance loss by using more than a teaspoon of sherry per cup of soup. Although the delicate fragrance of the sherry will escape into the air, the soup will be overpowered by the not so delicate sherry *taste*, which does not dissipate into the air so readily.

Yet another soup-making faux pas is to reach habitually for the sherry bottle. The ability of sherry to add charm to a soup is lost when it becomes familiar.

**Why should I add soup bones to the pot while the water is still cold?**

Your goal is to extract from the bones as much of their taste, aroma, color, nutrients, and thickening agents as you can. A sudden plunge into boiling water would partially seal these elements into the bones, and therefore fewer of them would leach out into the water.

**Why do many flambéed dishes smack too much of alcohol?**

Most flambéers — including black-tie restaurant captains — perform their pyrotechnic magic solely for its oohs-and-ahs value. They are not especially concerned about whether or not they have allowed enough time for most of the alcohol content in the beverage to burn away, and unless most of it does, the alcohol's assertive flavor will overpower the main ingredient.

When selecting the beverage to be flambéed, remember that the higher its proof the more readily it will ignite. Don't dally once you pour on the flambéing agent. Set it ablaze before too much of its alcohol has been absorbed by the food.

Another rule for successful flambéing is to preheat the alcohol to about 130°F before you strike the match, because an alcoholic beverage — unless it is of exceptionally high proof — will stubbornly refuse to ignite much below that temperature. Since lukewarm food and sauce, as well as a room-temperature serving dish, can quickly cool the alcohol upon contact, you should also make sure that the preparation has not cooled too much and that the dish is preheated.

**Why is it ludicrous to cook with champagne?**

What gives champagne its glorious character is its effervescence. Take away the bubbles and even a Dom Perignon will taste like a third-rate wine. (Prove it to yourself — the next time you have champagne, purposely let a small glass of it go completely flat, then sample.) When you cook with champagne, its bubbles disappear by the time the dish or sauce is cooked, so you will be flavoring your food with what is the equivalent of the concentrate of a third-rate wine. Though a dish served with "champagne sauce" has cachet, a preparation made with a decent, dry white still wine is more gastronomically and economically rewarding.

# 10

## O·I·L·S   A·N·D   F·A·T·S

### What is the difference between a fat and an oil?

An oil is a fat. However, it is common practice to use the term "fat" for those fats that are in a solid state while at room temperature. Those that are liquid at room temperature are called oils.

Fats from animals are solid and, generally, fats from vegetables are liquid at room temperature. The notable exceptions are vegetable oils from the coconut and palm kernel. Chemically speaking, there is less difference between animal and vegetable fats than most people would suspect. Even though their saturation and cholesterol profiles do differ, both fats are made up of a glycerol molecule linked with three fatty acids. They share the attributes of being water insoluble and having a greasy feel.

### What is shortening?

Shortening is classified as a fat because it is solid at room temperature. Shortening can be made with animal or vegetable fats, or a combination of them. Those based on vegetable oil are made solid by hydrogenation.

Read the label. If it says "pure vegetable shortening," the product is exactly that. The phrase "pure shortening" means that either animal or vegetable fats, or both, could have been used. If the word "pure" is missing, the manufacturer has included additives to lengthen the shortening's storage life or improve some of its cooking properties. Those additives, incidentally, lower the smoke point.

## Can baked goods be made with oil?

One of the failings of oil is that, unlike fats such as butter or lard, it is inclined to collect instead of remaining uniformly distributed through the baking dough. For that and other reasons, your baked goods will tend to be too grainy, an effect that is undesirable except in a few specialties. Fat gives your baked items a fluffy, moist texture and, as a bonus, a commendable flavor.

We do not recommend the all-purpose oils, the type that have been engineered to be suitable for both baking and deep-frying. These products do not give the best of both worlds: good baking properties plus a high smoke point for deep-frying. In order to give the oils improved baking quality, the food processor must use additives that appreciably lower the oil's smoke point. An all-purpose oil, therefore, is a compromise, noticeably inferior both to regular oils for frying and to fats for baking purposes. No matter how hard the food technologists may try, their laboratory quest for a truly all-purpose oil will be futile.

## Why does fat make some meats taste better?

Fat does more than add flavor and keep the cooking meat moist. It makes steaks more succulent because fat spurs salivation. It also lubricates the meat's muscle fibers, making it easier for your teeth to tear the fibers apart.

## Is fat consumption unhealthful?

We must eat fat to stay alive. What is harmful to good health is over- and under-consumption of fat. Thanks to the barrage of warnings from the mass media, most people know the dangers associated with eating too much fat: obesity and coronary heart disease, to name two. However, overcautious people who go to the other extreme (consuming as little fat as possible) unwittingly risk their health another way.

Fat is the vehicle that transports fat-soluble vitamins (A, D, E, and K) through the body. Without a fresh supply of fat as an energy source, and if your body has used up its stored fats and carbohydrates, it is forced to resort to its supply of protein, an organic compound that is far better utilized for other missions, such as building body tissues. However, fat, too, has its building chores; it is essential for cell development. Besides its nutritive value, fat adds flavor and interest to prepared dishes, and because it takes longer to digest than protein or carbohydrates, helps keep the stomach satisfied between meals.

Authorities say that 20 to 25 percent of a normal adult's calories should come from fat. In practice, the figure is about 50 percent for the average American. As these figures suggest, most Americans need not fret about a fat shortage in their diet. They should worry about the other peril, excess fat intake.

### Is cholesterol unhealthful?

Cholesterol, an alcohol, is not a dire threat to good health, per se. It is essential for bodily functions, including the building of cell membranes and sex hormones. You can get your necessary supply of cholesterol from your liver (where it is produced) and by eating foods of animal origin: meat (especially fatty cuts and organs), dairy products, and eggs. Although your body needs some cholesterol, an excess amount in your arteries can cause coronary heart disease and premature death.

If your serum cholesterol level is below 200 milligrams per deciliter of blood, you probably don't have to be concerned about lowering your level because you're classified in the "desirable blood cholesterol" group. If your level is between 200 and 239, you should give serious attention to reducing your level because you're in the "borderline high blood cholesterol" group. If your level is 240 or above, you're classified in the "high blood cholesterol" group — and failure to go on an immediate and strict cholesterol-lowering diet would be foolish if not ultimately fatal. Consult your physician.

## Is a vegetable oil or margarine that "contains no cholesterol" ideal for cholesterol watchers?

Many shoppers assume that if they buy a vegetable oil or margarine whose label says "contains no cholesterol," they run no risk of raising their serum cholesterol level. For the record, since cholesterol comes only from animal sources, these two vegetable-based foods never contain cholesterol. Therefore, the shopper shouldn't be paying attention to cholesterol. He should be minding whether the product contains saturated fat, and if so, how much. Saturated fat is harmful because it forces the liver to produce more low-density lipoprotein (more on this topic later).

## What is the structural difference between saturated, monounsaturated, and polyunsaturated fat?

A fat or oil is composed of one glycerol molecule linked with three fatty-acid molecules, hence the umbrella name triglycerides. A fatty-acid molecule is a chain of carbon, oxygen, and hydrogen atoms. The length and make-up of this hydrocarbon chain can vary, but there is a maximum number of hydrogen atoms that each carbon atom can have. If the molecule has its full capacity of hydrogen atoms, it is called saturated. The diagram below depicts the middle of such a molecule:

$$\cdots - \underset{\overset{\displaystyle |}{H}}{\overset{\overset{\displaystyle H}{|}}{C}} - \underset{\overset{\displaystyle |}{H}}{\overset{\overset{\displaystyle H}{|}}{C}} - \underset{\overset{\displaystyle |}{H}}{\overset{\overset{\displaystyle H}{|}}{C}} - \underset{\overset{\displaystyle |}{H}}{\overset{\overset{\displaystyle H}{|}}{C}} - \underset{\overset{\displaystyle |}{H}}{\overset{\overset{\displaystyle H}{|}}{C}} - \underset{\overset{\displaystyle |}{H}}{\overset{\overset{\displaystyle H}{|}}{C}} - \underset{\overset{\displaystyle |}{H}}{\overset{\overset{\displaystyle H}{|}}{C}} - \underset{\overset{\displaystyle |}{H}}{\overset{\overset{\displaystyle H}{|}}{C}} - \underset{\overset{\displaystyle |}{H}}{\overset{\overset{\displaystyle H}{|}}{C}} - \underset{\overset{\displaystyle |}{H}}{\overset{\overset{\displaystyle H}{|}}{C}} - \underset{\overset{\displaystyle |}{H}}{\overset{\overset{\displaystyle H}{|}}{C}} - \underset{\overset{\displaystyle |}{H}}{\overset{\overset{\displaystyle H}{|}}{C}} - \underset{\overset{\displaystyle |}{H}}{\overset{\overset{\displaystyle H}{|}}{C}} - \underset{\overset{\displaystyle |}{H}}{\overset{\overset{\displaystyle H}{|}}{C}} - \underset{\overset{\displaystyle |}{H}}{\overset{\overset{\displaystyle H}{|}}{C}} - \underset{\overset{\displaystyle |}{H}}{\overset{\overset{\displaystyle H}{|}}{C}} - \underset{\overset{\displaystyle |}{H}}{\overset{\overset{\displaystyle H}{|}}{C}} - \cdots$$

Otherwise, the molecule is unsaturated (the number of missing hydrogen atoms is always divisible by two). If the molecule has exactly two fewer hydrogen atoms than it is entitled to, it is called mono-unsaturated. Notice the double bonding of two carbon atoms and the corresponding absence of two hydrogen atoms:

$$\cdots -\underset{H}{\overset{H}{C}}-\underset{H}{\overset{H}{C}}-\underset{H}{\overset{H}{C}}-\underset{H}{\overset{H}{C}}-\underset{H}{\overset{H}{C}}-\underset{H}{\overset{H}{C}}-\underset{H}{\overset{H}{C}}-\overset{H}{C}=\overset{H}{C}-\underset{H}{\overset{H}{C}}-\underset{H}{\overset{H}{C}}-\underset{H}{\overset{H}{C}}-\underset{H}{\overset{H}{C}}-\underset{H}{\overset{H}{C}}-\underset{H}{\overset{H}{C}}-\underset{H}{\overset{H}{C}}-\underset{H}{\overset{H}{C}}- \cdots$$

If the molecule has room for four or more extra hydrogen atoms, it is called polyunsaturated:

$$\cdots -\underset{H}{\overset{H}{C}}-\underset{H}{\overset{H}{C}}-\underset{H}{\overset{H}{C}}-\underset{H}{\overset{H}{C}}-\overset{H}{C}=\overset{H}{C}-\underset{H}{\overset{H}{C}}-\underset{H}{\overset{H}{C}}-\underset{H}{\overset{H}{C}}-\underset{H}{\overset{H}{C}}-\overset{H}{C}=\overset{H}{C}-\underset{H}{\overset{H}{C}}-\underset{H}{\overset{H}{C}}-\underset{H}{\overset{H}{C}}-\underset{H}{\overset{H}{C}}- \cdots$$

Animal fats contain a lot of saturated fatty acids, some mono-unsaturated fatty acids, and scant amounts of polyunsaturated acids. Except for the tropical oils, the opposite is true for vegetable oils.

## Why is saturated fat unhealthful?

Saturated fat forces the liver to produce more low-density lipoprotein (LDL), a microscopic vehicle that carries cholesterol through the arteries. LDL promotes build-up of atherosclerotic plaque, deposits on the artery walls that inhibit blood circulation. This can cause a stroke or heart attack.

Cholesterol watchers are warned not to buy products with high oil content if the label merely states "pure vegetable oil" rather than listing the oil's specific name. "Pure vegetable oil" is likely to be made in large part from highly saturated coconut or palm oil because they cost less than the widely available mono-unsaturated or polyunsaturated oils. Nondairy creamers, in general, are another source of highly saturated oils parading under the "pure vegetable oil" banner.

### Why are mono-unsaturated and polyunsaturated fats considered beneficial?

Neither fat fosters excess low-density lipoprotein (LDL). In fact, both tend to lower the amount of LDL in your body. Keep in mind, however, that since both are fats, they become unhealthful if excessively consumed.

Which fat is better, mono-unsaturated or polyunsaturated? A decade ago scientists believed that the polyunsaturated kind was more desirable. Now, researchers are voting for the mono-unsaturated variety. Like polyunsaturated fat, it decreases the amount of LDL in the bloodstream. Unlike polyunsaturated fat, it doesn't decrease the amount of high-density lipoprotein (HDL) in the bloodstream. HDLs are highly beneficial because they tend to remove excess cholesterol from the circulatory system. This helps explain why olive oil has become the pet among informed cholesterol watchers — approximately three-fourths of its oil is mono-unsaturated.

### Is a 100 percent peanut or other vegetable oil free of saturated fat?

Just because a vegetable oil is classified as mono-unsaturated or polyunsaturated doesn't mean it doesn't contain saturated fats. This classification is based on the predominant oil. All oils are a combination of saturated, mono-unsaturated, and polyunsaturated oils. What's most important to the cholesterol watcher is the percentage that is saturated. The worst offenders are the tropical oils, including the widely used coconut and palm kernel oils. They even contain a higher percentage of saturated fats than does butter (respectively, 92 percent and 84 percent versus 63 percent).

The following chart shows you the percentage breakdown of fat types in thirteen popular vegetable oils. Figures are averages (the exact figures vary by growing region, season, etc.). Oils are listed in ascending order of saturation.

| OIL | Saturated (%) | Mono- unsaturated (%) | Poly- unsaturated (%) |
|---|---|---|---|
| Canola/Rapeseed | 6 | 65 | 29 |
| Walnut | 9 | 28 | 63 |
| Safflower | 10 | 13 | 77 |
| Sunflower | 12 | 19 | 69 |
| Corn | 14 | 28 | 58 |
| Soybean | 15 | 24 | 61 |
| Sesame | 15 | 41 | 44 |
| Olive | 15 | 73 | 12 |
| Peanut | 18 | 49 | 33 |
| Cottonseed | 27 | 19 | 54 |
| Palm | 54 | 38 | 8 |
| Palm kernel | 84 | 14 | 2 |
| Coconut | 93 | 6 | 2 |
| Averages | 28 | 32 | 40 |

**Is a margarine made with oils that are high in mono-unsaturated and polyunsaturated fats good for cholesterol watchers?**

Contrary to popular belief, margarine contains significant amounts of saturated fats (which, according to many studies, can raise blood cholesterol level). The misconception arises because margarines are generally made with vegetable oils that are high in unsaturated, low in saturated, fats. In order to solidify the oils into a spread and to increase shelf life (saturated fats are less susceptible to oxidation, and therefore rancidity, than unsaturated fats), the margarine manufacturer hydrogenates his oils. Hydrogenation adds hydrogen atoms to a mono-unsaturated or polyunsaturated fatty acid's hydrocarbon molecular chain, and the addition of new hydrogen atoms converts unsaturated oil molecules into saturated ones.

Therefore, do not be hoodwinked by a company's sales pitch that its product is made totally with unsaturated oils. What counts is not the absence of saturated fatty acids in the oil when it entered the margarine factory, but the presence of saturated fatty acids in the product when you melt it over your steaming corn on the cob. If you see the word "hydrogenated" preceding "vegetable oils" in the ingredient list, you know the product contains saturated fats. On the other hand, if you do not see the "hydrogenated" qualifier, do not automatically assume that the food has not been hydrogenated.

Another indicator of degree of saturation is the margarine's firmness. Generally, the harder the margarine, the more saturated fats it contains. Therefore — other factors being equal — a pourable margarine is less saturated than a tub margarine, which in turn is less saturated than a stick margarine.

### What are sucrose polyesters and why are they nonfattening?

Sucrose polyesters (SPE) are man-made fat substitutes. Their taste and mouth-feel imitate those of natural oils. The SPE molecules are too large to be absorbed into the bloodstream through the intestinal walls, so they pass completely through your digestive track, with calories intact.

**What happens when you deep-fry a food at too low a temperature? Or at too high a temperature?**

When, for instance, chicken is submerged in sufficiently hot cooking oil, the breaded or batter-coated surface quickly forms a protective shield. This wrapping prevents the oil from penetrating to the chicken and therefore helps keep it from becoming greasy. The chicken cooks by indirect, rather than direct, heat. Conduction is the word for this type of heat transfer.

If the oil is not hot enough, unwanted oil will reach the chicken before the outer protective layer can form. If the oil is too hot, the breaded or batter-coated wrapping will be burned by direct heat before the chicken has had time to cook by conduction. The proper temperature varies by the kind of oil and the type and thickness of the food. As a general rule of thumb, the magic number for cooking breaded or batter-coated foods in vegetable oil is about 375°F.

**Why should I not crowd a pan with food when I am deep-frying?**

It is unsatisfactory to deep-fry in oil that isn't hot enough, and since the addition of room-temperature food will surely lower the temperature of a hot oil, it stands to reason that you should not deep-fry too much food at one time. The less food you add to the oil, the smaller the drop in oil temperature and the quicker the temperature recovery time. For each volume of food, use at least six volumes of oil.

We have a tip that will allow you to minimize the problem of the oil dropping below its desired temperature. Preheat your oil about 15°F above its optimal deep-frying temperature. If the ideal temperature is 375°F, preheat to 390°F. Why can't one preheat the oil even higher and deep-fry an even larger batch, you may ask. Because you risk ruining the oil's cooking effectiveness by chemically altering its molecular structure. A temperature of 400°F or higher taxes even an oil with a 450°F smoke point. It also increases the number of fat molecules that vaporize into the air and make a greasy landing on your kitchen cupboards.

Here is another deep-frying tip: Warm your ingredients to at least room temperature before you add them to the hot oil. Otherwise, the oil temperature can drop into the "greasy" 300° to 325°F zone — and probably will not have a chance to regain its proper temperature level before the food is cooked.

**Why should a breaded food be allowed to rest before cooking in hot oil?**

Binding the breadcrumbs to the food is vital. If they fall off into the oil, they will burn, imparting a bitter flavor to the food and lowering the smoke point of the oil. Though there is no sure-fire way to keep every breadcrumb from coming loose, you should do everything possible to prevent it.

Most breaded foods are coated with three layers: seasoned flour, lightly beaten egg, and breadcrumbs, in order of application. For the egg to perform one of its chief functions — binding the breadcrumbs to the food — it must partially dry before cooking. This is best accomplished by placing the uncooked breaded food on a cake rack for twenty to thirty minutes at room temperature. Resting the breaded food in the refrigerator, as some cookbooks advise, is not recommended, because your food will pick up odor during its stay. Wrapping the breaded food before placing it in the refrigerator does not solve your problem, because though you keep out the refrigerator odor, you simultaneously keep in the egg moisture. And whether or not you wrap the breaded food, it will be cold when you remove it from the refrigerator and can, therefore, worsen the temperature drop problem.

Other helpful hints for keeping the breadcrumbs attached include:
- Using room-temperature eggs
- Not overbeating the eggs, because bubbles are poor binders

- Using small breadcrumbs because they adhere better than large crumbs
- Preparing homemade crumbs, which cling better than the store-bought variety because of their coarser texture

### Why is it a good idea not to salt foods before you deep-fry them?

Salt can draw moisture to the surface of the food and therefore increase the possibility of splattering when you place the food in the hot oil. It can also lower the smoke point and hasten the chemical decomposition of cooking oils. The more you plan to reuse a cooking oil, the more important it is not to presalt your foods (or at least to minimize presalting), because the effect is cumulative.

### Why do many short-order cooks prefer to deep-fry in used oil?

More than thrift encourages these chefs of the coffee shop circuit to favor secondhand oil. As food cooks, it dyes the oil, gradually imparting a deep honey pigmentation that can be transferred to the next batch. This cosmetic benefit comes at the expense of proper flavor and aroma, as you undoubtedly have noticed if you have taken a bite of one of those photogenic french fries served at your neighborhood greasy spoon.

### Why is an electric deep-fat fryer unsuitable?

When deep-frying, you will sometimes have to adjust the temperature quickly. The conventional pan-on-a-flame method gives you a reasonable amount of this flexibility, but there is too long a lag between the time you reset the electric deep-fat fryer's thermostat and the time the oil reaches the desired temperature. Deep-frying with a pan on an electric range causes almost as much trouble as the electric pan method.

## Why is knowing the smoke point of an oil important?

The smoke point of an oil is the temperature at which it starts to smoke. When an oil smokes, it begins to decompose, and — say some experts — many of its unsaturated fatty acid molecules become saturated. What is known for sure is that the chemical breakdown of the glycerol molecules in the fat creates acrolein, an obnoxious-smelling compound that can inflame the cook's respiratory system.

Knowing an oil's smoke point can also save you money because each time you deep-fry with an oil, you lower its smoke point irreversibly. If you buy an oil with a smoke point not very far above 375°F (the normal deep-frying temperature), chances are its smoke point will drop to below 375° after its first use. If you want to save money by reusing an oil as many times as possible, select one with the highest smoke point.

The smoke point for any given vegetable oil varies from brand to brand, but approximate averages for the leading oils are 510°F for safflower, 495°F for soybean, 475°F for corn, 440°F for peanut, 420°F for sesame, and 375°F for olive. The figure is roughly 375°F for vegetable shortening (solidified oil).

## What are flash and fire points?

Even higher than the smoke point are two other critical points: flash and fire. An oil reaches its flash point (about 600°F, for most oils) when tiny wisps of fire begin to leap from its surface. If the oil is then heated to its fire point (which averages slightly under 700°F for most varieties), its surface will be a blazing inferno.

Never use water to put out an oil fire. If you do, the water will splatter the burning oil and spread its destructive reach. Smother the flames with a tight-fitting lid or a sheet of foil wrap (kept handy for such an emergency). If the grease fire has spread outside the pan, suffocate it with baking soda or the foam of a fire extinguisher that is formulated for an oil fire, if you have one.

**How can I prolong the useful life of an oil?**

First, select the right pot. Opt for a stainless steel rather than an iron pot because the latter will hasten rancidity. For the same reason, choose a tall and narrow, rather than a squat and wide, pot to minimize surface area. Oxygen is an enemy of oil.

The longer an oil is heated, the more quickly it will decompose. Therefore, do not preheat the oil any longer than is necessary. If you are cooking more than one batch of food, add each new batch without delay (unless time is needed to adjust the cooking temperature). Turn off the heat immediately after removing the last batch from the oil.

Some cookbooks recommend heating the oil until a slight haze appears on the surface. This is poor advice because smoke indicates that your oil is decomposing — and it does not reveal the exact temperature, which is the information you want. The best way to ascertain temperature is with a quality deep-fat frying thermometer. We recommend its use even if you have a rheostat on an electric deep-fat fryer because such thermostatic controls are seldom sufficiently accurate.

Your oil can be tainted by the breadcrumbs and other particles that are scorched within a minute after they detach themselves from the frying food. Shake off loosely attached crumbs before adding the food to the oil. When crumbs do fall off the food into the oil, remove as many as possible with a small strainer or slotted spoon before they have a chance to burn.

As soon as the oil cools to a safe temperature for handling (about 140°F or so), funnel it through several layers of cheesecloth into its original bottle or, preferably, into a clean glass jar. Choose a storage container whose volume approximates the volume of the oil because the more ullage (the air space between the lid and the liquid), the quicker the oil will oxidize, and, therefore, the quicker it will become rancid.

Light also damages oil, so keep your supply tightly covered in a dark, cool cupboard. Better yet, refrigerate the oil once it has been opened.

## Doesn't refrigeration cloud an oil?

It is perfectly natural for an otherwise sound oil to develop a cloudy appearance (and, for some oils, a solid consistency) when stored at refrigerator temperature. The oil suffers no damage and should become clear again when brought to room temperature.

## What are the signs of a deteriorated oil?

Visual clues include changes in color and viscosity, the presence of impurities, and a lowered smoke point.

An oil perceptibly darkens with use — and especially with misuse — because the molecules of both oil and food burn when subjected to high or prolonged heat. Because sugar caramelizes, sugar-rich foods can particularly deepen the oil's color.

The more you use an oil, the more slowly it will pour. This decrease in fluidity is mainly caused by an alteration of the oil's molecular structure, but also by the accumulation of loose, absorbent food particles, which can be seen as sediment or suspended flecks.

When smoke appears on the oil's surface before the temperature reaches 375°F, your oil will no longer deep-fry effectively.

An oil's downfall is also indicated by rancidity, primarily caused by prolonged contact with air. Rancidity can best be described in sensory terms by comparing it with the taste and smell of a stale potato chip (there are plenty of those around).

If the oil's natural odor and flavor have been unduly contaminated by foods cooked in it, the oil should be discarded. The same is true if it tastes burnt or inordinately oily.

## Why are the Italian olive oils from Sicily more robust than those from Tuscany?

More than the warm Mediterranean sun gives Sicilian olive oil its characteristic rich, full flavor and aroma. In deference to local palates, Sicilians tend to harvest their olives when they are riper and, during processing, take pains to retain more of the original olive flavor than do their fellow countrymen, the Tuscans.

Which olive oil rates higher is a matter of epicurean debate. Some cooks prefer the delicacy of the Tuscan oil, and others couldn't live without the lusty quality of the Sicilian oil. Be your own judge, but to be fair, taste the best from both regions. It is generally acknowledged that Tuscany's and Sicily's best growing areas are, respectively, Lucca and Castelvetrano. Look for their names on the label.

Also look for the phrases "virgin" and "cold-pressed." A virgin olive oil is the liquid of the first pressing (later pressings require more pressure, which releases some of the undesirable flavor of the olive skins and seeds). "Cold-pressed" means that no heat (or virtually none) was used to extract the oil. Olive oil makers who use heat sacrifice quality for quantity.

You may also want to compare the superior Lucca and Castelvetrano oils with American olive oils (and even with some of the less expensive imported Italian varieties). You may be surprised to learn how insipid most of our best-selling brands are. The same comparison can be made with other vegetable oils. A case in point is Chinese peanut oil, which, unlike its highly refined American cousin, smacks of peanuts.

# 11

## B·A·K·I·N·G

**H**ow does baking powder leaven baked goods?

Perhaps you recall from your high-school or college chemistry class experiments that carbon dioxide bubbles are generated whenever water is poured over a dry acid and alkali mixture. Well, that is exactly what happens when you use baking powder, because this cooking ingredient is essentially a blend of acid (calcium acid phosphate, sodium aluminum sulfate, or cream of tartar, to name three) and alkali (sodium bicarbonate, popularly known as baking soda). Add water to this mixture and a chemical reaction results, producing carbon dioxide. The gas generated creates minuscule air pockets, or enters into existing ones, within the dough or batter. When placed in a hot oven or on a hot griddle, the dough or batter rises, primarily for two reasons. First, the heat helps release additional carbon dioxide from the baking powder. Second, the heat expands the trapped carbon dioxide gas and air and creates steam. The resulting pressure swells the countless air pockets, which in turn expand the food being baked.

**Does baking powder lose its potency over a period of time?**

Yes. You can easily determine whether you need a fresh supply by conducting this simple chemical experiment: Pour one-quarter cup of hot tap water over one-half teaspoon of baking powder. The fresher the baking powder, the more actively this mixture will bubble. If the chemical reaction is weak or does not occur, your baking powder will not properly raise whatever you are planning to bake.

**Can I make my own baking powder?**

Yes. The standard home recipe for making the equivalent of one teaspoon of commercial baking powder is one-half teaspoon of cream of tartar, one-quarter teaspoon of baking soda and — if you plan to store your supply — one-quarter teaspoon of cornstarch. The cornstarch absorbs moisture in the air and therefore prevents a premature chemical reaction between the acid and alkali. When using homemade baking powder, work quickly, because the carbon dioxide gas is released more quickly and at a lower temperature than is the case with the commercial double-acting powders.

**When substituting buttermilk for sweet milk in a baking recipe, why should I substitute baking soda for all, or some, of the baking powder in the recipe?**

In order for a chemical leavening agent to release the optimal quantity of carbon dioxide gas into the dough or batter, the acid and alkali must be in proper proportion, as it is in the case of baking powder. When you substitute buttermilk for sweet milk, you incorporate extra acid into the batter or dough, and you therefore upset the proper proportion of acid to alkali that was worked out in the original recipe. That extra acid will reduce the amount of carbon dioxide generated and, accordingly, inhibit the leavening process. To counteract the hyperacidity, the cook needs only to substitute baking soda (an alkali) for some or all of the baking powder in order to maintain the necessary quantity of alkali.

For each cup of buttermilk that you use in place of sweet milk, reduce by two teaspoons the amount of baking powder called for in the original recipe and replace it with one-half teaspoon of baking soda.

## How does yeast leaven bread?

Yeast *(Saccharomyces cerevisiae)* is made up of minute one-cell fungi that rapidly multiply if given their favorite foods (sugar or starch) in a moist environment. The ideal temperature for growth is 110° to 115°F, though for bread-leavening purposes, 80° to 95°F yields the best product. When the yeast cells feast on the sugar (or the starch that a yeast enzyme has converted into glucose, a simple sugar), a chemical reaction takes place: The sugar ferments and, as a result, is converted for the most part into alcohol and carbon dioxide. As with baked goods made with baking powder, the carbon dioxide — along with trapped expanding air and steam — leavens the food.

Teetotalers and the squeamish need not fret about consuming alcohol and live yeast cells. The heat of the oven or griddle evaporates the first ingredient and kills the second.

## Are dry and compressed yeast products interchangeable?

Yes. One packet (about one scant tablespoon) of active dry yeast has the leavening power of one standard cake of compressed yeast. Since compressed yeast contains 70 percent moisture (compared to only 8 percent for dry yeast), it must be stored in the refrigerator — and even then it loses its leavening effectiveness in about two weeks. Dry yeast need not be refrigerated but it must be stored in an airtight container lest it absorb water from the atmosphere, raising its moisture content. That would reactivate the yeast's metabolic enzymes, awakening the dormant yeast cells.

## How can I test the vitality of yeast?

Just before using the yeast, mix some into one-quarter cup of lukewarm water that has been enriched with one-quarter teaspoon of sugar, the food for the yeast. If the yeast mixture does not start to bubble within five to ten minutes, your microorganisms are dead or enervated and will not leaven your dough or batter.

## How do air and steam leaven baked goods?

When heat builds up the pressure of the air trapped within the tiny air pockets in the dough or batter, these cavities expand, and therefore so do the baked goods. Dough- or batter-inflating pressure is also generated when heat converts some of the food's water content into steam. Popovers and cream puffs are prime illustrations of this process.

## What prevents baked goods from collapsing back to their original size once their leavening gas escapes or cools?

Baked goods acquire a firm structure principally because the heat of the oven or griddle coagulates the protein and gelatinizes the starch in the batter or dough. If it were not for this firming action, the weight of the food's mass would cause many of the air pockets that were formerly supported by the pressure of the carbon dioxide, steam, or hot air to cave in.

## Why should I use less yeast or baking powder when baking at high altitudes?

Since the atmospheric pressure is lower at, say, 5000 feet than at sea level, the carbon dioxide gas generated by the yeast or baking powder encounters less resistance from the surrounding air. Therefore, a given quantity of carbon dioxide expands with greater force, and the dough or batter is leavened more quickly and to a greater volume at higher altitudes. Unless the baker cuts back the quantity of leavening agent used, the baked goods may have a rough texture that would be more suitable for Rocky Mountain goats than for discriminating Denverites.

**Why must I be prepared to vary the amount of flour that I use for a particular bread recipe?**

The flour you use today may have either more or less moisture than was in the supply you used yesterday, last week, or last year. Flour tends to lose moisture the longer it is stored. Also, moisture content usually varies with the brand of flour and the season, and a flour will pick up moisture if you knead it on a humid day.

For these reasons, you must sometimes make adjustments in the amount of flour you use (or, if it is possible, in the liquid), in order to keep the dough or batter's flour/liquid ratio in proper balance. If your flour has more than an average amount of moisture, use more flour. If it is on the dry side, use less.

**What are the pros and cons of whole wheat versus white wheat flour?**

Whole wheat flour contains all the edible parts of the wheat berry: the starchy endosperm, the nutritious germ (embryo), and the outer bran layer. To produce white flour, the miller removes most or all of the germ and bran.

White wheat flour has three principal advantages over whole wheat flour. First, it does not become rancid as quickly and easily, and therefore has a longer shelf life. It is less vulnerable to rancidity because it does not contain the germ, the component of the wheat berry that contains the fat that causes rancidity. Second, white wheat flour leavens better because it contains more gluten per weight. Third, white wheat flour is more digestible. Finally, from the marketer's viewpoint, white wheat flour has greater salability: Most Americans have been conditioned since childhood to prefer baked goods made with white wheat flour.

Whole wheat flour has its advantages, too. First and foremost, it is significantly more nutritious because nearly all the vitamins, minerals, protein, fat, and fiber of the wheat berry reside in the germ and bran. One must not be fooled into thinking that enriched white bread is the nutritional equal of whole wheat bread, because far more nutrients are removed during the milling of white flour than are replaced in the enrichment process. One should also not be hoodwinked by the term "wheat bread" on the label. For flour made from the whole berry, look for the term "whole," or "100 percent whole," before the phrase "wheat bread." If the list of ingredients says "whole wheat flour and wheat flour," the bakery used a blend of whole and white wheat flours.

To discerning palates, whole wheat bread is also superior to white wheat bread because it has a more interesting flavor and texture.

### What is the difference between ordinary whole wheat and graham flour?

The various wheat berry components of regular whole wheat flour are ground more or less uniformly. In the milling of graham flour, the outer bran layer is ground to a coarser texture than are the endosperm and germ.

### Why is all-purpose flour a poor compromise for most baking tasks?

All-purpose flour is a blend of hard and soft wheat flours. Each of these flours is ideal for specific tasks. Hard flour is perfect for bread making because of its high content of gluten, a substance that provides structure for the expanding dough. Soft wheat flour is the better choice for baked goods that do not need to rely upon a high gluten content — most biscuits, pastries, and cakes, for example. When you use all-purpose flour for bread making, your bread lacks sufficient gluten. When you use all-purpose flour for most cakes and other delicate baked goods, their texture will be tough because of too much gluten. We strongly recommend that you leave the all-purpose flour on the supermarket shelf and buy both pastry (sometimes called cake) flour and bread (sometimes called baker's) flour. If a food is best made with a blend of the two flours, as is the case with popovers, the home baker can create a suitable mixture.

If you are forced to use all-purpose flour because pastry and bread flours are not sold in your area, remember that a recipe calling for all-purpose flour will yield different results in different regions of the country. Reason: The major national flour processors use different blending formulas to take into account regional baking preferences. Since a Southerner tends to bake more biscuits and the Northerner, more bread, the Southern formula has a larger proportion of soft wheat and the Northern formula has a higher proportion of hard wheat.

## Is unbleached flour preferable to bleached flour?

Unbleached flour has a more natural taste because it has not been tainted with the chemicals used to process bleached flour. Millers treat their bleached product with chemicals for more than one reason. The most obvious is cosmetic: Bleaching agents whiten the flour. But just as important, millers cut their costs with chemical processing. Flour must be aged to strengthen its gluten content, and natural aging of unbleached flour requires keeping the product in a warehouse for several months. Flour processors discovered that they could avoid that storage expense by using chemicals to age the flour artificially.

When you purchase unbleached flour, look for an established brand, your assurance that the flour has been sufficiently aged.

## Is sifting flour necessary?

Unless the recipe says to sift, it is usually wiser not to. Reason: Most modern baking recipes are based on the measured volume of unsifted flour, partly because the flour sold today is not as compacted as it was in our grandparents' day. But even if the flour of yesteryear didn't need sifting for lightness, it probably would have been best to sift it anyway to remove insects and other impurities.

**How does the choice of liquid affect the dough?**

Bread made with water has a chewier texture and crisper crust than one made with milk. However, milk helps produce a more delicate texture and, because of its protein and sugar (lactose) content, a deeper-hued crust. Adding milk, potato water, or beer furnishes the yeast with hearty food and the diner with added nutrients, calories, and flavor.

**Why is a sourdough baguette denser and more acidic than a standard baguette?**

The sourdough yeast *(Saccharomyces exiguus)* multiplies at a significantly slower rate than does common baker's yeast. A more compact and less airy loaf results.

Sourdough bread is more acidic because, unlike baker's yeast, sourdough yeast cannot digest maltose sugar. Bacteria are, therefore, free to digest it — and a certain type native to the San Francisco area does. In the process, a highly acidic by-product is formed, one that helps give sourdough bread its characteristic flavor.

**What is the function of sugar, honey, and molasses in bread making?**

Although these sweeteners are not essential, they can make the bread more tender because they postpone protein coagulation and thus allow the dough or batter to swell to a greater volume before heat stabilizes the structure. They can also add flavor, deepen the color of the crust, and extend the bread's shelf life.

On the negative side, they add calories and, if too much is used, their caramelization can discolor the bread. A superabundance of these sweeteners can also slow down the yeast's growth enough to keep the dough from rising properly.

When substituting molasses or honey for sugar, remember that your dough will require a little extra flour to keep the optimal balance between the dry and liquid ingredients.

**What function does salt serve in bread making?**

Though salt is not an essential ingredient for bread making, it does give bread a firmer crumb and crust. This more appealing texture is due to the salt's having slowed down the growth of yeast, thereby helping to prevent the dough from expanding too quickly. Salt also contributes flavor to bread.

**What is the function of egg in a yeast bread?**

Eggs are not required in yeast bread making, though they do bestow color, flavor, nutrients, increased volume, and an over-all richness. However, for baked goods such as popovers — or the pâte à choux–based cream puffs, éclairs, and profiteroles — egg yolks are essential. Without the support given by heat-coagulated egg protein, these baking specialties could not maintain their steamed- and puffed-up shapes.

**Why will bread made with a fat like butter stay fresher longer than one made without fat?**

When bread dries out, it stales. The fat content in a bread slows down moisture loss. The French buy their bread supply twice a day because authentic French bread is fatless and therefore stales quickly.

**What else does a fat contribute to bread?**

Should a baker want to give a bread a softer and smoother texture, fat can help because it retards gluten development (the greased gluten strands have a more difficult time latching on to each other and therefore are less effective in forming a structural network). A fat also adds flavor, richness, nutrients, calories, and, if it is butter or lard, saturated fatty acids. Butter and margarine also lend color.

**What bread-baking steps produce a soft crust? A hard crust?**

For a soft crust, brush butter (or other fat) over the top of the bread before it is baked or while it is in the oven. Reason: Fat retards the drying out of the exposed surface.

For a hard crust, brush the top of the baked goods with cold water either before placing it in the oven or while it is baking. Alternatively, create a steamy baking environment by placing a pan of water in the bottom of the oven.

**Why does yeast dough need to be kneaded?**

The most obvious reason is to distribute the yeast cells and other ingredients uniformly throughout the dough. One result of the uneven dispersal of yeast cells is that the dough will rise faster in some places than in others.

It is equally important to develop a firm gluten that will provide a supporting framework for the expanding dough. Gluten is a mixture of proteins in the flour that, when kneaded, becomes a cohesive network of elastic strands. As the carbon dioxide gas develops, it becomes trapped inside the gluten structure. The trapped gas finds a home in the countless minute pre-existing air pockets within the dough or creates its own minuscule cavities. As more gas develops, pressure builds up within these spaces. This pressure stretches the elastic gluten strands, increasing the volume of the dough.

Not everyone is blessed with strong hands and a will to knead, or a machine equipped with a dough hook. If you fall within this category but love to bake your own bread, there are no-knead bread recipes. You don't have to knead because you work with a batter rather than a dough; you must, however, beat the batter well to distribute the yeast. Unfortunately, no-knead recipes produce a gummy mixture that tends to stick to the baking pan unless you grease the pan very generously (and even then, the baked item may stick). Moreover, the bread may have a coarser texture than you might like. Your bread will also have a shorter storage life than a kneaded bread.

**What happens if yeast dough rises too little? Too much?**

Both extremes produce a tough-textured bread. In the case of insufficient rising, the air pockets in the dough do not expand enough to give the bread a light, airy texture. When a dough over-rises, the strength and elasticity of the gluten strands are irreparably weakened, and therefore the dough's structure is doomed to collapse.

**If the yeast bread dough did not rise sufficiently, what went wrong?**

One possibility is that the dough was too cold to foster yeast growth (80° to 95°F is the best temperature range for leavening bread). Another likelihood is that the yeast was "liquidated" when the baker mistakenly mixed it with water that was too hot — a temperature of 140°F or more will usually kill yeast. It is also possible that the yeast was D.O.A.

**Why should I slightly underblend my pancake batter and then let it rest for an hour or two before using it?**

If you mix pancake batter too energetically or for too long, you will overdevelop the gluten in the flour and your pancakes will be tougher than necessary. Excess blending can also cause the premature formation, and escape, of the carbon dioxide that you need for leavening the pancakes.

A much better strategy is to stop mixing the ingredients just before all the tiny lumps of flour dissolve and then let the process automatically complete itself as the batter sits undisturbed in your refrigerator. The cold refrigerator temperature not only retards bacterial attack and growth, it impedes gluten development and hinders the yeast or baking powder activity.

A smooth batter produces more than just desirable texture. It also helps to brown your morning masterpieces more evenly because a greater area of the bottom surface will rest flat on the hot griddle.

**How does sugar help give pancakes a rich brown color?**

As the pancake cooks on the griddle, the sugar melts and then caramelizes. The more sugar you add to the batter, the greater the browning effect of caramelization. Many recipes from popular cookbooks and magazines, however, specify so much sugar that the pancakes could almost be better served as a dinner dessert than as a breakfast food.

**Why is the butter of America inferior to that of France for making *pâte feuilletée* (puff paste)?**

*Pâte feuilletée* consists of layers of rolled-out, butter-coated thin sheets of dough. It is used to make such famous pastry as napoleons and *vol-au-vents*. When *pâte feuilletée* bakes, the water in the butter steams and helps separate the individual layers, raising the pastry to many times its former height.

If the butter contains too much moisture, too much steam will be generated and the pastry will cook too rapidly and expand too much. The result will be misshapen and will lack the light, delicate texture of a *pâte feuilletée* made with a butter that has the proper moisture content. Most French butters have about 10 percent moisture, and typical American butter has over 15 percent — too much for this use.

Some American bakers reduce the moisture by placing the domestic butter in a kitchen towel and forcing some of its water content out and into the towel with a rolling pin. Though this technique may solve the excess moisture problem, the pastry will not have the heavenly flavor of a quality French butter, such as the glorious one churned in the Normandy village of Isigny.

**How do I prevent ingredients like nuts and dried fruits from settling to the bottom of a batter or dough during baking?**

Sprinkle them with flour before mixing them into the batter or dough. The coating absorbs some of the surface oil and water that exudes from these ingredients during baking and therefore reduces their tendency to slip downward through the batter or dough.

## Why do my cakes develop unwanted domes?

Likely, your cake batter has too much flour. If your batter were thinner, all its liquid molecules would have more time to circulate before the batter near the pan's edges would set. Once that occurs, the amount of heat transferred to the liquid center is reduced because the molecules near the pan's edges will no longer be in motion. Therefore, the center will take longer to solidify, giving it extra time to rise, creating the dome effect.

## Why do different baked goods require different baking temperatures?

Ideally, these foods should be baked at a fairly high temperature (in the 425° to 450°F range) so that the expanding internal gases can adequately increase the dough or batter's volume before the coagulating protein sets the food's structure. Because of their small size, most biscuits can be successfully baked in or near that temperature range. A lower temperature (about 400°F) is necessary for baking bread loaves because the higher temperature would burn the outside of the bread before the heat could reach and bake the inside. Well-sugared breads must be baked at an even lower temperature (325° to 375°F) because the sugar would caramelize too much at a higher temperature and blacken the crust.

## Why are black baking pans usually superior to the shiny variety?

A dull, dark, or black surface absorbs more of the radiant energy coming from the oven walls than a bright, shiny, or white surface, which reflects much of it. A black pan (carbon steel, for instance) will therefore become hotter and transmit heat more quickly than an otherwise identical uncoated stainless steel or aluminum pan in the same oven. This phenomenon explains why white suits and dresses are popular in hot, sunny weather. (A Harvard University study in the Middle East found that the surface of an outfit made with black cloth is about 10°F hotter than one of white cloth because the black cloth absorbs two and one-half times more radiant energy from the sun than the white.)

On the average, a shiny pan is 15°F cooler in a 350°F oven than its black equivalent, and that 15°F can make a crucial difference. Because the shiny pan's temperature is lower, you must either extend the cooking time or increase the baking temperature. Neither of those two alternatives is totally satisfactory. No matter what the cooking temperature or how long the cooking time, chances are that either the exposed crust will receive too much heat, or the crust that lines the pan will absorb too little heat.

Shiny bakeware is not all that bad. It can be beneficial at times. Some delicate cookies require a very hot oven, but are apt to burn on the bottom when baked on a dark, dull cookie sheet. A glistening cookie sheet, on the other hand, reduces the heat reaching the cookies' undersides.

If you do bake with a shiny pan, it pays to use a scouring pad to keep its surfaces free of dark stains, or they will tend to become mottled. When you bake with such a pan, the portion of the food resting on a black blotch may burn by the time the food on a bright area is properly baked.

In one of our experiments, we purposely baked a loaf of bread in a shiny metal steel pan that was tarnished in spots with accumulated oven grease stains. The light-and-dark color pattern on the bottom and side crusts of the baked bread came close to duplicating that of the stained pan's outer surface.

**Does food bake more quickly in a glass than in a metal container?**

Yes. This is because the transparency of glass allows radiant heat to pass directly through it, absorbing comparatively little of that energy in the process. Cooks using a recipe based on figures for a dark-surfaced pan and baking in one made of oven-proof glass must either shorten the baking period or lower the oven temperature by 10°F. When the recipe is designed for a shiny pan and you use a Pyrex container, decrease the temperature 25°F.

**Why should a baking pan be at least one and a half inches clear of the oven walls and any other pans?**

When the width of a river decreases, the speed of its current increases. The same phenomenon occurs with currents in your oven except that, in this case, the flowing substance is air rather than water. If there is a narrow gap between a pan and an oven wall or another pan, the air currents that flow upward through it will move faster than those that flow upward through less restricted areas of your oven. And since a faster moving hot air current cooks food faster than one that moves more slowly, uneven baking results. Air current A, depicted in our accompanying illustration, will cook the food on its side of the pan faster than air current B will cook the food on its side.

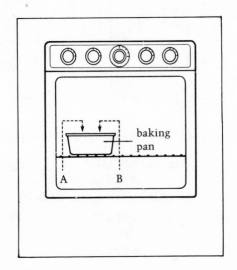

Uneven baking also occurs because food on the left side of the pan is bombarded with more of the radiant heat (see relevant discussion on pp. 27–29) that emanates from the oven's walls.

**When baking on more than one oven shelf, why should I stagger the pans?**

In the following illustration, the pans in oven A are staggered so that air can reach the tops and bottoms of both pans. In oven B, the bottom of the food in pan 1, as well as the top of the food in pan 2, will undercook because insufficient hot air currents will reach the area between the two pans.

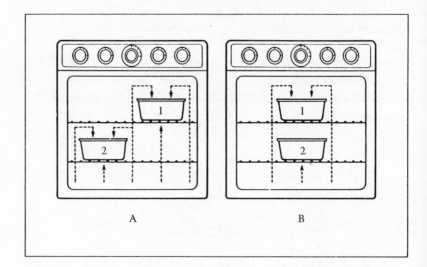

A                                        B

**What is the best temporary filler when baking a pie shell blind?**

Some people use beans or rice, and some use metal pellets when baking a pie shell blind — that is, before adding the filling. Though both the manufactured and the natural weights are heavy enough to keep the empty pie dough flat on the pan while baking, the metal pellets are better heat conductors.

Therefore, the upper surface of the pie shell is less likely to be underbaked. Moreover, you don't have to worry about serving your guests an off-scented crust.

### Why is it helpful to brush beaten egg on a pie crust before adding the filling and baking the pie?

This technique helps prevent soggy pie crusts because the egg protein forms a shield between the dough and moist pie filling. Since the coagulating temperature of the egg mixture is lower than the jelling temperature of the filling, you reduce the period in which the water in the filling comes in direct contact with the crust.

### Why should quiches made with onions and mushrooms be served fresh from the oven?

Because these foods have a high water content, they lose an appreciable amount of moisture as they cool. This moisture can give a quiche two undesirable characteristics: a weeping surface and a soggy crust.

### Why should breads and cakes be unmolded from their pans soon after they are removed from the oven?

When a bread or cake comes out of the oven, it is permeated with trapped steam. As it cools, the steam either escapes into the air or converts to water, which the solids quickly absorb. If too little steam dissipates into the air, the bread or cake will become soggy.

To prevent sogginess, first let the baked product rest in the pan for several minutes until it has settled, then promptly unmold it and place it on a cooling rack. This maximizes the surface area from which the steam can escape. It also eliminates the possibility that moisture will condense and accumulate in the space between the bottom of the bread and the pan.

**Why does bread usually stay fresher in a breadbox than in a refrigerator?**

Two reasons. First, the relatively dry refrigerator air draws more moisture out of foods than does normal room temperature air. Second, the bonding between the starch and water molecules is weaker at refrigerator temperature than at room (and freezer) temperature. Consequently, bread will turn stale more quickly in the refrigerator. On the other hand, if the bread is not located in a cool, dry place and is not kept in an airtight bag, it might be attacked by airborne mold spores. If so, mold could develop on the bread's surface at such an accelerated pace that the bread would have been better stored in the refrigerator, despite the staling factor.

For optimal long-term storage, freeze the bread (it freezes well). Whatever storage medium you choose, be it breadbox, refrigerator, or freezer, minimize moisture loss by keeping the bread well wrapped.

# 12

## B·E·V·E·R·A·G·E·S

Which has more caffeine, tea or coffee?

A pound of tea — on the average — has twice the caffeine of a pound of roasted coffee. However, since that weight of tea typically yields about 160 cups, whereas the pound of coffee brews about 40 cups, the net result is that the cup of tea has roughly one-quarter the caffeine of a cup of coffee.

The exact amount of caffeine in coffee or tea can vary appreciably according to such factors as the bean or leaf type, grind or leaf size, and brewing time and temperature. Parents who forbid their young children to drink coffee should be aware that a twelve-ounce bottle of a typical cola has approximately one-quarter the caffeine of an average cup of coffee — and many times more of it than found in a cup of decaffeinated coffee.

**Why does a late night cup of coffee keep some people awake more than others?**

The frequent coffee drinker develops a greater tolerance to the stimulating kick of caffeine than does the occasional java imbiber. Also, people are born with varying degrees of tolerance. Psychosomatic considerations come into play, too. Chances are you will toss and turn in bed at night if you think that insomnia is the inevitable consequence of a nocturnal cup of coffee.

**Should coffee and tea drinkers forgo those Styrofoam cups stocked by most office coffee wagons and fast-food outlets?**

At the very least, people shouldn't be drinking two or three cups a day out of those containers, as some office workers do. The acid in coffee, and especially tea, dissolves some of the cup's polystyrene into the brew, a disintegration that doesn't benefit your taste buds or health. Cup erosion is most pronounced when hot tea is flavored with lemon, an acid.

**Why is hot tap water a poor choice for brewing coffee or tea?**

Hot tap water extracts too many of the metals, chemicals, and impurities embedded in the pipes and boiler. These off-flavors come through the cold-water tap, too, but to a much lesser extent. We know of some coffee lovers who eschew even cold tap water and use distilled water. If one's local water supply has a disagreeable off-taste (as some do), then this approach would make sense.

**Is it always advisable to use freshly boiled water for brewing coffee or tea?**

For best results, the answer is yes. Water that has been boiled, then cooled, and then reboiled has lost enough of its oxygen content to give a slight flat taste to the brewed coffee or tea.

**What is the ideal temperature for brewing coffee and tea?**

The ideal brewing temperature for coffee strikes a balance between extracting the maximum amount of caffeol compounds and the minimum of polyphenol compounds. Caffeol (not to be confused with caffeine), is responsible for most of the characteristic rich flavor and aroma of coffee, and polyphenols (tannins) give coffee a tang, a desirable quality, if not excessive. Most coffee professionals place the optimal temperature somewhere in the 185° to 205°F range. If the brewing temperature is too low, the coffee grounds will not release enough of their caffeol compounds. If the temperature reaches the boiling point — and especially if it remains there for more than a brief period — the grounds will yield too much of their polyphenol content and thus will likely create a displeasing bitter taste. It should be pointed out that the best-known coffee component — caffeine — is desirable or undesirable depending on whether or not you relish its stimulating effect. Caffeine plays only a minor role in defining the taste of coffee.

Recommended brewing temperatures for tea are more hotly debated by the experts. Our experiments show that, in most instances, green teas are best brewed between 180° and 200°F, oolong teas between 185° and 205°F, and black teas between 190° and 210°F. Also, within each of the three categories, the better the quality of tea, the lower the brewing temperature should be.

### Why does percolated coffee taste bitter?

Not only has percolated coffee been boiled, it has been boiled for approximately seven to fifteen minutes. Little wonder that the resulting coffee tastes bitter. Another drawback is that the percolator method exposes the coffee's aromatic agents to the air prematurely and excessively, so that too much of the aroma escapes into the kitchen air long before the coffee is ever poured. A coffee scent in the room, though evocative, does not compensate for a deficiency of fragrance in the cup.

Of the most popular coffee-brewing processes, the drip method is by far the best.

### What determines ideal grind size?

Coffee style helps dictate the size of the grind. Beans used for making espresso should be ground finer than those for American-style coffee. Turkish coffee demands an even finer grind.

The brewing method also helps influence grind size. The ideal grind size for American-style coffee is what is known as "drip grind" because it has the optimal surface area for making a brew that is rich but not bitter. Despite the taste advantage of using drip-style coffee grains, you cannot use them in a percolator because the grains would fall through the perforations in the basket and into the brew.

## Can the grind size for drip coffee be too small or too large?

Yes. If the coffee grains are undersized, the water takes longer than necessary to filter through. Also, the increase in the exposed surface of the grains allows the water to extract too many polyphenols. Result : The coffee is bitter.

If the coffee grains are oversized, the water will pass through them too quickly. And because of the limited surface exposure of the grains, the water will extract fewer caffeol compounds. Result: Either the coffee will be weak, or the cook will be forced to use extra grains and the coffee will be more expensive than need be.

## Why should coffee be brewed soon after it has been ground?

Ground coffee deteriorates noticeably within a few days — as opposed to two to three weeks for coffee beans — because such a large surface area is exposed to air. This allows volatile flavoring compounds to escape easily. In addition, the increased surface area hastens oxidation and rancidification of the coffee's essential oils. As coffee grains sit around, they also lose some of their carbon dioxide, a gas that contributes to the brew's body and bouquet.

Coffee processors often sell their ground product in so-called vacuum-packed metal containers in order to keep volatile aromatic coffee substances in and oxygen and moisture out. Still, time brings some deterioration in quality because every coffee can contains some oxygen, despite the vacuum claim. Once the can is opened, the coffee grains are vulnerable to even more oxygen and moisture. To minimize flavor loss and delay rancidity, keep out as much oxygen and moisture as possible, and cover the container promptly after use. Storing the covered coffee in a cool place — such as your refrigerator — also increases its shelf life.

Whole beans are less susceptible to oxidation. However, be wary of coffee displayed in open wooden barrels. Unless the merchant does a brisk coffee business and he doesn't replenish partially filled barrels by dumping the new beans on top of the old ones, some of his beans may be overexposed to oxygen.

For the best cup of coffee, buy whole beans from a conscientious merchant with a fast turnover and grind them yourself as needed. If you must store your coffee bean supply for more than several weeks, freeze it in a well-sealed moisture-proof container. Beans can go directly from freezer to grinder to coffee maker.

## Why should I serve coffee immediately after brewing?

As the coffee sits on the warming device, its volatile aromatic compounds flee the liquid. Moreover, the heat that keeps the coffee warm simultaneously develops a bitter flavor in the coffee's essential oils.

## Why can I sip coffee that is hot enough to burn my skin?

In sipping a very hot cup of coffee, you probably suck in more air than you normally do when sipping a not-so-hot cup. This stream of room-temperature air lowers the liquid's temperature through convection and evaporation. Also, the saliva that coats your mouth partially insulates your oral tissue from the hot coffee.

## What is the difference between an Italian, French, and American coffee roast?

These roast classifications refer to the length of the roasting period and not to different kinds of beans. American roasts get the least time in the coffee roaster, while those labeled Italian (or espresso) are given the most time. A French roast falls between the two.

An Italian roast (and, to a lesser extent, a French roast) brews a stronger-flavored and slightly more bitter cup of coffee than an American roast because of its longer roasting period and its finer grind.

### What is the rationale for the mocha-java blend?

The java coffee beans that are cultivated on the Indonesian island of that name have a rich, mellow flavor and aroma but lack enough acid to give balance to a cup of coffee. Just the opposite occurs with mocha coffee beans, a product that is transported from the Middle Eastern port of that name. Mocha beans are deficient in rich flavor and aroma but have surplus acid. Centuries ago someone came up with the idea of blending the two types of beans to produce a balanced cup of coffee, and the idea was a success.

Nowadays, what is sold as mocha-java is really mocha-java–style coffee because few beans come from the Yemen port of Mocha and many of the "java" beans in the mix come from lands beyond Java.

### What is the essential difference between a black and green tea?

All tea is plucked from the same botanical species, *Thea sinensis*, and is classified black or green depending on how the harvested leaves are treated.

Black tea leaves — the type that are most popular in America and Great Britain — are first partially dried (withered). This is done by spreading them in layers on racks for about a day. Then the leaves are passed through rollers that rupture their cells in order to release some of the internal juices, which contain enzymes that trigger fermentation. Several hours later, the fermenting process is brought to a halt by heating and drying (firing) the leaves in an oven or, more traditionally, with sunshine.

Green tea leaves are not fermented — and therein lies the

salient processing difference between the black and the green. To prevent fermentation, the freshly plucked leaves undergo a steaming rather than a withering process. The heat of the steam renders the enzymes in the leaves incapable of causing fermentation. The lack of fermentation is largely responsible for the great contrast in color and taste between a cup of black tea and a cup of green tea. Green tea is typically less pungent as well as much lighter and more yellowish green in color, though exceptions to the rule do exist.

Oolong tea, the third major category, has a character that falls between those of black and green teas. Oolong tea leaves go through the same processing steps as black teas, except that the fermentation period is appreciably shorter.

The world's finest black tea is vintage (not plain) Darjeeling from India, while the blue ribbon in the realm of green tea goes to the April-picked, Grade One (sixteen grades exist) Dragon Well from the People's Republic of China. Though oolong teas can be good, a great specimen has yet to be produced.

**For a strong tea, which is preferable, a longer steeping period or more tea leaves?**

If you prefer strong but not bitter tea, increase the amount of tea leaves, not the steeping period. The longer the water and tea remain in contact, the more bitter your drink will be because more polyphenols are extracted from each leaf.

**Why is it necessary to cover a steeping cup or pot of tea?**

The lid does more than minimize the water's heat loss. It also traps steam, which dampens any unsubmerged tea leaf and sends it to the bottom.

Another way to prevent heat loss while steeping is to preheat the cold teapot by pouring plain boiling water into it and letting the container stand for several minutes before discarding its contents.

**Should I add milk to tea?**

If a brew is of mediocre quality, you may have a scientific reason for adding milk. Mediocre teas tend to be more astringent than quality teas. Milk lowers their astringency because some of the astringent tannic acids in the brew bind chemically with the milk's protein molecules. And, there is another benefit: With fewer free tannins, tea is less constipating. However, tea connoisseurs are right in saying that adding milk to a quality tea is the gastronomic equivalent of "throwing the baby out with the bathwater" because the milk masks the tea's subtle aromas and flavors.

**What's wrong with drinking milk directly out of the carton?**

Hygiene is the obvious consideration, especially for other people who may subsequently drink the milk. However, even if only one person will be drinking the milk, he might be affecting his wallet because he will be decreasing storage life. A human's mouth is a repository of many forms of bacteria that can sour the milk prematurely.

**Will frozen orange juice concentrate last a week in the refrigerator once thawed and mixed with water?**

Because of its high acid content, the juice should still be potable after a week in the refrigerator, but its nutritional value will suffer. Oxygen is the primary agent that destroys the sought after vitamin C content in the orange juice, and is introduced in several ways. Tap water contains dissolved air, and ambient oxygen is incorporated into the juice during mixing and each time the pitcher is opened.

If a large can of frozen concentrate lasts you as long as a week, consider purchasing a smaller container if vitamin C is a priority. Keep the container covered as much as possible. Also, minimize the duration that the prepared orange juice is out of the refrigerator because the lower the temperature, the slower the vitamin C loss.

### Is the "White wine with white meat, and red wine with red meat" dictum fallible?

That maxim is an oversimplification because it does not take into account the many exceptions to the rule that stem from the marked differences in the characteristics of both wines and recipes. Roast chicken is a case in point. Because of its hearty flavor, it would be better married to a red wine, as long as the beverage is dry and light-bodied.

### Are some ingredients incompatible with wine?

Not all ingredients have an affinity with wine. High-acid liquids such as vinegar and citrus juice, for instance, give wine a disagreeable off-flavor. The sulfur content of egg yolks does the same deed. Other enemies of wine include artichokes, asparagus, chocolate, onions, pineapples, and tomatoes. For a detailed exploration of the broad and complex world of wine-food affinities, see Howard Hillman's *The Diner's Guide to Wines* (New York, Hawthorn, 1978).

### When is cork the best material for a wine bottle stopper?

A wine that is unpasteurized and is to be aged in the bottle requires a cork because the wine is still "alive" with the microorganisms that helped it to mature. For optimal results, the maturation process should be slow — and it is the amount of oxygen available to the microorganisms that largely determines that rate. If the cork is too porous (as a result, for instance, of drying out because the bottle wasn't stored in a horizontal position), the wine will soon sour. If the cork is manufactured from a nonporous metal or plastic, the microorganisms inside the bottle will be denied sufficient oxygen. A moist quality cork is the happy medium.

If a wine has been pasteurized (as most domestic jug wines are), the microorganisms have been killed. A stopper made of noncorrosive metal or plastic can therefore be just as suitable as one made of cork, because there is no need for it to breathe. And because this kind of stopper is cheaper, the savings can be passed along to the consumer. Another plus is that you need not store the metal- or plastic-stoppered bottle in a horizontal position.

**What are those tiny glasslike particles that sometimes cling to the bottom of a wine cork?**

Contrary to the belief of some horrified wine drinkers, these crystalline bits are seldom, if ever, broken glass. They are, in all likelihood, malic acid crystals that have solidified from the wine and are evidence of an inferior, though not necessarily unwholesome, wine-making process.

**Is air the greatest enemy of leftover wine?**

Yes. As soon as you pull the cork or unscrew the cap of a fresh bottle of wine, the bacteria-laden air in the room starts souring the wine. Let us say you have just finished a delightful dinner and there, sitting on your table, is a half-empty, standard-sized wine bottle. Don't just cork the bottle for tomorrow's meal, even if you put it in the refrigerator. Pour the liquid into a clean, empty half-sized bottle (saved for this purpose), then cork and store. This will decrease the ullage, the amount of air space ly ng between the wine and the cork. By so doing, you slow down the wine's deterioration because you decrease the initial count of wine-destroying bacteria, as well as diminishing the volume of oxygen needed by these bacteria.

**Why is wrapping a bottle with wet layers of newspaper a good way to cool a picnic wine on a scorching day?**

Cooling occurs because, when water molecules change from liquid to gas, they absorb heat calories from their surroundings.

In the case of the picnic wine, the day's heat evaporates the water in the newspaper, and some of the heat calories from these wrappings are thus transferred to the air. The newspaper, now colder, assimilates some of the heat calories from the glass bottle, which in turn removes some of the heat from the wine. As a result, the wine cools. It works.

**Why does beer stay colder in a glass bottle than in an aluminum can?**

The heat from your living room or from your guest's clutching hand takes longer to reach the chilled beer through the glass than it does through the aluminum because not only is the glass considerably thicker, it is also a much poorer conductor of heat.

**Why do most knowledgeable beer drinkers prefer draft to bottled or canned beer?**

All beer is susceptible to spoilage caused by microorganisms. This problem is not often serious for draft beer dispensed from kegs because generally it is consumed long before the microorganisms can ruin the brew. Beer sold in bottles and cans, on the other hand, takes such a slow route from brewery to belly that unless it is pasteurized, it would likely be undrinkable upon opening. This pasteurization process — which is not used for genuine draft beer — partially cooks the beer and therefore negatively alters its flavor. Because a growing number of people recognize the difference in taste between pasteurized and unpasteurized beer, you might consider buying a suitable-size barrel of unpasteurized beer for your next party.

**How do I make crystal-clear ice cubes?**

The air dissolved in tap water is usually the cause of noncrystal-clear ice cubes. To rid the liquid of this excess baggage, boil the water for at least several minutes. Let the water cool, pour it gently into the trays and freeze it. As a bonus, your cubes will last slightly longer because they are denser. A less labor-intensive but more costly method is to use pure distilled water.

### Why should ice cubes be rinsed?

As ice cubes rest in their container in your freezer compartment, they pick up F.O. (our pet abbreviation for "freezer odor"), which can debase an iced drink. Fortunately, unless your cubes are over a week old, most of the damage is only surface-deep because few of the foul-smelling molecules have had enough time to penetrate the ice. A quick rinse of the cubes under cold running water just before you use them dispatches the malodorous molecules down your drain rather than your gullet.

Every refrigerator has F.O. If your best friends cannot believe that their spick-and-span refrigerators are afflicted, suggest to them that they compare two glasses of water, one chilled with rinsed cubes and the other with some that are unrinsed.

### Am I more likely to become dehydrated in the summer or winter?

Though your body loses more water during warm months, you are more likely to become dehydrated during the cold months because you are less conscious of the need to drink water. You lose water through sweating in the winter, but that loss is less apparent. The sweat doesn't linger on your skin as long because the moisture is absorbed quickly by the dry atmosphere in heated rooms and by your absorbent cold-weather clothing.

### Is thirst an accurate indicator of my body's need for water?

Thirst is an imprecise warning system. Your body usually needs water replenishment long before thirst begins and well after it ends. This means that if you are thirsty, you had better make it a priority to drink some water as soon as possible (dehydration can be harmful). You should also continue to drink water after your thirst disappears.

### Which is better for slaking thirst, plain water or soft drinks?

Water is considerably superior for quenching thirst because regular soft drinks contain sugar. Your small intestine requires extra water to digest sugar and has to "steal" it from other parts of your body. The result is counterproductive: In thirty or so minutes you end up thirstier than you were before.

### Should I drink iced or room-temperature water to quench my thirst?

Even a young child knows that iced water is more refreshing and cools the body better than does room-temperature water. Few of us are aware, however, that there is another reason to choose iced water when we are thirsty. Iced water quenches thirst faster because the cold water lowers the stomach's temperature, causing it to constrict. This action forces the water more quickly into the small intestine where it can be absorbed rapidly into the bloodstream.

### Do we need to drink more water at higher altitudes?

You may have to drink at least several more glasses a day in, for example, Denver than San Francisco. Water evaporates faster through your skin pores at higher altitudes because the atmospheric pressure is lower and the air is drier. We also exhale more moisture because the thinner air increases our breath rate. (The best way to appreciate that we exhale water is to think about the vapor we emit on a wintry day.)

### How is carbonated water produced?

Naturally carbonated water is created when acidic subterranean water chemically interacts with limestone to form carbon dioxide. This gas is dissolved into the water under high pressure in the underground environment. Artificially carbonated water is created by dissolving the carbon dioxide gas into the liquid under high pressure in aboveground tanks.

### Why do champagne and soda pop fizzle when opened?

Before the cap is opened, the pressure inside the bottle is sufficiently high to keep the carbon dioxide gas that is dissolved in the liquid within the liquid. When the cap is removed, the pressure drops to the room-temperature pressure level, which is insufficiently high. The carbon dioxide in the liquid begins to escape in the form of small, rising bubbles. Eventually, the exposed liquid will go flat.

### Why does a person get higher quicker on champagne than wine?

Carbonation speeds the absorption of the alcohol into your bloodstream.

### Does alcohol affect drinkers more on hot days?

The higher the environmental temperature, the more a given quantity of alcohol will affect you. However, alcohol is usually more dangerous in subfreezing weather. The alcohol dilates the blood vessels under the skin, giving drinkers a false sense of bodily warmth and increasing the amount of heat escaping from the body. They are thus more prone to frostbite and the deadly dangers of hypothermia.

### Does alcohol affect women more than men?

Yes, but the reason is usually the difference in weight, not sex. The average woman has less tissue to absorb alcohol than the average man. Incidentally, a woman is most susceptible to the effects of alcohol just prior to her menstrual period, when her metabolic rate slows down.

## Why does alcohol lower inhibitions?

Alcohol is a narcotic that "numbs" some of the brain cells that regulate a person's defenses and sense of propriety. For example, people tend to take more physical risks, to be more easily aroused sexually, and to be more outspoken with a couple of drinks under their belt. A large quantity of alcohol, however, can numb those cells so much that the person conks out.

## Does coffee sober up a drunk?

No. Like the cold shower, it simply turns a drunk into a wide-awake drunk. Once the alcohol enters the bloodstream, it must be metabolized. Sometimes this will takes hours, so give a drunk ample time to sober up before allowing him to drive home.

## Can I freely switch drinks without fear of getting a hangover?

Contrary to popular notion, people do not get a hangover simply because they switch from a dry martini to a scotch and soda to a glass of wine. What will cause tomorrow's throbbing headache is primarily one or more of the following ten factors:

- The quantity of alcohol imbibed. Of all ten causes, this is usually the chief culprit. Other considerations being equal, larger people have a greater drinking capacity.
- The type of alcohol consumed. Congeners are by-products formed during the distilling and aging process. These "impurities" give various liquors a distinct flavor, but they also help produce headaches. Drinks like scotch and brandy have many congeners, whereas vodka has relatively few. Among wines, Chianti has far more than average.
- The quality of alcohol drunk. Premium brands are better filtered and better processed, and thus have fewer congeners than the "Old Tennis Shoe" labels.
- The rate at which you pour it down the hatch. The body of an average drinker can comfortably absorb approximately one drink per hour.

- The ingredients of the drink. Lots of syrupy additions will make a stomach revolt, with or without the aid of alcohol.
- One's level of tolerance to alcohol in general, and to the type of drink in particular. Steady drinkers have an advantage in this category over the now-and-then imbiber.
- The quantity of food in your stomach. The folk saying "Never drink on an empty stomach" is definitely true because alcohol stimulates the stomach's secretion of gastric juices. When the stomach is empty, these juices have little else to do except irritate the stomach lining.
- The quality of food in your stomach. Many merrymakers gorge themselves with sickening hors d'oeuvres or overeat at the dinner table — and then blame the next day's results solely on the alcohol.
- Hygiene. Some busy party givers recycle the glassware with a quick rinse, which does little to wash away pathogenic bacteria.
- Self-fulfilling prophecy. If a person thinks a hangover will result, chances are it will.

# 13

# F·O·O·D   S·T·O·R·A·G·E

How is food preserved?

Food can be preserved by eliminating or reducing spoilage-causing microorganisms — such as bacteria, yeast, and molds — or by creating an environment unconducive to their growth. Food can also be preserved by destroying enzymes or by forestalling chemical processes (oxidation, for instance) that would otherwise alter its essential characteristics.

There are five major food preservation techniques: drying, salting, pickling, refrigerating, freezing, and canning. Some foods, like ham, are preserved by a combination of two or more of these methods. Though one need not necessarily use chemical additives to preserve a food by any of the five basic techniques, modern food processors generally use these agents liberally, in order to extend shelf life, among other reasons.

Drying (removing up to 99 percent of the food's water content) is an effective preservation method because no known form of earthly life (save W. C. Fields) can thrive without water. Enzymes, too, are thwarted without a sufficient $H_2O$ supply. Since desiccated foods can readily assimilate moisture from the air, it is advisable to store them tightly wrapped in a low-humidity environment. Placing the food in a cupboard near a stove is not the answer because water molecules from the steaming pots can be greedily absorbed by the "thirsty" food.

Freeze-drying is a special form of drying: The selected food is frozen before its water content is removed. The water is first changed to ice, and then directly into water vapor, a process called sublimation. The middle phase, liquidity, is skipped.

Salting (curing) draws much of the moisture from the food either by simple absorption or by osmosis. Salt also creates an adverse environment for microorganisms. One salting technique is dry-curing: The food is coated or buried in salt. A second popular technique is to immerse the food in brine, a salt-and-water solution. A variation of the second method is to inject brine into the food, for instance by pumping the saline solution through the blood vessels.

Pickling involves treating foods such as cucumbers with vinegar or other acidic liquids that are hostile to the well-being of microorganisms. A pickling solution usually also contains water, sugar, salt, and spices; certain chemicals can also crop up in the formula. Marination is, among other things, a pickling process.

Refrigerating a food will not kill most of the microorganisms present, but it retards their growth enough to preserve the food. Freezing, of course, is an even better deterrent. For optimal results, a freezer's temperature should be no higher than 0°F (−18°C), a level that is beyond the capability of the freezer compartments in the majority of home refrigerators. Enzymatic reactions continue at low temperatures, although at a very slow pace, and they do not cause problems except when freezing fruits and vegetables (see "Why must vegetables be blanched before freezing?" later in this chapter).

Canning requires two major steps. The first is heating the food hot enough and long enough to kill most of the microorganisms and all of the potentially more dangerous ones, such as the bacterium *Clostridium botulinum.* The second step is sealing the food in an airtight, sterile can or jar to protect the contents from any onslaught by a new supply of microorganisms or oxygen, and to keep the food from drying out.

There are many other preservation techniques in addition to the five described above. For example, sugar helps prolong the storage life of jams, and smoke does the same for hams. Radiation uses gamma and other electromagnetic waves to kill microorganisms.

## What is the temperature "danger zone" for bacterial growth in foods?

According to the U.S. Department of Agriculture, most bacteria thrive at temperatures between 60° and 125°F. The growth of microorganisms will be prolific unless other precautionary steps, such as marinating, have been taken to make the food unfavorable to bacterial growth.

It is important to note that we use the phrase "most bacteria." There exist certain cryophilic (cold-loving) bacteria and other microorganisms that can do nicely, thank you, at temperatures below 60°F. Likewise, our world has thermophilic (heat-loving) microorganisms that flourish at temperatures above 125°F. For these reasons, more cautious experts place the danger zone between 40° and 140°F — and some expand it even further.

## Does freezing diminish the quality of food?

The answer is an undeniable yes. When the frozen food thaws, some of its stored water seeps out of its cells, and consequently the cells lose their plumpness and the food its firmness. The water loss is caused by the creation of ice crystals and the loss of osmotic capability.

Osmosis, in simple terms, is the natural passing of liquid through a semipermeable membrane (in this case, the cell wall) to equalize the concentration of liquid on both sides of the membrane. Since the dissolved solids inside the cell make the water in the cell more concentrated than that on the outside, water will flow into the cell, swelling it in the process. The swelling increases the pressure of one cell against the other, and thereby the food's rigidity. Freezing, however, diminishes the osmotic capability of the cells, and thus their capacity to absorb and retain water.

Ice crystals, the second major cause of flabbiness, form inside and around the cells when the food is frozen. These crystals take up more space than the original water, and the expansion bursts many of the cell walls and pushes some of the cells apart, giving the seeping liquid an easy escape route.

A simple experiment will conclusively prove that freezing does give a mushy texture to foods with a relatively high water content. Buy two identical steaks, freeze one and refrigerate the other. After the steak is frozen (four to eight hours), thaw it in the warmest part of the refrigerator (this should take about ten to fifteen hours). Then bring both steaks to room temperature (about one hour) and grill or sauté them. The difference in texture will be quite obvious.

Another drawback to freezing most foods is that when liquid flows out of the ruptured cell walls, it carries with it some of the food's original flavor and nutrients. Still another negative feature is that most frozen foods, if stored long enough, will pick up foreign odors from the freezer.

Vegetables generally survive the freezing ordeal better than meat, seafood, and fruit. Peas, spinach, and lima beans are among the vegetables that suffer the least deterioration (though, to be sure, some damage occurs). Vegetables like cauliflower and broccoli are poor freezers because the process ruins their desirable texture.

### Why are certain freezing methods better than others?

The key to maintaining a food's quality is speedy freezing. The faster the food is frozen, the smaller will be the ice crystals that are formed in and around its cells. These tiny crystals do not cause as much tearing as the larger ones formed by slow freezing. The food's texture, therefore, will suffer less damage. Another related benefit is that the food — particularly meat —

will not lose as much of its juices during thawing because its cell walls remain relatively intact.

Most commercial food processors quick-freeze their products by methods such as immersion in a cold solution or exposure to frigid air blasts. The process is, of course, faster than any possible in a home freezer. Yet there are steps that can be followed to ensure that an individual home unit freezes food as quickly as possible. Avoid overloading your freezer, because crowding prevents cold air from circulating properly. When possible, add only a few room-temperature items at a time to a partially filled freezer because a large volume of unfrozen food will appreciably raise the freezer's temperature and capability, and some of the food already in the freezer is likely to partially thaw and then refreeze, forming larger ice crystals in the process.

**Are there some foods that are less suitable for freezing?**

As people who have sprinkled salt on icy sidewalks know, salt lowers the freezing point of water. So if a prepared food has been presalted (most have), the food will not freeze as well as it would if unsalted and will thus have a shorter minimum freezer storage life.

Fat does not freeze as well as protein and carbohydrate and consequently has a shorter freezer storage life than its two companion nutrients. The implication is clear: If you plan to freeze a cut of meat for a long period, you would probably be wise to trim off all or most of its excess fat before freezing it.

Since salt pork and bacon are both fatty and salty, their freezing properties are poor.

**Is a full freezer more energy-efficient than a half-empty one?**

It uses less energy because frozen foods retain cold far better than does air. As a bonus, your food will stay frozen longer in the event of a blackout. Don't, however, keep your refrigerator full. Air circulation is essential for helping preserve the scent and freshness of some nonfrozen items.

### Does a chest freezer have an energy-saving advantage over an upright freezer?

A chest freezer will not lose as much cold air each time you open it because cold air is heavier than warm air. The cold air in the four-walled chest has only one avenue of escape — upward. In contrast, cold air easily cascades out of an upright freezer each time you open its fourth wall, the door.

### Why does chicken have a shorter freezer and refrigerator life than beef?

It has a higher unsaturated-to-saturated fat ratio. Unsaturated (especially polyunsaturated) fats are more prone to oxidation, and therefore rancidity, because oxygen molecules can more easily bind with their molecules.

### What is the best way to store surplus pan juices?

Take advantage of a basic law of nature: Fat has a lower specific density than water, the principal ingredient of pan juices. After liquid fat and pan juices are mixed together, the fat — because of its lower specific density — gradually rises to form a distinct upper layer, while the pan juices settle. Therefore, to store pan juices, pour them into a container, cool to near room temperature, cover, and refrigerate. When the fat layer has solidified, you can easily remove it, leaving the pan juices behind. However, we do not recommend removing the fat layer until you are ready to use the stored pan juices because the fat serves as a functional seal that helps prevent bacteria and foreign odors from reaching the juices as they sit in your refrigerator.

**Why should I wrap meat tightly before storing it in the freezer?**

Freezing does not halt evaporation of the meat's fluids, it only retards it. Therefore, if the entire surface of the meat is not carefully covered with a moistureproof (or at least moisture-resistant) wrap, some of the food's water, which is temporarily in a solid state, will evaporate. This direct transformation from ice to water vapor is termed sublimation, and it results in what cooks call freezer burn.

The meat's covering should be sealed securely to prevent oxidation and to help ward off rancidity. Although the fat in any meat will eventually become rancid if stored long enough, the grace period is certainly long enough for normal requirements if the food is kept solidly frozen and is not exposed to excess oxygen. A tight wrapping is also a precaution against the meat's absorbing freezer odors.

**Why should food that is to be frozen not be wrapped in aluminum foil?**

Aluminum foil usually helps maintain a food's temperature — whether high or low — because it retards the transfer of heat from the food to its surroundings and vice versa. Thus, a food protected by foil will retain heat and not freeze as quickly as it would in, say, plastic film.

Although aluminum foil is not the best choice for freezing, you can profit in other ways from its properties. Some examples: A food, or section of a food, can be wrapped with foil for slow thawing. If serving must be delayed, you can keep a hot food warm, or a cold food cool, longer in aluminum foil. Because a shiny surface reflects radiant heat, you can preserve heat by facing the shiny surface of the foil inward toward the hot food. By the same token, when keeping a food cold — perhaps for a picnic lunch — face the shiny side outward so it can reflect radiant heat away from the food.

**Why should I not wrap salty or acidic foods in aluminum foil?**

Salt and acids react chemically with aluminum, forming a powdery white substance on the surface of the foil and food. Though harmless in small doses, this coating is undesirable in terms of flavor and cosmetic appeal. If you want to take advantage of the storage virtues of aluminum foil, first cover the exposed food with plastic wrap.

**Why does chocolate sometimes develop a white discoloration?**

The bloom (as this discoloration is called) is almost always caused by improper storage and is usually one of two substances. It could be cocoa fat that rose to the surface of a solid chocolate mixture that was stored too long at room temperature. Or, it could be sugar that was drawn to the surface by the condensation of a loosely wrapped, refrigerated chocolate mixture; the moisture extracts sugar from the mixture's interior. In either case, the bloom is unaesthetic but harmless.

**Why must vegetables be blanched before freezing?**

Obvious changes in color, texture, and taste take place in a vegetable that is left out on a table or in the refrigerator. The vegetable's own enzymes are largely responsible for that transformation. The extremely cold temperatures of freezing slow down the changes, but do not completely stop them. In fact, some enzymatic activity has been observed at $-100°F$, and the temperature in most home and commercial freezers is not below $0°F$.

Extreme heat, on the other hand, inactivates enzymes and sets color and flavor. For this reason, most vegetables should be blanched before they are frozen. The process involves partially cooking the food in boiling water or steam for up to several minutes. Some cooks choose to boil or steam their vegetables as they would before serving. However, blanching is preferable to full cooking because it does less damage to the vegetable's texture, color, and taste.

**Why is sugar syrup customarily added to frozen fruits?**

Fruits are also candidates for blanching as they, too, are susceptible to deterioration caused by enzymes. However, a more effective alternative to blanching fruit is to preserve color, flavor, texture, and nutrients by adding an antioxidant, such as ascorbic acid or sugar syrup, before freezing. This technique deactivates enzymes and blocks oxidation.

Sugar also serves at least two other important functions. When it comes to freezing, slightly unripe fruits are better than ripe ones — and sugar's sweetening power helps mask the acidic flavor in unripe fruits. Sugar also lowers the freezing point and, thus, helps prevent the formation of large ice crystals that could rupture the fruits' cell walls and membranes. Punctured cells are undesirable because flavorful juices would seep out, making the texture mushy when the mixture thawed.

**How can I tell if a wrapped piece of meat sitting in the butcher's display case has been frozen?**

A large pool of juices in the tray package is probably a result of the rupturing of cell walls, caused by freezing.

**Why are certain methods better than others for thawing meat?**

Two primary aims when thawing are to minimize damage caused by the ice crystals melting in the meat and to avoid bacterial contamination as the meat's temperature rises. However, the cook faces what seems to be a contradiction. On the one hand, rapid thawing causes more of the meat's juices to be lost and more deterioration in texture. On the other, rapid thawing — if done properly — reduces the threat of bacterial contamination.

The problem can be resolved by transferring the meat from the freezer to the refrigerator, where the temperature is high enough for the meat to thaw and cold enough to allow the process to progress at a slow pace while preventing bacteria in and on the meat from increasing dangerously. Thawing in the refrigerator can take as little as several hours for a thin steak or as much as several days for a colossal turkey.

Sometimes the cook does not have the time to defrost meat in the refrigerator and must leave it out at room temperature. This usually doesn't present a problem if the meat is a thin cut, because the time it takes to thaw is not long enough to pose a health risk. But the surface of a thick piece of meat will completely thaw long before the inside and therefore affords ample opportunity for bacterial growth. If meat must be defrosted quickly and is a little too thick to risk thawing at room temperature, place it in a tightly sealed waterproof bag and leave it in a tub or sink filled with cold water.

Wherever you choose to thaw meat, keep it securely wrapped as a precaution against moisture loss and contamination from the environment.

We don't recommend thawing meat (especially a thick cut) in a microwave oven. The meat's exterior will be mushy and overcooked long before the meat's interior begins to thaw. As we explained in Chapter 1, a microwave oven can heat molecules in the liquid, but not the solid, state.

### Is it safe to refreeze a food?

Yes, if the food is not dangerously contaminated at the time of refreezing and is handled properly afterward. The only detrimental effect will be the one normally associated with freezing, a loss in texture and flavor — and it may be amplified.

The "do not refreeze" warning gained its prominence when Clarence Birdseye, the father of the frozen-vegetable industry, included the phrase on his company's packages. Business logic stood behind his decision. Birdseye did not want to be held responsible for any mishandling once the product reached the consumer's hands. If the customer repeatedly removed a package from the freezer, only to return it there after deciding it wasn't needed, the resulting textural damage would certainly discourage future sales. The frozen-food company also wanted to prevent customers from encouraging bacterial growth by subjecting the product to room temperatures for an extended period of time.

Some food writers interpreted the "do not refreeze" as a not-to-be-questioned health precaution, and the misapprehension quickly spread. We do not mean to suggest that foods should be randomly thawed and refrozen. Caution should always be exercised, especially since the injuries a food suffers during freezing and thawing make it more vulnerable to deterioration. Generally, you can safely refreeze a food that still has ice crystals, or that has been no warmer than 40°F and has been out of the freezer for no more than twenty-four to forty-eight hours. Shellfish, dishes containing cream, and cooked goods are among the foods that are particularly susceptible to bacterial growth. In most cases, they should not be refrozen once they have thoroughly thawed.

**Should I think twice about buying a frost-coated package of frozen vegetables?**

Yes. This is too often a sign that the frozen food has thawed to some extent at least once before you saw it. The source of the frost is usually moisture that has escaped from the food inside the package. But even if the ice crystals are caused by moisture from another package, its existence portends deterioration, because if one package inside a shipping container has thawed, then chances are that some of the contiguous packages have also.

Sometimes thawing occurs in the store's display unit. Our research in several dozen supermarkets indicates that the surface temperatures of the topmost frozen-food packages in open display units are sometimes above 32°F. We've also observed a similar problem for refrigerated items like meat and milk that are stored in open display units. The temperatures of the topmost (or foremost) refrigerated packages are occasionally higher than they should be. This condition reduces storage life and, likely, now and then creates a health hazard. Moral: Select deep.

**Are certain foods natural storage enemies?**

Yes. Onions, for example, should never be stored with potatoes — they emit gases that negatively alter the flavor of the potatoes. However, some storage relationships are symbiotic, as is the case with oranges and bananas. Oranges give off ethylene gas, which accelerates the ripening of the bananas.

**Why should you not store fruits and vegetables in sealed air-tight bags?**

Fruits and vegetables are alive. Like animals, they breathe in oxygen, expel carbon dioxide. Eventually, in an airtight environment, they will use up all the available oxygen, and suffocate. Damaged cells spell loss in color, flavor, texture, and nutrients.

**Why should I not refrigerate jars of dried herbs?**

Condensation forms inside the cold jar each time you open the container in the room-temperature kitchen. This moisture shortens the dried herb's storage life.

**Why do I have to defrost my refrigerator less in the winter than in the summer?**

The frost build-up comes primarily from the moisture-laden air that flows into the refrigerator each time you open it. In winter, less moisture flows in because the room air is drier and you don't open the door as frequently for ice cubes and cool drinks.

Delaying the defrosting chore can be expensive in this day of high energy costs. The coating insulates the tubing, forcing the refrigerator to work longer to cool to the desired temperature.

**Can a person cool a room by leaving the refrigerator door open?**

We hear stories about people doing this when their air conditioner breaks down on a sweltering day. Their solution is counterproductive. The room gets warmer because a refrigerator is not a 100-percent-efficient machine — it produces more heat than coldness. Few people realize how much heat is expelled through the refrigerator's rear exhaust vent.

### Why does a vacuum storage bottle maintain the temperature of beverages better than a thermal bottle?

The heat of a stored hot beverage is mainly lost to the colder air around it through conduction, and a cold beverage will gradually gain heat from the environment in the same way. A thermal or a vacuum bottle retards the transfer of heat (in either direction) between food and its surroundings by placing a poor heat-conducting medium between the two.

The basic difference between the vacuum and thermal storage bottles is the chosen medium. With a vacuum bottle, the medium is a near-vacuum, which is hermetically sealed between the unit's inner and outer glass liners. In the case of the thermal bottle, the medium is a solid material that is a poor conductor of heat, but not as poor as a near-vacuum. Consequently, the vacuum bottle more efficiently impedes heat transference — and this capability is most pronounced when storing a hot beverage. (Just in case there is any confusion, allow us to point out that the Thermos brand employs a vacuum and not, as its name might suggest, the thermal method.)

A thermal storage bottle does have a convincing selling point: It is less breakable, a pragmatic consideration when the user is a lunch-toting child.

### Why is a pressure cooker a must for most home canning?

To kill the bacteria that can produce the deadly botulism toxin in low-acid canned foods, you have two options. You can cook the food at or near the boiling point for a ridiculously long time, a process that cooks the food to death before it kills the bacteria. Or you can use a pressure cooker, which better preserves the texture, color, flavor, aroma, and nutrients of the food because it can reach a temperature of about 250°F and thus appreciably shorten the required cooking time.

### Does an animal's state of mind during its final hours affect the storage life of meat?

Yes. If a mammal (or fish) is agitated, afraid, startled, or otherwise psychologically disturbed, its body automatically starts to convert the carbohydrate glycogen stored in its tissues into sugar for quick energy. This natural biological reaction gives the animal greater strength to fight or take flight, thus increasing its chances for survival. However, should the animal die, any conversion that occurred will shorten the meat's storage life. After death, the glycogen remaining in the muscles converts into lactic acid, a substance that retards bacterial growth. It follows that the lower the glycogen level, the less lactic acid is produced, and therefore that the meat will not stay fresh as long.

Every experienced deer hunter has heard the so-called chestnut that the venison will be more tender if the arrow or bullet is well targeted, slaying the animal instantly. This advice is not only humane but also sound, because if the deer struggles, runs, and enters a state of shock before dying, it will use up much of the glycogen in its muscles. When this happens, the venison meat cannot safely be hung for very long, and therefore it will not become as tender as it should be. But even if the meat is not aged, any lactic acid that is in the flesh will have a direct tenderizing effect on the meat, in the same way an acid-rich marinade chemically softens connective tissue (see relevant Q&A on pp. 49–50).

For the same reasons, modern slaughterhouses kill — be it with an electric probe or whatever — with such surprise and swiftness that an animal barely has time to contemplate its fate. Some slaughterhouses go one step further and try to maintain an environment that is as serene as possible for the animal. One creature's sense of tranquillity may not be another's, though. Classical music, which lulls some humans into blissful repose, seems to upset cattle's equanimity, if we are to believe an article printed in a Finnish newspaper. An ensemble of musicians had to stop rehearsing in a room in a slaughterhouse because the management believed that the music made the animals tense, and therefore diminished the quality of the meat.

# 14

## N·U·T·R·I·T·I·O·N
## A·N·D  H·E·A·L·T·H

**D**oes chicken soup help cure colds?

Yes, but this therapeutic magic is not chiefly due to its ingredients, as many people believe. The primary credit belongs to heat. The higher the temperature, the more fluid the mucus becomes and the more quickly it exits the respiratory tract. This is beneficial because mucus harbors cold-causing microbes. Chicken soup is not the only remedy. Another hot liquid such as a cup of tea would also serve the mucus-ridding purpose.

If you do use chicken soup, make it from scratch. Commercial soups and bouillon cubes tend to be very salty, to the point where the soup will partially dehydrate you. That would be counterproductive because when you have a cold, your body needs an extra supply of water to combat and flush out the microbes and unwanted by-products.

**Can diet, cigarettes, or medication affect a person's vitamin requirements?**

Yes. What you put in your body can sometimes sap the strength of certain vitamins or can undermine your body's ability to process or manufacture them. Whenever this happens, you will probably need to consume more than the U.S. recommended daily allowance of vitamins (although these allowances are more than ample for most people).

Chain smokers, for instance, need extra vitamin C, and boozehounds and sugar fiends require more of the B complex vitamins than their moderate companions. Additional B complex vitamins are also recommended for people using antibiotics for extended periods of time, and for women taking birth control pills (who also need extra vitamin C).

However, lack or loss of vitamins need not be offset by supplementary vitamin pills. Increasing one's intake of fruits and vegetables usually accomplishes the same mission more efficiently.

**Why are manufactured vitamins no different from natural vitamins, as far as the body is concerned?**

Most vitamins are actually surprisingly simple configurations of basic elements such as carbon, hydrogen, oxygen, and nitrogen, and they can be flawlessly duplicated in the laboratory. Your body cannot discern any difference between, for instance, ascorbic acid (synthetic vitamin C) and rose hips (natural vitamin C) because the two have an identical chemical makeup. The argument for natural vitamin supplements is faulty — although lucrative. If you shop around for vitamins or vitamin-fortified foods, you will notice that the natural vitamins usually cost considerably more than the synthetic.

However, any vitamin supplement, whether it be natural or synthetic, is no substitute for a balanced diet. Scientists may be able to successfully manufacture the vitamins that have so far been identified, but they have neither the knowledge nor technology to manufacture all the subtle components of a complete diet.

**What should cooks know about water-soluble vitamins?**

Unlike the four fat-soluble vitamins (A, D, E, and K), the eight B vitamins and vitamin C dissolve in water. Though your body can for weeks store in its fat cells the fat-soluble vitamins it needs, your reserve of water-soluble vitamins is relatively short-lived. The primary reason is that the B complex and C vitamins easily flee our bodies in our perspiration and urine. Consequently, you need to replenish your supply of water-soluble vitamins on a daily basis. Here lies the wisdom of drinking a daily dose of orange juice (high in vitamin C) at breakfast and eating ample portions of vegetables (high in various B vitamins and, sometimes, in vitamin C) for lunch and dinner.

Because of their water solubility, the B complex and C vitamins leave vegetables as easily as they do your body. One way to reduce their loss is to cook your vegetables in as little liquid as possible in order to minimize the quantity of vitamins that leach out into the cooking medium. Steaming your food in a scant amount of water, therefore, is preferable to boiling it. And when you do steam (or if you must boil), use the leftover cooking liquid. Another vitamin-saving technique is to cook foods as quickly as possible, which is why Chinese woks are so highly touted by nutrition-conscious cooks.

**Are fresh vegetables more nutritious than frozen ones?**

When referring to vegetables fresh from the farm, the answer is a resounding yes. However, a frozen-food product is likely to be more nutritious than nonfrozen vegetables that have meandered along a time-consuming route from earth to palate. Typically, a slow truck transports vegetables from the farm to a warehouse, where they wait until they are shipped to the supermarket, where they wait until a customer takes them home to the refrigerator, where they wait again until the home cook decides to use them. When this journey is long-drawn-out, as it usually is, the vegetables lose more vitamins than if they had been fast-frozen.

Under these circumstances, the product found in the super-market's frozen-food section is often more nutritious because if food processors are going to preserve their vegetables successfully, they must select only the freshest, those in the best condition, and must normally freeze them within hours after they have been harvested, if not sooner. In addition, their freezing process is extremely cold and quick. (A shortcoming of freezing, of course, is that it deteriorates texture.)

### Is spinach more nutritious raw?

Though most vegetables are more nutritious when eaten raw, there are exceptions, and carrots and spinach are two. Many of their vitamins and minerals pass unused through the body because the human digestive system — unlike that of ruminant creatures — cannot sufficiently disintegrate the comparatively tough cellular walls of these vegetables and therefore cannot extract all the nutrients.

### Are most of a potato's vitamins in the skin?

Vitamins in potatoes and most other vegetables are not concentrated in the skin (as some health food faddists believe), but in the pulp just under the skin. However, since it is impossible to peel a potato without scraping away some of the vitamin-rich pulp, it makes sense to cook and serve it with its skin. Besides, the skin does have some nutrients and adds flavor, texture, and color contrast.

### Should a nutrition-conscious cook use iron pots?

Although it is true that iron pots can bolster your diet with extra iron, this metal can annihilate some of the vitamin C in the food you cook. We are not against iron pots per se (some of our favorite pots are cast iron), we just do not believe that anyone should use them for the iron-intake rationale. If you need extra iron (many women do), plan on eating more iron-rich foods such as dark green leafy vegetables, legumes, egg yolks, and whole cereal grains. If you suffer from an acute iron deficiency, iron-supplement pills are available.

## What is the best container for milk?

There is no definitive answer. A glass milk bottle has two chief advantages over the now-popular rectangular wax-coated paper carton. It is reusable and does not impart a flavor and foreign matter to the milk. A glass bottle's chief drawback is that its transparent material allows light rays to reach the milk — and light zaps some of the milk's vitamins.

As children, we did not know this fact and therefore were unable to appreciate why conscientious dairies supplied their customers with a light-shielding metal case in which the milkman placed the bottles. Less concerned dairies instructed their milkmen simply to set the bottles on the doorstep. Unless the customer brought the bottles inside the house before the rooster's first crow, the early morning light attacked the milk. The longer the bottles remained on the doorstep, the greater the deterioration.

## What is an essential amino acid?

Amino acids are the building blocks of proteins that your body needs to construct and replenish tissue, red blood cells, and enzymes. Of some twenty required amino acids, your body can manufacture all but eight of them (some authorities say nine). These select eight are called essential amino acids.

Proteins in meat have all eight essential amino acids and thus are referred to as complete protein. Vegetables, with the notable exception of soybeans, do not possess all the essential amino acids, and therefore their proteins are termed incomplete.

Fortunately for vegetarians, one does not have to eat a complete protein food to obtain the amino acids the body cannot produce. Strict vegetarians can instead plan a meal consisting of foods that collectively contain the essential eight. Whole cereal grains and legumes are the most famous of such complementary foods whose proteins add up to form a complete source. There is one salient condition, however. The two must be eaten at the same meal. Thus, the traditional peasant dish of rice and beans or the American Indian mixture of lima beans and corn (succotash) are good sources of protein.

Lacto-ovo vegetarians need not be as concerned about consuming their required share of complete protein because dairy products and eggs contain all eight essential amino acids.

People who, for economic or personal reasons, eat a scant quantity of meat, eggs, and dairy products combined with large portions of whole cereal grains are nutritionally safe, too, because animal protein has a surplus of the essential amino acids that cereal grains lack. This pairing partially explains why millions of peasants in southern China can remain healthy on a diet consisting of a high proportion of rice (which, like other cereal grains, is particularly low in the amino acid lysine) while usually eating no more than a meager serving of seafood (high in lysine).

### Which is better, iodized or plain salt?

Iodine is essential in the diet because without it, your thyroid gland could not manufacture thyroxine — a hormone necessary for bodily functions such as growth, and the prevention of goiter. Because some Americans (particularly those in the so-called goiter belt in the North Central states) suffer from iodine deficiency, the U.S. government encourages table salt processors to fortify their product with potassium iodide to help assure that everyone receives enough of the mineral.

However, some medical authorities believe that if you eat a lot of seafood or food grown in iodine-rich soil (commonly associated with coastal areas), or drink water that has acquired the mineral from such soil, you may be overdosing on iodine if you also regularly use iodized salt. The iodine-fortified product makes more sense for people who live great distances from a seaboard.

## Why does a candy bar provide a quick energy boost?

Candy is rich in simple sugars that can be quickly digested and absorbed into your bloodstream, so you may feel an extra lift soon after eating a candy bar. In contrast, your body must take the time to convert more complex carbohydrates (such as are found in a potato or piece of bread) into glucose before they can be used for energy.

On the negative side, a typical candy bar consists of empty calories and does not provide your metabolism with valuable vitamins and minerals. Nor does it furnish long-lasting energy; in an hour or so after munching on the candy bar, you may be hungry again or feel a psychological and physical letdown because of the sudden drop in your blood sugar level.

## What do all the additives listed on a food package do?

The accompanying chart describes briefly the principal uses of some of the additives that are most frequently listed on packages in supermarkets. Bear in mind that our list is far from comprehensive. The food industry uses hundreds of additives, too many to itemize in this book. We had to be selective.

| ADDITIVE | PRINCIPAL USE AND COMMENTS |
|---|---|
| Acetic Acid (Ethyl Acetate) | Flavoring agent found naturally in many fruits. Synthetic version used in baked goods, beverages, chewing gum, gelatin, ice cream, liquor, and puddings. |
| Ascorbic Acid (Vitamin C) | Antioxidant that can also serve as a color stabilizer and nutrient. Helps preserve such foods as beer, bread dough, frozen fruit, jellies, and |

milk. Prevents loss of redness in cured meats and provides a source of vitamin C in drinks and breakfast foods.

**BHA (Butylated Hydroxyanisole)** Similar to BHT (see below) in function and use. BHA, however, is considered less of a health risk.

**BHT (Butylated Hydroxytoluene)** Antioxidant for retarding rancidity in fat and oils. Commonly used in foods such as breakfast cereals, cake mixes, potato chips, sausages, snacks, spices, and vegetable cooking oils. Some people experience allergic reactions.

**Calcium, Sodium Propionate** Preservatives used to fight growth of mold and bacteria. Calcium also acts as a diet supplement. Found in foods such as breads, cakes, pies, poultry stuffing, rolls, Swiss cheese.

**Carrageenan (Irish Moss)** Derived from seaweed, therefore a natural additive. Primarily used as a thickening agent in such foods as coffee creamers, cottage cheese, ice cream, jelly, and sour cream. Also used to stabilize oil-water mixtures and foam in beer.

**Casein, Sodium Caseinate** Nutritious proteins used to thicken and bleach. Often found in coffee creamers, frozen custard, ice cream, and ice milk.

*(Continued)*

| | |
|---|---|
| Citric Acid, Sodium Citrate | Used as antioxidants and flavoring agents. Produced both naturally (in citrus fruits and berries) and synthetically. Used as a fruit flavor in such products as candy, carbonated beverages, chewing gum, ice cream, and instant potatoes. |
| Disodium Phosphate | Chelating agent (traps trace amounts of metal ions that would lead to spoiling and color loss). Used in processing evaporated milk, pork products, sauces, and as an emulsifier in various cheeses. |
| Gums (Various Types Including Arabic, Ghatti, Guar, Karaya, Locust Bean, and Tragacanth) | Natural thickeners and stabilizers. Primarily used as firming agents in prepared food. They also stabilize beer foam, act as emulsifiers in salad dressings, and prevent the formation of crystals on ice cream and candy. |
| Hydrogenated Vegetable Oil | When hydrogen is added to liquid vegetable oil, a new solid compound is created. This process changes most of the polyunsaturated oil to saturated fat. Hydrogenated vegetable oil products include margarine and shortening. It is used nowadays in many processed foods. |

|                                       |                                                                                                                                                                                                                                                                                      |
| ------------------------------------: | ------------------------------------------------------------------------------------------------------------------------------------------------------------------------------------------------------------------------------------------------------------------------------------- |
| Hydrolized Vegetable Protein (HVP) | Used to enhance the flavor of food. Composed of vegetable protein, which has been broken down chemically into amino acids. The protein is then more easily digested. Commonly found in canned chili, frankfurters, gravy and sauce mixes, and instant soups. |
| Monosodium Glutamate (MSG) | See pages 179–80. |
| Sodium Benzoate | Preservative that fights the growth of bacteria and other microorganisms in acidic foods. Frequently used in carbonated drinks, jams, margarine, pickles, preserves, and salad dressings. Cranberries and prunes are natural examples of this additive. |
| Sodium Bisulfate, Sulfur Dioxide | Preservatives and antibrowning agents used in beverages, corn syrup, dehydrated potatoes, dried fruits, soups, and wine. Destroys vitamin $B_1$ (thiamine) in food. |
| Sodium Chloride | Chemical name for salt, the world's number-one additive. Used to flavor and preserve a wide range of processed foods. |
| Sodium Nitrate, Sodium Nitrite | Preservatives and coloring agents used to inhibit the growth of botulism-producing bacteria. Can produce carcinogenic nitrosamines |

*(Continued)*

| | when combined with natural stomach and food substances called amines. Found in most cured meats including bacon, bologna, frankfurters, ham, salami, and sausages. |
|---|---|
| Sorbic Acid, Potassium Sorbate | Naturally and synthetically produced. Prevents mold and, to some extent, bacteria growth in such foods as baked goods, cheese, dried fruits, mayonnaise, soft drinks, syrup, and wine. |
| Sugar | See next Q&A. |

**If the word "sugar" is absent from the ingredients list on a label, can the food still contain sugar?**

Keep an eye out for the suffix "-ose." Dextrose, fructose, lactose, maltose, and sucrose, for instance, are all forms of sugar. Sugars are used as sweetening and sometimes preserving agents. As explained in Chapter 9, there is little nutritional difference among the various types of sugar — all provide empty calories. While artificial sweeteners such as sorbitol and saccharine have few, if any, calories, they also have no nutrients.

**Why does sugar cause tooth decay?**

Sugar is food for plaque-residing bacteria colonies. They convert the sugar into acid that corrodes tooth enamel, causing tooth decay. The degree of decay is dependent more on how long the sugar remains in contact with the bacteria colonies than on the amount of sugar consumed. For this reason, a pure caramel candy usually does less damage than a sugary cookie made with starch. The latter substance helps bind the sugar to the tooth.

## Why do I need fiber in my diet?

Fiber, also known as roughage or bulk, refers to undigestible carbohydrates found in whole cereal grains, fruits, vegetables, seeds, legumes, and nuts. These undigestible substances facilitate digestion and elimination by carrying other waste products along with them as they leave the digestive tract and by absorbing fluids that make wastes soft enough for easy passage.

Many doctors lay partial blame for various malfunctions and diseases of the bowel, colon, and rectum on a deficiency of fiber in the diet. Without adequate fiber, the intestines and bowel work sluggishly, and the wastes that result from the digestive process remain in your system longer than they should. A lack of dietary fiber has even been linked to diseases ranging from circulatory disorders to arthritis, but the evidence is inconclusive. In recent times, oat bran has become a popular breakfast cereal ingredient because some evidence indicates that it lowers serum cholesterol levels.

Fiber-conscious Americans and inhabitants of other countries where highly refined foods glut the market usually must strive to consume enough fiber. Unfortunately, some weight-conscious people do not consume enough fiber because they mistakenly believe that carbohydrates per se are fattening. Dieters should also be aware that most fiber passes through the body without being absorbed, and, according to medical evidence, it can help keep weight down in two distinct ways. First, it is believed to help rid the digestive tract of some fats and carbohydrates that otherwise would eventually be absorbed into the body. Second, fiber's chewy texture and heaviness create a full feeling, making you less tempted to satisfy yourself with refined high-calorie foods.

Too much fiber is bad, too. It can cause intestinal gas and, it hinders your body's ability to absorb certain minerals. How much is too much fiber? Some experts recommend a maximum of about 35 grams per day for the average adult male.

## What is the theory behind eating a varied diet?

Science has identified over forty different essential nutrients — and no one food ingredient offers them all. Moreover, our body probably needs some nutrients that food scientists know nothing or little about. A diet rich in variety therefore stands a better chance of providing all the necessary nutrients. A varied diet also lessens the possibility of consuming an unhealthy amount of any single nutrient. Likewise, such a diet reduces the magnitude of exposure to unwholesome substances such as toxins and pathogenic microorganisms that any single food might harbor.

## Why are fast eaters more prone to stomachaches?

Food gobblers increase their chances of heartburn in two ways. First, they swallow a lot of air. Belching typically follows. The rising air sends acidic digestive juices flying up to the esophagus. Second, since wolfers don't have time to chew their food into easily digestible pieces, their stomachs are forced to release extra acidic digestive juices to break down the abnormally large pieces. This higher than usual quantity of acid can cause heartburn.

The type of food matters, too. Most chronic heartburn sufferers know that high-acid foods can trigger the condition. So can alcohol and coffee — and lying down after a meal. It's not common knowledge that fatty foods can also activate heartburn. Indirectly, they relax a valve in the esophagus which normally prevents the acidy gastric juices from backing up into the esophagus.

Some diners take antacid pills to relieve heartburn because their alkaline ingredient helps neutralize the acid. One should not use this remedy on a steady basis without seeking medical advice because antacid pills alter the body's acid-base balance.

An oft overlooked remedy is a glass of plain water. It dilutes the acid.

## What is the most dangerous room in a home?

The kitchen. More accidents occur there than in any other room, including the living room, dining room, bathroom, bedroom, playroom, closet, and garage. Think of the many accidents waiting to happen because of hot stoves, sharp knives, waxed floors, flimsy stepping stools, heavy packages stored above eye level, and toxic housecleaning chemicals kept under the sink, within easy reach of young children. And don't forget food poisoning (see next Q&A's).

## What is the single greatest cook-induced source of bacterial contamination in the kitchen?

Usually it's the humble can opener. Although many cooks wash their cutting board surface dutifully after each use, they forget to do the same to the can opener. Even if just one tiny food particle sticks to the blade, it can make an excellent medium for pathogenic microorganisms. This bacteria would have ample time to multiply by the time the cook uses the can opener the next day.

## Why should you not set a hot pot on a butcher block or other cutting surface?

The primary harm is usually not damage to the cutting board surface but an increase in bacterial contamination. The board absorbs heat from the pot and can retain it for up to thirty minutes. During this time, any pathogenic bacteria that are on the board will multiply faster than if the board were at room temperature.

## How does trichinosis attack the body?

You can contract this disease when you eat pork or pork products that contain live worms that are round in shape and microscopic in size and are called trichinae. (Although most people associate trichinosis with pig meat only, other animal flesh, including deer and bear, can also be contaminated.) After you eat infected meat, the parasites lodge and reproduce in your intestines. Their larvae enter the bloodstream and travel to your muscles, and while growing there, cause pain, fever, muscle deterioration, and sometimes death.

Trichinosis is not found around the entire globe. Southeast Asians eat raw pork, and Europeans consume raw hams — for example, the celebrated prosciutto of Parma — without dire health consequences. In the United States, the medical profession nowadays sees relatively few cases of trichinosis, due to increased public awareness and the widespread adoption of precautionary measures. For instance, garbage — favored by trichinae and pigs — is now cooked before it is fed to the animals. Most municipalities have instituted laws requiring that butchers within their jurisdiction use a separate meat grinder for pork, or that they sterilize the grinder before changing from pork to nonpork. In this way, the chance of contaminating other foods is minimal or nil. Government standards help assure the consumer that cured ham and precooked sausages produced by responsible meat processors are free of trichinae.

Whenever you eat any other American-produced pork, it is wise to assume that it contains live trichinae, even though the actual chances that this is so are incredibly small. Why play what amounts to Russian roulette in the kitchen? Remember that a government inspection seal is no protection against trichinosis because the examiners do not check for the microscopic worms. Take the same precautions that your butcher should: Never taste-test uncooked pork mixtures. Always wash thoroughly — with hot water and soap or detergent — your hands or any utensil that touches raw pork. If you grind the pork, sterilize the machine with boiling water afterward.

Cooking the meat to an internal temperature of at least

137°F, or freezing it at a temperature below −10°F for several weeks, will kill any trichinae present. (Freezing, however, alters the meat's cellular structure, making it mushy when cooked.)

Intelligent safeguarding is not the same as overreacting, which is what many cookbooks are doing when they recommend cooking pork to a temperature between 170° and 185°F. If you follow those directions, your meat is bound to be less palatable and nutritious, and furthermore, prolonged cooking causes excess shrinkage. On the other hand, you don't want to cook your pork to just 137°F, because the meat's flavor would not develop fully. For pork that is both rewarding and safe to eat, we recommend cooking it to an internal temperature of 160°F (a 23°F safety margin).

### Is an uncooked canned ham trichinosis-proof?

Federal law dictates that all ham must be cooked to an internal temperature of at least 140°F before being canned. Since a temperature of 137°F kills the deleterious parasites, a can of ham is not a threat, whether labeled uncooked or fully cooked (the latter must be cooked to a minimum interior temperature of 148°F).

### What causes botulism?

A person can be stricken with botulism after ingesting the toxin produced by the bacterium *Clostridium botulinum*. The bacterium can form the toxin only in the absence of oxygen, so canned goods and products like meat that are wrapped in airtight casings are potential sources of botulism.

The pernicious toxin is more likely to be generated in low-acid food, such as mushrooms, peas, corn, or beans, than in a high-acid food like tomatoes. However, some new tomato hybrids are not acidic enough to prevent the bacteria from creating the toxin, so home canners beware. Food destined for canning must be heated to a temperature high enough and for periods long enough to kill any toxin-producing bacteria present.

If toxins have developed in a food that has been stored under anaerobic conditions, they can be made innocuous by boiling the food for thirty minutes. Nevertheless, any suspect food product — such as one with a swollen can or jar lid — should be discarded untasted.

Botulism symptoms include malfunctioning of the nervous system. Vision, speech, and swallowing are impaired. Death results in cases where the respiratory muscles are paralyzed.

There is an antiserum, but there is also a catch to its use. It is most beneficial when given before the patient's symptoms are apparent, and most people do not have any idea that they have eaten contaminated food until they are physically affected. Once a person does exhibit symptoms, quick diagnosis and treatment is crucial to survival.

### What causes staphylococcal poisoning?

"Staph," as this common food-borne disease is nicknamed, is caused by a toxin produced by the bacterium *Staphylococcus aureus.* That microorganism creates the toxin most readily in the 40° to 120°F temperature zone, particularly in low-acid foods. Custard-filled foods are notorious sources of staph. Foods such as this should not be left out of the refrigerator for long.

For the record, mayonnaise has been given a bum rap: It's not the underlying reason why chicken and other mayonnaise-dressed salads become contaminated under the hot sun at picnics. In fact, the relatively high salt and vinegar/lemon content of commercially prepared mayonnaise slows down bacterial growth. The real culprits are low-acid ingredients such as the chicken. (Please note, however, that homemade mayonnaise usually *is* too low in acid and salinity to retard the bacterial growth.)

Not to be confused with staphylococcal food poisoning is the toxic reaction caused by the various *Salmonella* bacteria sometimes found in food. Unlike staph and botulism, the disease-producing agent is the bacterium itself and not the toxins generated.

**Does a special anti-impurity filter that one attaches to the kitchen sink's water tap or pipe do more harm than good?**

Unless you frequently replace the filter or thoroughly clean it, you risk unsafe bacterial build-up. In some filtering systems, the bacteria multiply so rapidly that within a couple of weeks the number of microorganisms that flow into your drinking glass may exceed the quantity that would have traveled unhindered through your tap.

Even if a filter is changed frequently, there remains the question of the effectiveness of the various brands. With most, the water gushes through the filter too quickly to kill as many microorganisms as the unwary buyer is led to expect. Perhaps an even more important issue is whether your water supply is as dangerously contaminated with pathogenic microorganisms, additives, impurities, and other demons as some alarmists — and filter hucksters — claim. Check the local facts before investing in a filter apparatus.

**Can I get lead poisoning from glazed pottery kitchenware?**

Each year, a number of people die or become seriously ill from lead poisoning caused by the lead that leaches out of improperly glazed pottery kitchenware.

By U.S. law, glazed pottery designed for culinary use must be fired at a high enough temperature to fuse the lead component of the glaze into the container permanently. Some glazed kitchenware pottery that is brought into this country illegally, or in the hands of returning tourists, falls well short of the federal standards. If used to store or cook foods (and especially highly acidic foods), the lead will likely migrate from the walls of the vessel to those of the diner's stomach. This lead build-up in the body can cause damage to internal organs as well as to the immune, cardiovascular, and other systems. Children can also suffer learning and behavioral disorders.

A California family was severely stricken by lead poisoning after having habitually stored their orange juice over a period of years in a glazed pitcher that was purchased as a souvenir in Tijuana, Mexico. The amount of lead that leached out each day was minuscule, but since lead poisoning is cumulative, the outcome nearly proved lethal.

The type of tin cans that are sealed with lead solder are another potential source of lead poisoning. It is a sound policy never to store an open can of a high-acid food, such as grapefruit juice, in the refrigerator. Instead, transfer the contents to a glass jar or similar unleaded, noncorrosive vessel.

### Is food wrapped in newspaper safe to eat?

There should be no danger to your health if the newspapers are at least one week old and come in contact with the food for less than an hour. The ink of a recently printed newspaper, however, is not completely dry and may transfer some of its harmful chemicals to the food. Particularly noxious are the chromatic inks splashed across Sunday's comic strips. Such pages should never be used — even if they are dated December 2, 1956.

### Is alcohol drinking unhealthy?

The answer depends mainly on how much you drink. Studies indicate that the average moderate drinker (who consumes the equivalent of two glasses of wine a day) lives longer than the average teetotaler. Of course, that teetotaler far outlives the average heavy drinker.

Heavy drinking can create a host of serious if not fatal problems. For example, it can cause heart disease and cirrhosis of the liver, impair immunological responses, disrupt metabolism of needed nutrients, add pounds with empty calories, reduce sexual performance, foster impotency, impede restful sleep, and cause accidents. The list goes on.

# 15

## D·I·E·T·S

We've included this chapter because cooks play a major role in determining the success of weight-reduction and other diets. Special diets are also discussed elsewhere, including in the cholesterol-related items in Chapter 10.

### What are food calories and how are they measured?

What do food scientists mean when they say an apple has 300 calories? They are specifying the potential energy (heat) that the apple can generate as it passes through the body. Each food calorie is equal to the amount of energy required to raise the temperature of 1 kilogram (1 liter or 2.2 pounds) of water by 1°C at 1 atmospheric pressure. This calculation is based on a kilogram rather than a gram, so a food calorie is one thousand times greater than the normal calorie, the one commonly used in physics and chemistry.

Scientists calculate the food-calorie value with devices such as the bomb calorimeter, a sealed compartment in which a specific weight of food is completely burned. Sensitive instruments measure the amount of energy generated by the burning food.

## How many calories do we need?

The average man burns roughly 1700 calories per day for basal metabolism, the average women roughly 1325 calories. These are the calories the body burns for basic life-support processes including breathing, digesting, thinking, circulating blood, replacing cells, and maintaining body temperature. These basal metabolic functions take place even if one is sitting perfectly still.

In addition, your body needs calories for physical activity. For instance, the typical per hour calorie expenditure rate beyond the basal metabolic rate is practically zero for watching TV, 300 for casual walking, 400 for leisurely cycling, 500 for unhurried swimming, and 600 for moderate-paced jogging. Children, in addition, need extra calories for growing. Calories you consume beyond the basal metabolic, physical activity, and growing requirements are converted to body fat.

## Why do humans and other animals have fat?

The body's fuel is glucose (sugar). It is stored as glycogen (for quick energy) and fat (for longer-term needs). Converting glycogen into the needed glucose is a relatively fast process. Converting fat into glucose, however, is considerably slower and more complex. Why, then, does the body need fat? Wouldn't it be simpler if the body used glycogen exclusively for its energy reserve? Glycogen has a shortcoming. It's a carbohydrate that, like protein, contains only 4 food calories (energy) per gram. Fat, in contrast, contains 9 calories per gram. To substitute glycogen for four pounds of fat, the body would need to carry around nine pounds of glycogen. That's an extra five-pound burden.

## Do fat people need more calories than thin people to maintain their weight?

A 300-pound fat person burns more calories than does a 150-pound thin person because he requires more energy to move his body weight around, pump blood, and perform other functions. Don't conclude, however, that this fat person needs twice as many calories. On a pound-for-pound basis, the average fat person burns fewer calories than the average thin person, for three reasons. First, he has a thick adipose fat layer, which insulates the body, reducing heat loss and therefore reducing the number of calories needed to regulate body temperature. Second, a fat person is typically less active than a thin person. Third, a fat person has a higher fat-to-muscle ratio. This means he needs fewer calories because fat cells require fewer calories than protein-rich muscle tissue to function and survive.

### Does a woman require fewer calories than a man of the same weight?

If 1500 calories per day is just what a male needs to maintain his weight, the same number of calories would likely cause a female of the identical weight to gain extra pounds. A female requires fewer calories on a pound-for-pound basis because her basal metabolic rate is slower than a male's. Hormonal differences between the sexes are partially responsible — so is the difference between their bodies' fat-to-lean-muscle ratios. This ratio is higher for females (as explained in the previous item, fat burns calories at a slower rate than does lean muscle tissue).

### Can a successful dieter return to his old weight-maintaining calorie intake?

The less you weigh, the lower your basal metabolic rate. If your "no gain, no loss" calorie intake level was 1400 calories before you lost weight, that intake level would now be too high to maintain your new weight.

### Why do so many people end their weight-reducing diets several days after they begin?

Typically, the weight watcher is elated during the first few days of his diet. His scale shows a dramatic weight loss. Then, the rate of loss dramatically decreases or vanishes. Discouragement sets in and motivation wanes. What few dieters realize is that much of the initial decrease is due to water loss, not fat loss, the real goal.

Dieters usually lose a lot of water through urination during the first few days, for several reasons. First, when the body discovers that it doesn't have enough carbohydrates to convert into glucose for energy, it goes to reserve sources, including the glycogen stored in the liver. Since water is stored with this glycogen, the body will lose water when the glycogen is used.

Second, the body will continue to lose water even after the available glycogen is depleted. At that point, the body begins to convert water-plentiful muscle tissue into the needed glucose. Several days into the diet, the body smartens up — it stops consuming its own muscles and switches to stored body fat for its energy source. Since far less water is stored with fat than with glycogen or muscle tissue, far less water will be lost as calories are burned.

Third, salt plays a major role in the noticeable weight loss during the first few days. Since a dieter usually reduces the quantity of food (especially junk food) he normally eats, his salt intake will probably also be reduced. This lowers the body's water-retention capacity.

So, the next time you begin a diet, don't pay too much attention to your scale during the first few days. The lion's share of any weight drop will be water. Measure the long-term progress of your diet against your third-day weight.

Once you've been on your diet for several days, don't necessarily be disheartened if one morning the scales report that you've gained two or three pounds overnight. The gain is mostly water (for it to be fat, you would have to consume an extra 3500 calories for each gained pound — that adds up to over 10,000 calories for a three-pound gain). Chances are that the food you ate yesterday was inordinately salty, which would increase the quantity of water your body retains. Go back to a normal salt intake and the extra pounds will be eliminated within a couple of days.

**A pound is a pound, so what's wrong with losing water?**

Don't be motivated or discouraged by water-related fluctuations. Though you could shed an extra pound or two of water with tactics such as drinking only a modicum of water each day, it would be unhealthy. Never dehydrate yourself, because your body needs a certain amount of water for vital functions such as flushing out toxins and other waste by-products. They remain in the body unless the kidney has sufficient water to flush them out. In fact, you will probably need to increase your water intake because dieters usually produce more waste by-products than nondieters — the extra by-products are formed when the body converts stored fat into energy. The extra water can also help alleviate constipation, which some dieters experience when they reduce their food intake.

The average person needs to consume about eight glasses of water a day. This person doesn't necessarily have to drink eight glasses because most of the foods we eat are mainly water.

**Is it better for a weight watcher to reduce the intake of protein or fat than to curtail carbohydrates?**

Usually, yes. A person needs to consume adequate carbohydrates because they are the most efficient source of fuel for the body. If, for instance, your body is denied the carbohydrates sufficient for quick energy and other functions, your metabolism will start breaking down protein for these purposes. The protein could be better used for functions like tissue construction and maintenance.

To correct a common misunderstanding, carbohydrates are not inordinately fattening. Their calorie count per unit of weight is equal to that of protein (about 4 calories per gram) and is half that of fat (about 9 calories per gram). What give potatoes, rice, pasta, and bread their girth-inflating reputation are the butter, sour cream, rich sauces, sugar, and other calorie-laden embellishments that frequently accompany these food staples.

Certain carbohydrates also provide needed fiber (see the Q&A on fiber in Chapter 14, pp. 263–64) and are belly fillers. And since the chief sources of excess calories are protein and fat, rather than carbohydrates, it stands to reason that one should focus calorie cutting on those two areas. One should, however, cut back consumption of highly refined carbohydrates like sugar because these foods provide empty calories.

**Why should weight watchers eat slowly?**

When we eat, our blood glucose levels rise temporarily. Our blood glucose receptors perceive this change and signal the brain that the body has consumed enough food. It takes about twenty minutes for this signal to reach the brain. Therefore, it's easy to pass the point of satiation without realizing it.

This problem is especially acute for fast eaters. Within the twenty-minute duration, they can consume a lot of food, many more calories than they really need, leaving them with an uncomfortable, bloated feeling. If they had chewed and eaten slowly, they wouldn't have ingested as much food by the time the brain transmitted the "full" signal.

**Should a weight watcher skip breakfast?**

Some dieters do, but they do not save as many calories as they may think. Skipping breakfast (or any meal) lowers your basal metabolic rate. Your body will then burn calories at a slower rate than if you had eaten breakfast.

Eating breakfast offers other benefits. With something in your stomach, you'll be less likely to be ravenous when lunch comes around and won't be as tempted to overeat. This added energy in the morning improves your concentration and problem-solving skills and increases your ability to get along with coworkers. And, if you're eating only so many calories a day, and you eat most of them at night, you would be better off transferring some of those calories to breakfast. This gives your body a greater opportunity to burn calories as fuel instead of storing them as fat.

**Will overfeeding a baby dramatically increase his chances of being an obese adult?**

An adult's fat cells won't increase in number if he overeats. He grows fatter because the size of his existing fat cells increases. However, according to one study, if an infant is overfed, the number of his fat cells does increase and will remain with him for life. When he reaches adulthood, he'll have a greater capacity to "balloon out" because there will be more fat cells that can expand.

**Should a baby be weaned on skim milk?**

This is undesirable for most babies because they need a relatively high concentration of calories in their diet to sustain their extraordinary growth rate. Whole milk provides a higher concentration because it has more fat (which has more than twice as many calories per gram as do protein and carbohydrates). Fat also contains essential nutrients for the baby that are lacking or deficient in proteins and carbohydrates.

Older children don't require such a high concentration of calories in their diet. But since they are still growing, they probably should be drinking whole rather than skim milk unless otherwise advised by a doctor or registered dietician.

**Should the elderly eat less than they did during their prime?**

Suppose a person weighed and exercised the same at sixty-five as he did at twenty-five. His body would require 10 percent fewer calories than he did in his youth, partially because his fat-to-muscle ratio decreased as he grew older. Body fat requires less energy than protein-rich muscle.

A senior citizen also needs fewer calories because his basal metabolic rate has decreased. He burns fewer calories.

The need for vitamins and other essential nutrients does not decline as much as an older person's caloric requirements. Consequently, the aged have little room in their diets for empty-calorie foods, such as sugar and alcohol, that they may have enjoyed in their earlier years. For health's sake, they must make every calorie count.

**Why is it difficult to begin a low-sodium diet if the dieting person is used to consuming a lot of salt?**

If a heavy salt user suddenly reduces his salt intake to the recommended 1 to 2 grams per day, his foods will probably taste unappetizingly bland. Consequently, he may be tempted to quit his diet at the onset.

His foods will taste insipid at the beginning of his low-sodium diet because his taste buds have become accustomed to high salt levels. A pinch of salt to a 5-gram-a-day person tastes considerably less salty that it would to a 1-gram-a-day person. If he doesn't quit his new diet, his food will once again taste flavorful after a few weeks because his taste buds will have become used to the lower salt level.

A resolve to stay on the diet isn't enough. The dieter must approach processed food products cautiously because many contain high levels of hidden sodium. The culprits include bouillon cubes, ketchup, fast-food burgers and fried chicken, meat sauce condiments, meat tenderizers, mustard, olives, pickles, potato chips, salad dressings, soups, soy sauce, and TV dinners. Even if the ingredient label specifies the exact quantity of salt per serving portion, the shopper must be on the lookout for other sodium sources such as sodium bicarbonate, monosodium glutamate, sodium nitrate, and sodium propionate.

**Why can people on low-sodium diets use sour salt?**

Sour salt is citric acid, not sodium chloride. This white, tart crystalline compound, which looks like salt, is used as a substitute by some salt watchers because it adds needed zest to saltless foods and its saltlike appearance makes it psychologically satisfying. Sour salt may make sense when a low-sodium dieter dines out because it can be conveniently toted to the restaurant. At home, the individual could just as easily opt for another acidic flavoring agent, such as lemon juice or vinegar, and usually with much more interesting gustatory results.

Many food packagers use potassium chloride as a salt substitute. Its molecular structure is similar to salt's (substitute a potassium atom for the sodium atom in sodium chloride and you have potassium chloride), but that doesn't mean the two molecules will have similar flavor profiles. They don't. It's best to use flavoring agents like herbs and spices as salt substitutes because potassium chloride doesn't have a gratifying taste and excessive dosages are dangerous to some people.

### Does an athlete's food need extra salt?

Few athletes need extra salt, either in their foods or from salt tablets. Their regular diet usually provides sufficient salt for their needs. Consuming extra salt could dehydrate and upset the stomach. Worse, it could thicken the blood, risking clotting.

### Is the "big, juicy steak" diet valid for athletes?

Some athletes still think so, but the consumption of an excessive amount of protein either in the form of meat or supplements doesn't help build muscles as well as complex carbohydrates do. Neither does protein provide fuel for the muscles — carbohydrates and fats do it.

To be sure, the athlete needs some protein. A meat-rich diet, however, isn't going to do anything dramatic except, perhaps, raise his serum-cholesterol level or damage his kidneys.

### What should an athlete eat before training or competing?

He should avoid fats because they take up to six hours to digest. Proteins are digested more quickly but should be limited because they increase the body's need for water. Carbohydrates are the best bet. They are digested the fastest and, as we explain in the next item, can be converted into quick-energy glycogen. The carbohydrates should be the complex, not the simple, variety. Sugar, for example, dehydrates and increases insulin production.

The meal should be light and consumed several hours before the activity. If the athlete eats a heavy meal or doesn't give the food time to digest, the digestive system saps some of the body energy needed by the muscles.

**What is the principle behind the marathoner's carboloading diet?**

The goal is to build up for the race as much glycogen as possible in the muscle tissue. Glycogen is the best fuel for a long-distance runner.

Glycogen build-up is achieved by consuming large quantities of carbohydrates such as pasta for several days prior to race time. The runner must not work out too strenuously during this period lest he burn up the glycogen he's storing for the race.

Some authorities argue that the body will build up even more glycogen if the athlete depletes his stored glycogen reserve before beginning the carboloading diet. To accomplish this, the athlete is supposed to train rigorously and avoid carbohydrates during the days immediately preceding the high-carbohydrate regimen.

**Does the menstrual cycle influence calorie intake?**

Dieting females should watch their portion and calorie count with extra attention during the ten days after ovulation. Studies show that females tend to consume about 500 calories more per day during that span than they do during the ten days preceding ovulation.

## Should a pregnant woman eat more than the normal three meals a day?

As the baby begins to fill the abdomen, the mother will have less room for her own digestive tract. Consequently, some females will no longer be able to eat as large a meal as they did during their prepregnancy days. Some experts recommend that pregnant women spread their food intake over more than the traditional three meals a day — as long as all their nutritional needs are met.

Whether the expectant mother is eating three or more meals a day, she needs to increase her daily calorie intake because, as the saying goes, she will be eating for two people. Her body requires more calories because it will be developing the maternal life-support tissues and fluids as well as the fetus. On the average, her weight will increase by about 20 percent.

## Should an ulcer sufferer also eat more frequently?

Ulcers are more likely to act up on an empty stomach, so trying to keep at least some food in the stomach makes sense. Bland foods work best. Spices, fats, coffee, and alcohol exacerbate the condition. So does stress.

Gastric ulcers occur and are aggravated when an excess quantity of acidic digestive juices builds up in the stomach. These juices eat away areas of the stomach lining, causing the ulcers.

## What foods cause allergic reactions?

There's hardly a food or additive that doesn't cause someone to begin sneezing or wheezing, to develop hives or rashes, to become dizzy or nauseated, or to behave abnormally. However, some food substances are more common culprits than others. These include chocolate, citrus fruits, corn, eggs, milk and other dairy products, peanuts and other legumes, shellfish, strawberries, and wheat.

A cook must be aware of a diner's allergies because some can be fatal. We know of one person who risks death if he eats peanuts. The potential tragedy for him is that a cook could thicken a sauce with ground peanuts and he might not know it until it was too late.

Food substances called allergens do the damage. They are harmless to most people, but when the allergy sufferer consumes them, they trigger an abnormal defense reaction in his body. His immune system produces an overabundance of antibodies, which induce his cells to release too many mediators. An excess amount of those allergen-fighting chemicals causes the symptoms.

### Do some foods lessen the effect of pharmaceutical drugs?

When given a prescription, it's a good idea to ask your physician or pharmacist whether certain foods could sap the drug's therapeutic value. Some do. For example, spinach is rich in vitamin K, which can undermine the benefits of anticoagulant drugs.

# 16

# P·O·T·P·O·U·R·R·I

## How does the body perceive taste?

Most of what people discern as taste is really smell. You know, for example, how food "tastes" bland when you have a cold. The chief reason it does is that mucus blocks many of the food odors from reaching the olfactory receptors in your nasal chamber.

Another way to demonstrate how taste buds receive more credit than they are due is to take our suggested test. Close your eyes, hold your nose, and let a friend give you unidentified samples of familiar foods such as raw apples and onions, as well as various flavoring agents and cooked meats. Chances are you will instantly recognize few, if any, of the foods that you thought you could "identify blindfolded."

Even onions are difficult to recognize with this test, though the interval between taking the first bite and the time you shout "eureka" will be relatively short. The highly volatile oils of the onion will reach your olfactory receptors through the back door — that is, they will traverse the internal passageway that connects your oral and nasal cavities.

Eaters also sometimes erroneously ascribe the sensory perceptions of sight, touch, and hearing to taste. As tests have proven, hamburger that has been dyed a bright green will not taste like hamburger to most people. And if you could take the crispness out of a raw apple, most people would say, "It just doesn't taste right," rather than correctly conclude, "It doesn't feel or sound right."

Our taste buds do, nevertheless, contribute much to our perception of foods. Surprisingly, we sense an infinite variety of flavors through the interaction of just four primary types of taste buds. While their intensity and location on the tongue vary from person to person, they are generally concentrated as shown in the illustration below.

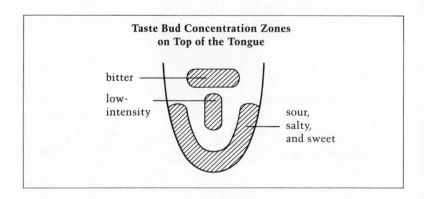

**Taste Bud Concentration Zones on Top of the Tongue**

bitter

low-intensity

sour, salty, and sweet

Some of your 9000 taste buds are also found on other parts of your mouth, including lips (usually very salt-sensitive), underside of the tongue, and inner cheeks. The most overrated area is the roof of your mouth, your palate.

You can map your own taste buds with our easy experiment. Place in front of you four clean glasses, each partially filled with one ounce of room-temperature water. Add, and thoroughly stir, one tablespoon of sugar into the first glass, one tablespoon of lemon juice into the second glass, one teaspoon of salt into the third glass, and two teaspoons of bitters, such as the Angostura variety, into the fourth glass. After tasting each sample, note the place(s) where the specific flavors are the most intense.

## Why does ice float?

Water has three phases: solid, liquid, and gas. In the solid phase, its oxygen and hydrogen molecule components bind in a looser fashion, creating niches in the intermolecular crystalline structure. Liquid-phase water lacks these niches, so it's denser. Therefore, the liquid-phase water sinks or, you could say with equal logic, the less dense air floats.

## What makes a soufflé rise? What makes it fall?

Beaten egg whites make the soufflé rise to the occasion of your dinner party. They are also responsible for its (the soufflé's, not your dinner party's) downfall.

Egg whites (albumen), when beaten, consist of countless minute air bubbles. When the air inside them is heated in the oven, it expands and enlarges the albumen bubbles, which in turn inflate the entire soufflé. When the air inside the bubbles cools, the soufflé deflates.

The soufflé also decreases in volume when a force such as a moving spatula punctures some of the air bubbles. Though many a cook has blamed the collapse of a soufflé on the spouse who slammed the kitchen door, the force of the shock waves from that deed is too weak to pop more than a few air bubbles, if any at all. The culpable party, if truth be told, is the cook who made one or more culinary errors in the science of soufflé making (for a successful soufflé, see recipe that follows).

PRINCIPLE-ILLUSTRATING RECIPE

### Macadamia Cheese Soufflé

(4 servings)

The basic soufflé is no more than a thickened, flavored sauce (or purée of meat, seafood, vegetable, or

*(Continued)*

fruit) that has been lightened with beaten egg whites and then baked. Once you learn the reasons why you follow certain procedures and avoid certain others, soufflé making is child's play — you'll end up with a glorious soufflé each and every time.

3 yolks of large eggs
4 whites of large eggs
3 tablespoons unsalted butter
⅝ cup finely chopped or grated Gruyère cheese
3 tablespoons white wheat flour
1 cup whole milk
4 tablespoons finely chopped macadamia nuts
¼ teaspoon salt
⅛ teaspoon black pepper
pinch of cayenne pepper
pinch of cinnamon
pinch of nutmeg
Optional: ⅛ teaspoon cream of tartar

STEPS
*Tips and Insights in italic*

1. Bring eggs and milk to room temperature.

*Your soufflé will rise to great heights only if you whip the egg whites to their maximum volume — and to accomplish that goal, you must use room-temperature, rather than cold, eggs.*

2. Grease the inside of a 6-cup soufflé dish with 1 teaspoon of the butter and then coat it with 1 teaspoon of the cheese (shake out and discard any cheese particles that do not stick). Cover and chill the prepared dish in the refrigerator for 20 to 30 minutes. Preheat the oven to 400°F.

*Thoroughly grease the inside of the dish, and espe-
cially the side walls, because without the butter lu-
bricant, the soufflé mixture will stick to the dish
and not rise freely. Chilling the dish keeps the butter from melting prematurely and sliding to the bottom during baking.*

3. Separate the eggs (all four whites in one bowl;
three egg yolks in the other).

*Reserve the surplus egg yolk for other purposes. If
used in this recipe, the extra protein supplied by the
yolk would cause the baking soufflé to set and
brown prematurely. (Important: For this step and
Step 5, review the first five questions in Chapter 6
for tips on beating egg whites.)*

4. Prepare a *roux* with remaining butter and flour,
then incorporate milk. (Important: See Steps 1 to 4
of the Mornay Sauce recipe in Chapter 8.) Stir in
beaten egg yolks. Add remaining cheese and stir until melted. Add nuts. Season with salt and spices.
Turn off burner, stir well, and let the sauce cool to,
or near, lukewarm (115°F). This will take about 15
minutes.

*To prevent yolks from curdling when you add
them to the hot sauce, first warm them by mixing
into them one or two tablespoons of the hot sauce.
And once the eggs are in the sauce, keep the sauce
comfortably below the simmering point. The finer
the cheese is grated or chopped, the more quickly it
will melt.*

(Continued)

5. Add cream of tartar to egg whites and beat.

*Under- or overbeating reduces volume and sabotages delicate texture. (Review the Q&A's on beating egg whites in Chapter 6, starting on p. 118.)*

6. Fold egg whites into lukewarm sauce. But first, lighten the sauce base by mixing into it about one-third of the beaten egg whites. Then, gently spoon the remaining beaten whites on top of the mixture. Using a rubber spatula, cut directly downward through the middle of the mixture. Scrape the spatula across the bottom and up the side of the bowl and then give it a polite flip. Slightly rotate the bowl and repeat. Keep repeating until nearly all the beaten whites have been incorporated into the mixture.

*If the sauce is too warm or too cold when you fold in the egg whites, your soufflé will not inflate to its maximum volume. Do not fold for more than a minute. Your soufflé will suffer less from having some lingering specks of egg white than it will from not having sufficient volume because it was excessively folded.*

7. With a delicate touch, spoon-pour the mixture into the chilled soufflé dish. If you have beaten the egg whites properly and incorporated them carefully into the sauce, the mixture should almost reach the rim of the dish.

*You need not tie a paper collar around the soufflé dish, as some recipes specify, because if you have followed our guidelines, your soufflé will not topple.*

8. Place the soufflé dish on a rack set just below the middle of the oven. Immediately turn down the oven thermostat to 375°F. Without once opening the oven door, bake for 22 minutes (for a moist

center) to 27 minutes (for a firmer but still moist center). Your soufflé will have risen two to three inches and will have acquired an attractive golden brown crust.

*Some food writers say you need not immediately place the uncooked preparation in the oven — not so, if you want a full-volume soufflé. The best soufflé has a moist center. Some recipes suggest overcooking the soufflé beyond the moist-center stage to give it added structural strength. If a soufflé is correctly prepared, that is unnecessary.*

9. Serve immediately.

*A soufflé is not only ethereal — it is ephemeral. Five minutes out of the oven is long enough to cool the air inside the soufflé appreciably and therefore enough to shrink your culinary triumph noticeably.*

**Variations on a Theme**

1. Reserve a teaspoon of both the nuts and the cheese to sprinkle on top of the soufflé mixture before it goes into the oven. Experiment with other cheeses, such as Emmentaler and Appenzeller. If freshly grated and used in a blend of milder cheese, Parmesan cheese can give your soufflé pleasant zest.
2. Cheese is just one of numerous possible main ingredients. Should you incorporate meat, seafood, fruits, or vegetables and want to take precautions against having the food pieces settle during the baking period, consider chopping them fine or puréeing them. If your pieces are slightly larger — which would be true of crab meat chunks — construct your soufflé in three layers. First, place half of your soufflé mixture in the dish, then add the star ingredient

*(Continued)*

(being careful that the pieces do not touch the sides of the dish), and then cover with the remaining half of the soufflé mixture.

If your main ingredient needs to be cooked, partially cook it before you add it to the soufflé mixture. Otherwise, it will not be cooked enough by the time your soufflé comes out of the oven.

3. Spices can also be varied, within reason, to suit your whims. Never make the same soufflé twice — do at least one thing differently each time.

4. You can give your soufflé a decorative dome. Using the end of a wooden spoon or a finger, make a half-inch-deep groove in your mixture, following the circumference of the dish, just before you place the soufflé in the oven.

### Why is semolina flour preferred by quality pasta makers?

Semolina flour, which is made from part of the durum wheat berry, has a very high level of protein and cellulose, substances that help keep the cooked pasta relatively firm. Pasta made with other flours tends to become mushy when cooked. Semolina flour also tastes better and is more nutritious than its leading rivals.

### Why should I simmer rather than boil egg-flour dumplings?

The combination of the 212°F boiling temperature and the resulting water turbulence will overcoagulate the egg protein and toughen your dumplings.

**What do ecologists have against fluorocarbon-propelled aerosol whipped creams?**

Once released from the metal canister, the lighter-than-air fluorocarbon chemical propellants drift upward into the stratosphere, where the sun's strong rays break down the fluorocarbon compounds into various substances, including chlorine. Soon, the chlorine attacks the stratospheric layer of ozone, an unstable form of oxygen that absorbs much of the sun's ultraviolet rays, which can cause skin cancer and other ailments.

But hold on; there is another potential danger to mortals on terra firma. A significant increase in the number of ultraviolet rays that penetrate the ozone layer would increase the temperature of the earth, which would cause the polar ice caps to melt, which would raise the sea level by forty feet, which would inundate every coastal city and village around the world, which would . . .

**Should cookbooks be stored in the kitchen?**

It's a practical site, but if you're talking about a rare or irreplaceable cookbook, the kitchen is too hostile an environment. First, you run the risk of the book being attacked by mildew-causing fungi, which flourish in humid kitchens. Second, if your kitchen is lit with fluorescent lighting, the tubes may leak enough ultraviolet rays to cause a damaging chemical reaction on the book's pages, cover, and binding.

**What is the best way to treat a burn?**

Ninety-nine percent of burns that occur in the kitchen are first-degree burns and usually require only home treatment. A first-degree burn is slightly red or discolored and causes only mild swelling and pain. If the burn is more severe than this, or if it covers an extensive area of the body, call a doctor or emergency medical center.

The best way for you to treat a first-degree burn is to cool the burned area quickly by lightly pressing an ice cube against it. This step minimizes the extent of cellular damage.

Next, place several ice cubes in a clean plastic storage bag and gently apply it to the burned skin. As soon as the ice feels unbearably cold to you, remove the bag. As soon as the pain returns, place the ice-cube bag over the burned area. Keep repeating until the pain subsides.

If the burn covers a wide or hard-to-reach area, soak the part affected in a suitable-size vessel or sink of water with plenty of ice cubes.

The ice-cube treatment is superior to the old-fashioned rub-with-butter method because ice cubes numb the pain. Moreover, butter can foster infection.

### Which will keep food warm longer, a glass or metal serving dish?

Assuming that both containers are identical in size, shape, and thickness, the glass one will keep food warm longer. Glass is a considerably poorer conductor of heat than is metal and, therefore, the rate of heat loss through the sides of the container will be slower. The same principle is true for glass's close relative, ceramic.

Many other variables also affect heat retention, including the food's fat and moisture contents. Fatty foods stay warm longer than lean ones. Ditto for solid foods versus liquidy ones like stews. Of course, the most influential variable of all is whether the food is covered.

### Why is it more important to preheat a dinner plate than a serving dish?

The mass of the room-temperature (70°F) dinner plate is usually much greater than that of the hot (say about 160°F) food. Consequently, an unheated plate will perceptibly cool the food before all of it has had a fair chance to be eaten and enjoyed. The cooling effect is almost as acute for a serving platter.

A deep-sided serving dish for a stew, soup, or vegetable poses less of a problem. The quantity of the heated food will usually warm the serving dish before the dish can appreciably cool the hot food.

### Why is the dancing-drop-of-water test used to measure heat for cooking hot cakes?

When the cooking surface of a pan is heated to about 325°F (the minimum temperature for properly cooking hot cakes) and cold tap water (not too much water, lest it cool the pan) is dribbled on top of it, enough steam will be generated under the water globules to launch them rocket-style into the air. After reaching a height of about one-sixteenth of an inch, the globules are pulled back to the pan's surface by the force of gravity, only to have the process repeated until all the water has been vaporized. This interplay between steam power and gravity gives the water molecules their up-and-down dancing motion.

If the pan's temperature is under 325°F (but over 212°F), the water will steam, though not with enough force to thrust the water globules above the pan's surface. If the pan's surface is above 425°F (too hot for pancakes), the steam will exert so much force that the water globules will be propelled helter-skelter on and beyond the pan, vaporizing before you can say the name of your local waterworks.

Since 400°F, and not 325°F, is the ideal temperature for cooking hot cakes, the dancing-drop-of-water test is not altogether an accurate criterion. Wait a couple of minutes after the water starts its dance performance before you pour the batter.

### How does soap help clean a dirty dish?

Soap (and detergent) reduces the relatively high surface tension of water and so enables the water molecules to penetrate better the pores of the food residue clinging to the dish. Unless that happens, some of the food particles — although surrounded by a sinkful of water — can remain dry, hard, and difficult to remove.

Soap helps clean dirty dishes in another way. Oil and water molecules naturally repel each other, and thus the water alone cannot effectively penetrate oil, or oil-coated food, on the dish. However, with the aid of an emulsifying agent, the water and oil will mix and travel down the drain together. Soap and detergent are such emulsifying agents.

A soap molecule is an emulsifier because of its split personality. One of its two ends is hydrophilic; it is drawn to water and shuns oil. The other end behaves in the opposite manner. It is hydrophobic — repulsed by water and attracted to oil. The soap molecule's hydrophilic end binds itself to the water, while the hydrophobic end attaches itself to the oil. A little elbow grease on your part, and the oil molecule glides off the plate. The oil-soap-water emulsion is not, however, permanent — as you can tell from the oil layer that sometimes lightly coats your hands.

In addition to its molecular properties, soap makes the water more viscous by its sheer physical presence. This increase allows the fluid to carry more and larger particles, so that freed soil floating in even relatively dirty water usually is not forced to take up residence on a soaking plate once again.

**Why is hot water a better dish-cleaning medium than cold water?**

Hot water not only makes oil and other food substances more fluid and therefore easier to dislodge, it also has a lower surface tension than cold water. Because of this, the hot water better penetrates the food, and, just as important, the soap or detergent can more readily form an oil and water emulsion. When rinsing a dish smeared with a raw flour paste, however, do not make the water too hot, lest the flour become instant glue.

**Why is flour so difficult to remove from pots and utensils?**

Flour is a starch and therefore can be quite sticky when exposed to water. Adhesive makers know this principle well, and starch is the basic material for many of their products.

Always rinse or soak a flour-coated pan or implement immediately after you use it. Use lukewarm water rather than hot, because temperatures higher than 140°F tend to cook, and therefore increase, the adhesiveness of a flour paste.


**How do I rid the inside of my teakettle of its deposit build-up?**

If you have been boiling only water inside your kettle, the hard deposit layer is mainly alkali compounds and minerals. Acid will dissolve such deposits. Fill the teakettle with a mixture of one part vinegar to six parts water, and let stand overnight. Next day, thoroughly wash out the kettle. If necessary, you can repeat the process.

In contrast, stains caused by acids like tea or coffee are best removed with an alkali such as baking soda.


**How can I remove a glued label from a new metal pot thoroughly and easily?**

Apply a little rubbing alcohol, paint thinner, or lighter fluid rather than water because they help loosen chemically the bonds between the metal and the glue. Or, if the label is on the outside of the pot, fill the utensil with boiling water and let stand. In most cases, the heat will loosen the glue's hold on the metal.

Whatever method you choose, be patient. Don't try to peel the label off the pot prematurely lest hard-to-remove remnants of the glue remain bonded to the metal instead of the label. Let nature separate the label and glue from the metal, in the slow, old-fashioned way. Overnight, if necessary.

## How do I separate stuck-together glasses?

The two glasses should part if you contract the inner glass and you expand the outer glass by subjecting them to cold and hot temperatures, respectively. Pour cold water into the inner glass, or use ice. Immediately immerse the outside of the outer glass in hot, but not boiling, water and carefully pull the two apart.


## Is the rule "Stir a mixture clockwise" nonsensical?

Some mixtures can be blended more quickly and easily and more uniformly if the cook stirs in only one direction. However, save for the negligible influences of human physiology and geodynamics, it doesn't make a hoot of difference whether you stir clockwise or counterclockwise (unless you believe in that old superstition that stirring counterclockwise brings bad luck).

Human physiology? Because of the anatomical design of the arm and hand (as well as force of habit), the vast majority of right-handers can more adroitly stir in a clockwise direction. The opposite is true for left-handers. Because right-handed chefs and recipe writers outnumber their southpaw colleagues by about nine to one, and because of the old superstition mentioned above, one can understand why the "stir clockwise" commandment became engraved in many cookbooks.

Believe it or not, geodynamics called the Coriolis force affects the ease of stirring, but again, to a minuscule degree. The rotation of the earth as it pirouettes through space creates an interesting phenomenon: Vortexes such as kitchen sink whirlpools and tropical storms generally spin counterclockwise north of the equator and clockwise on the lower half of the planet (unless the body of liquid or gas has strong countercurrents that could give the incipient vortex sufficient momentum to start swirling the wrong way). Ergo, a counterclockwise circular force — albeit minute — will be exerted on the fluid food in a bowl in a Northern Hemisphere city like Cleveland or Copenhagen. This bonus power will imperceptibly increase the velocity of the whirling mass if the Northern Hemispherean is stirring counterclockwise. Conversely, one who follows the "stir clockwise" superstition has to expend more energy — perhaps the equivalent of one calorie per century.

### How can I keep mosquitos from biting me while I'm barbecuing?

Sometimes the use of mosquito repellents and insecticides is insufficient. You need to take additional measures. Since mosquitos abhor smoke, you could always stand downwind from the barbecue unit, but your lungs and clothes wouldn't fare well.

Here are some practical tips. Be sure you've bathed recently. This helps remove the build-up on your skin of lactic acid, which lures mosquitos. Don't, however, put on perfume or don dark clothing — both attract mosquitos. Go low on alcohol because it dilates blood vessels and, therefore, increases the flow of blood near your skin. Banana daiquiris are definitely taboo because bananas contain a high level of serotonin, which attracts mosquitos.

### Is the saying "You're hungry an hour after eating Chinese food" true?

Yes and no is our answer. Many a typical American diner (let's call him Mr. Smith) receives hunger signals sooner than usual from his stomach because he has not eaten a genuine Chinese meal. A Chinese from Canton, for example, would eat a lot of rice complemented by smaller portions of vegetables (and even smaller portions of fish or meat, if any). Mr. Smith eats a lot of vegetables, while relegating the rice to a background role.

Adding even more to Mr. Smith's problem are the economics of some restaurant owners, who cut costs by serving a high proportion of watery vegetables (ingredients such as snow peas are expensive and therefore used sparingly, if at all). Since water quickly passes through the stomach, Mr. Smith may indeed have that ol' empty feeling within an hour or two.

Hunger pangs come about, too, because the average Chinese meal tends to be less rich in fats than the meals that Mr. Smith's stomach has come to accept as the norm. Since the digestive tract takes two or three hours longer to digest fat than it does carbohydrates and proteins, his stomach will start to rumble much sooner than if he had had his traditional high-fat American dinner.

Another factor is psychosomatic. In exactly sixty minutes, Mr. Smith's stomach may respond to his "hungry-in-one-hour" belief. Mind over matter.

### Are some foods sleep inducers?

Nearly everyone is familiar with the family holiday dinner syndrome. After eating your way through generous helpings of every dish gracing the table, you adjourn to the living room and sink into a comfortable chair, possibly to watch the televised football game. Long before the official gun marks the end of the first half you are in dreamland.

Your drowsiness is caused by more than the sheer bulk of food you consumed or by the dullness of the game or its commentator. Certain of the foods you are likely to eat on such occasions are rich in tryptophan, an amino acid that helps your body produce serotonin, a biochemical that has a soporific effect on man and other animals. Foods known to have high levels of tryptophan include turkey, beef, pork, and lamb — all traditional specialties for festive affairs.

Because carbohydrates also help produce serotonin, the gargantuan portions of starchy potatoes, yams, and bread you ate allowed the sandman to perform his miracle in a wink.

The type of food affects how long you will be sleepy. Your body digests fats more slowly than it does carbohydrates and proteins, so the higher your meal's fat content, the longer your doze.

Alcohol compounds the dozing problem. It anesthetizes brain cells that normally would keep you alert.

Naturally, if your food and alcohol intake is too much or too rich, your peaceful slumber may be short-lived when a nightmare or upset stomach gives you a rude awakening.

**Are some foods aphrodisiacs?**

Hardly any food — including garlic — has not been considered an aphrodisiac at some time or in one place or another. Among the foods that are currently in vogue in America as having the innate capacity to titillate the sexual appetite are: aromatic herbs and spices, artichokes, asparagus, avocados, caviar, chocolate, chili peppers, dates, eels, eggs, figs, ginger, honey, leeks, lobsters, mangos, mushrooms, nutmeg, oysters, papayas, passion fruit, quails, sesame seeds, saffron, and truffles.

Whether a particular food is aphrodisiac, however, is the subject of heated debate. Nearly all modern medical scientists scoff at the idea that any substance — except for a few that are proven, such as the potentially fatal Spanish fly (made from ground dried beetles) and the equally dangerous powdered bark of the yohimbine tree — can by itself sexually arouse the human body. Whatever effect a reputed aphrodisiac food may have, its potency is in direct proportion to the partaker's faith in its power. And even if you do not believe in a food's inherent erotic magic, a supposed aphrodisiac can usually bring the evening to a euphoric climax if accompanied by candlelight, soft music, and the object of your desire.

Alcohol acts as an aphrodisiac because it reduces inhibitions. Ogden Nash said it best: "Candy is dandy, but liquor is quicker." An excess of that love potion, on the other hand, can be a sexual depressant because, as William Shakespeare observed, alcohol "provokes the desire, but it takes away the performance."

# Further Reading

Of the many books we researched to write *Kitchen Science*, the following proved especially useful. We recommend them to anyone who wants to delve deeper into this exciting subject.

*Additives in Your Food,* by George Sullivan (New York: Cornerstone Library, 1976).

*Bakery Technology and Engineering,* 2d ed., by S. A. Matz (Westport, Conn.: Avi Publishing Company, 1972).

*Baking Science and Technology,* vol. 1, by E. J. Pyler (Chicago: Siebel Publishing Company, 1973).

*Basic Food Chemistry,* by F. A. Lee (Westport, Conn.: Avi Publishing Company, 1975).

*Biochemistry of Foods,* by N. A. M. Eskin et al. (New York: Academic Press, 1971).

*By-products from Milk,* 2d ed., by B. H. Webb and E. O. Whittier (Westport, Conn.: Avi Publishing Company, 1971).

*Cereal Crops,* by J. H. Martin and W. H. Leonard (New York: Macmillan Company, 1967).

*Cereal Technology,* by S. A. Matz (Westport, Conn.: Avi Publishing Company, 1970).

*Cheese,* by J. G. Davis (New York: Elsevier Publishing Company, 1965).

*Cheese and Fermented Milk Foods,* 2d ed., by F. V. Kosikowski (Ann Arbor, Mich.: Edwards Brothers, 1977).

*The Chemical Analysis of Foods,* by D. Pearson (New York: Chemical Publishing Company, 1971).

*Cold and Freezer Storage Manual,* by W. R. Woolrich and E. R. Hallowell (Westport, Conn.: Avi Publishing Company, 1970).

*The Complete Eater's Digest and Nutrition Scoreboard,* by Michael F. Jacobson (New York: Anchor Press, 1985).

*The Cook Book Decoder,* by Arthur E. Grosser (New York: Beaufort Books, 1981).

*Cooking with Understanding,* by H. L. Nichols, Jr. (Greenwich, Conn.: North Castle Books, 1971).

*The Cook's Book,* by Howard Hillman (New York: Avon, 1981).

*Dairy Technology and Engineering,* by W. J. Harper and C. W. Hall (Westport, Conn.: Avi Publishing Company, 1976).

*Dictionary of Food and Nutrition,* 4th ed., by A. E. Bender (New York: Chemical Publishing Company, 1975).

*A Diet for Living,* by Jean Mayer (New York: David McKay, 1975).

*Egg Quality: A Study of the Hen's Egg,* ed. T. C. Carter (Edinburgh, Scotland: Oliver and Boyd, 1968).

*Egg Science and Technology,* 2d ed., by W. J. Stadelman and O. J. Cotterill (Westport, Conn.: Avi Publishing Company, 1977).

*Elementary Food Science,* by J. T. R. Nickerson and L. J. Ronsivalli (Westport, Conn.: Avi Publishing Company, 1976).

*The Encyclopedia of Fish Cookery,* by A. J. McClane (New York: Holt, Rinehart and Winston, 1977).

*Encyclopedia of Food Engineering,* by C. W. Hall et al. (Westport, Conn.: Avi Publishing Company, 1971).

*Encyclopedia of Food Science,* ed. M. S. Peterson and A. H. Johnson (Westport, Conn.: Avi Publishing Company, 1978).

*Encyclopedia of Food Technology,* ed. A. H. Johnson and M. S. Peterson (Westport, Conn.: Avi Publishing Company, 1974).

*Experimental Study of Food,* by R. Griswold (Boston: Houghton Mifflin Company, 1962).

*Fish as Food,* vols. 1–4, ed. G. Borgstrom (New York: Academic Press, 1961–65).

*Food Additives Explained,* by Robert L. Berko (South Orange, N.J.: Consumer Education Research Center, 1983).

*Food and Man,* 2d ed., by M. E. Lowenberg et al. (New York: John Wiley & Sons, 1974).

*Food and the Consumer,* 2d ed., by A. Kramer (Westport, Conn.: Avi Publishing Company, 1977).

*Food and Your Well Being,* by T. P. Labuza (New York: West Publishing Company, 1977).

*Food-borne Infections and Intoxications*, by H. Riemann (New York: Academic Press, 1969).

*Food for Thought*, 2d ed., by T. P. Labuza and A. E. Sloan (Westport, Conn.: Avi Publishing Company, 1977).

*Food Fundamentals*, 3d ed., by M. McWilliams (New York: John Wiley & Sons, 1979).

*Food Microbiology: Public Health and Spoilage Aspects*, by M. P. deFigueiredo and D. F. Splittstoesser (Westport, Conn.: Avi Publishing Company, 1976).

*Food Oils and Their Uses*, by T. J. Weiss (Westport, Conn.: Avi Publishing Company, 1970).

*Foods*, 7th ed., by G. E. Vaill et al. (Boston: Houghton Mifflin, 1978).

*Food Science*, by H. Charley (New York: John Wiley & Sons, 1970).

*Food Science*, 2d ed., by H. Charley (New York: John Wiley & Sons, 1982).

*Food Science*, 3d ed., by N. N. Potter (Westport, Conn.: Avi Publishing Company, 1978).

*Food Theory and Application*, by P. C. Paul and H. H. Palmer (New York: John Wiley & Sons, 1972).

*Fundamentals of Dairy Chemistry*, 2d ed., edited by B. H. Webb et al. (Westport, Conn.: Avi Publishing Company, 1974).

*Fundamentals of Food Freezing*, ed. N. W. Desrosier and D. K. Tressler (Westport, Conn.: Avi Publishing Company, 1977).

*Fundamentals of Food Microbiology*, by M. L. Fields (Westport, Conn.: Avi Publishing Company, 1979).

*Fundamentals of Normal Nutrition*, by C. H. Robinson (New York: Macmillan Company, 1968).

*Introduction to Nutrition*, 3d ed., by H. Fleck (New York: Macmillan Company, 1976).

*Introduction to the Biochemistry of Foods*, by J. B. S. Braverman (New York: Elsevier Publishing Company, 1963).

*Introductory Food Chemistry*, by I. D. Garard (Westport, Conn.: Avi Publishing Company, 1976).

*Jane Brody's Nutrition Book*, 2d ed., by Jane Brody (New York: Bantam, 1987).

*Keeping Food Safe*, by H. Bradley and C. Sundberg (New York: Doubleday & Company, 1975).

*McGraw-Hill Encyclopedia of Science and Technology*, vols. 1–15 (New York: McGraw-Hill, 1977).

*Meat*, by D. J. A. Cole and R. A. Lawrie (Westport, Conn.: Avi Publishing Company, 1975).

*Meat Board Meat Book*, by B. Bloch (New York: McGraw-Hill, 1977).

*Meat Handbook*, 4th ed., by A. Levie (Westport, Conn.: Avi Publishing Company, 1979).

*Meat Hygiene*, 4th ed., by J. A. Libby (Philadelphia: Lea and Febiger, 1975).

*Meat Science*, 2d ed., by R. A. Lawrie (Oxford, England: Pergamon Press, 1974).

*Methods in Food Analysis*, ed. M. A. Joslyn (New York: Academic Press, 1970).

*The Microwave Oven*, by H. J. Van Zante (Boston: Houghton Mifflin Company, 1973).

*Milk, Cream and Butter Technology*, by G. Wilcox (Park Ridge, N.J.: Noyes Data Corp., 1971).

*Modern Food Microbiology*, by J. M. Jay (New York: Van Nostrand Reinhold Company, 1970).

*Modern Food Preservation*, by M. McWilliams and H. Paine (Fullerton, Calif.: Plycon Press, 1977).

*Modern Nutrition in Health and Disease*, 5th ed., by R. S. Goodhart and M. E. Shils (Philadelphia: Lea & Febiger, 1975).

*Nutrition for Your Pregnancy*, by Judith E. Brown (Minneapolis: University of Minnesota Press, 1983).

*On Food and Cooking*, by Harold McGee (New York: Charles Scribner's Sons, 1984).

*Poultry Products Technology*, 2d ed., by G. J. Mountney (Westport, Conn.: Avi Publishing Company, 1976).

*Practical Baking*, 3d ed., by W. J. Sultan (Westport, Conn.: Avi Publishing Company, 1976).

*Practical Food Microbiology and Technology*, 2d ed., by H. H. Weiser et al. (Westport, Conn.: Avi Publishing Company, 1971).

*Principles of Food Science*, vols. 1 and 2, by G. Borgstrom (New York: Macmillan Company, 1968).

*Principles of Sensory Evaluation of Food*, by M. A. Amerine et al. (New York: Academic Press, 1965).

*The Proteins*, vols. 1 and 2, by H. Neurath and R. L. Hill (New York: Academic Press, 1975).

*Proteins and Their Reactions*, by H. W. Schultz (Westport, Conn.: Avi Publishing Company, 1964).

*The Science of Food: An Introduction to Food Science, Nutrition and Microbiology*, by P. M. Gaman and K. B. Sherrington (Oxford, England: Pergamon Press, 1977).

*The Science of Meat and Meat Products*, ed. J. F. Price and B. S. Schweigert (San Francisco: W. H. Freeman & Company, 1971).

*Source Book for Food Scientists*, by H. W. Ockerman (Westport, Conn.: Avi Publishing Company, 1978).

*Starch and Its Components*, by W. Banks and C. T. Greenwood (New York: John Wiley & Sons, 1975).

*The Story of Food*, by I. D. Garard (Westport, Conn.: Avi Publishing Company, 1974).

*The Technology of Food Preservation*, by N. W. Desrosier and J. N. Desrosier (Westport, Conn.: Avi Publishing Company, 1977).

*Understanding Food*, by L. H. Kotschevar and M. McWilliams (New York: John Wiley & Sons, 1969).

# Index

Acetic acid, additive, 258
Additives and preservatives,
    258–62
Alcohol
    as an aphrodisiac, 299
    boiling point of water, effect
        on, 31
    consumption and hangovers,
        235–36; effect of coffee on,
        235
    drinking, effects of, 270
    in flambéed dishes, 186
    on hot days, effect of, 234
    and lowered inhibitions, 235
    men vs. women, effect of, 234
Allergic reactions to foods, 281–
    82
Aluminum foil, 243–44
Amino acids, essential, 256–57
Aphrodisiacs, 299
Apple(s)
    cellulose content of, 132
    seeds, poison in, 146
    wax treatment of, 131
Ascorbic acid (vitamin C),
    additive, 258–59
Asparagus, 133, 147

Athletes, diets for, 279–80;
    marathoner's carboloading,
    280
Avocados, 136
    discoloration of, 135–36

Babies
    fat cells in, 277
    weaning on skim milk, 277
Bacon, frying, 68; splatter, 68
Baked goods
    collapse of, 206
    nuts and dried fruits settling
        in, 215
    oils and fats for, 189
Baking, 203–20
    at high altitudes, 206
    vs. oven-roasting, 37
    pans, 215–17; placement in
        oven, 217–18
    at various temperatures, 215
Baking powder
    at high altitudes, 206
    homemade, 204
    as leavening agent, 203
    potency of, 203–4

Emulsified sauce(s), 149–51;
  stabilizing, 152
  in blender or food processor,
    152
  hollandaise, mayonnaise, etc.,
    149
  vinaigrette, 157–58
Enamel cookware, 13
Ethylene gas for ripening fruit,
    145
Exhaust fans, 17

Fat
  body, importance of, 272
  cells in babies, 277
  substitutes, sucrose polyesters
    (SPE), 195
Fat(s). *See also* Oils
  add flavor to meat, 189
  in the diet, healthy or
    unhealthy, 189–90
  saturated, monounsaturated
    and polyunsaturated, 191–95
Fiber in diet, 263–64
Fish, 75–89
  broiling, 88
  bruise marks on, 81
  caloric content of, 75–76
  contamination of, 85–86
  cooking, 86–87; various
    methods, 87–89
  cuts of, 78–79
  enhancing with "tripoly," 83–
    84
  farmed vs. natural
    environment, 78
  fat vs. lean, 74–76
  flavor of, 76–77, 81; affected
    by bones, 87
  flesh, color of, 79–81
  freezing, 85
  freshness of, 81–83
    and gill color, 82
    and odor, 82

and yellowing, 81
freshwater, bones in, 78
gills, removing, 88
myoglobin in, 79–80
river and lake, 77
serving promptly, 90
slimy look of, 83
storing, 84–85
subclassification of, 74
sushi, risks of eating, 86
tests for doneness, 89
and toxic mercury, 85–86
Flambéed dishes, 186
Flash and fire points of oil, 199
Flour
  all-purpose, 208–9
  bleached vs. unbleached, 209
  for bread, amounts of, 207
  instant vs. regular, 169
  removing from pots and
    utensils, 295
  semolina for pasta, 290
  sifting, 209
  for thickening sauces, 166–67;
    roux, 167
  whole wheat vs. graham, 208
  whole wheat vs. white, 207–8
Fluorocarbon propellants, danger
  of, 291
Food(s)
  allergic reactions to, 281–82
  as aphrodisiacs, 199
  bacterial growth in, 239
  calorie intake, 271–73
  freezing. *See* Freezing
  and pharmaceutical drugs,
    effects of, 282
  poisoning, 266–70
  preservation by canning,
    freezing, pickling, salting,
    etc., 238
  processors, budget-priced, 21
  processors, for making
    emulsified sauces, 152

Food (*cont.*)
  as sleep inducers, 298–99
  storage of, 237–51
  warming, 292; preheating
    dishes for, 292–93
  for weight watchers, 275–76
Freezer, energy-efficiency of,
    241; chest or upright, 242
Freezing
  food, aluminum foil for, 243–
    44
  fruits, adding sugar syrup to,
    245
  meat, wrapping tightly for,
    243
  methods of, 240–41
  for preservation of food, 238
  and quality of food, 239–40
  refreezing food, 246–47
  suitability of foods for, 241
  thawing meat, 245–46
  vegetables, blanching before,
    244
French fried potatoes, 139–41
Frozen vegetables
  buying, 247
  vs. fresh, 254–55
Fruits
  carotene content of, 135
  freezing, adding sugar syrup
    to, 245
  ripening at home, 145
  storing, 248
  sweeter part of, 146
  unprocessed, deterioration of,
    130–31
  and vegetables, 130–47
  wax treatment of, 131
  young vs. mature, 144

Garlic, sautéing with onions,
    137
Gas vs. electric range, 15–16
Gelatin
  rubbery skin on, 174

for thickening liquids, 173
  unflavored, dissolving, 174
Glass cookware (regular and
    treated), 13–14
Glasses, how to unstick, 296
Grocery bags, brown paper, 25
Gums (arabic, guar, etc.),
    additive, 260


Ham
  canned, refrigerated vs. room
    temperature, 67–68
  cooked, color of, 43
  iridescent sheen of, 67
  and trichinosis, 267
Hamburgers, meat for, 56
Heartburn, fast eating and, 264
Heat, for cooking food, 26–32
  conduction, 28
  convection, 28
  moist vs. dry, 29–30
  radiant, 27–28
  how transferred to food, 27–28
Herbs
  in cooking, when to add, 178
  dried, refrigerating, 248
Hollandaise sauce, 149
  curdling, 156
  delayed serving of, 156–57
  eggs in, 151
  recipe, 153–57
Hot cakes, cooking, 293
HVP (hydrolized vegetable
    protein), additive, 261
Hydrogenated vegetable oil,
    additive, 195


Ice, floating, 285
Ice cream
  ice crystals in, 116
  quality of, 116–17
  scooping, 117
  sugar content of, 115–16

and tooth decay, 262–63
white vs. brown, 183
Sushi, risks of eating, 86

Taste
  buds, concentration on
    tongue, 284
  perception of, 283–84
Tea (*Thea sinensis*)
  brewing temperature, 222–23
  caffeine in, 221
  insomnia and, 221–22
  milk, adding to, 228
  steeping, 227
  styrofoam cups, drinking
    from, 222
  varieties of (black, green,
    oolong), 227–28
  water for, 222
Teakettle, deposit, removing,
  295
Teflon nonstick coating, 11–12
Thermometer, meat, 23–24, 58
Thickening agents, 148–49. *See
  also* Sauces
  pectin, for jelly, 174–75
Thirst, quenching, 232–33
Tofu (bean curd), 143
Tomato(es)
  cellulose content of, 132
  serving cold, 145
  sex of, 146–47
Trichinosis, 266–67
Turnips, cooking, 133–34
TVP (textured vegetable protein),
  143

Ulcers, gastric, and food intake,
  281
USDA grades of beef, 66–67

Vacuum storage bottles, 249
Veal
  "anemic," 41

vs. beef (age), 46
bones vs. beef bones for
  making stock, 174
Vegetables, 130–47. *See also
  name of vegetable*
  acid and alkali, 132–33
  blanching before freezing, 244
  carotene content of, 135
  cellulose content of, 131–32
  cooking, 131–32
    amount of water for, 133
    covered or uncovered, 134
    moist heat for, 132
    time of, 133
  fresh vs. frozen, 254–55
  frozen, buying, 247
  and fruit, differences, 130
  green, cooking with baking
    soda, 134–35
  green, discoloration of, 134
  storing, 248
  tenderizing, 132
  unprocessed, deterioration of,
    130–31
  wax treatment of, 131
  white, turning yellow in
    cooking, 136
  young vs. mature, 144
Vegetarians, essential amino
  acids for, 256–57
Vinaigrette sauce, 157–58;
  recipe, 158–60
Vinegar, making, 183–84;
  "mother" or, 184
Vitamin(s)
  C (ascorbic acid), additive,
    258–59
  manufactured vs. natural, 253
  in potato skins, 255
  varying need for, 252–53
  water-soluble, 254

Water
  anti-impurity filter for, 269

Water (*cont.*)
carbonated, 233–34
cooking temperature,
importance of, 30–33, 34
in reducing diets, 274–75
simmering temperature of, 34
thirst and, 232–33
Weight watchers
eating slowly, 276
foods to eat, 275–76
skipping breakfast, 276
Whipped topping, dessert, 106
Wine(s)
cooking, use of, 184–87
cork, particles on, 230
foods incompatible with, 229
leftover, preserving, 230
red vs. white, 229

sherry, addition of, 185–86
stoppers for, 229–30
wrapping, to cool, 230–31
Wok-cooked foods, 17–18; for
nutrition-conscious, 254

Yeast
dry and compressed, 205
at high altitudes, 206
leavening action of, 205
vitality of, 205
Yeast dough
kneading, 212
rising, 213
Yogurt
commercial fruit-flavored, 115
homemade, 114–15

# About the Author

Howard Hillman is the author of more than twenty books, including *The Book of World Cuisines* (Penguin), *The Diner's Guide to Wines* (Hawthorn), *The Cook's Book* (Avon), *Kitchen Secrets* (Macmillan), *Great Peasant Dishes of the World* (Houghton Mifflin), and a series of epicurean guidebooks to major cities (David McKay). His books have been critically acclaimed and have earned many honors. Hillman's works have been selected by three book clubs, have been translated into braille and foreign languages, and have been named to the "Outstanding Reference Book" list of both the *Library Journal* and the American Library Association.

He has written food and wine articles for distinguished publications such as the *New York Times*, the *Wall Street Journal*, *Cook's*, *Medical World News*, and *Food & Wine*, and has critically rated restaurants for America's largest newspaper.

Howard Hillman is a culinary explorer who unabashedly loves wining, dining, and travel. He has journeyed more than a million miles to more than one hundred countries, shopping and cooking the local way in gourmet capitals (Paris and the like) as well as in locations off the beaten path (from Timbuktu to small villages in China). Altogether, he has investigated and prepared thousands of ethnic dishes. He has lectured on television and at universities, has been a guest on numerous radio and TV talk shows, and maintains one of the most extensive food and wine reference libraries.

His general background includes the presidency of the National Academy of Sports, a vice-presidency of the American Film Theatre, the editorship of *Quality Digest*, and the presidency of the Customer Satisfaction Institute. He is a Harvard Business School graduate.